WOMEN, RELATIONSHIPS, AND POWER: IMPLICATIONS FOR COUNSELING

Ellen Piel Cook, Editor
University of Cincinnati

AMERICAN
COUNSELING
ASSOCIATION

American Counseling Association
5999 Stevenson Avenue
Alexandria, VA 22304

Cover Design by Kay Bollen

Library of Congress Cataloging-in-Publication Data

Women, relationships, and power : implications for counseling / Ellen
   Piel Cook, editor.
        p.   cm.
   Includes bibliographical references and index.
   ISBN 1-55620-100-1
   1. Women—Psychology.   2. Sex role.   3. Women—Counseling of.
I. Cook, Ellen Piel, 1952–
HQ1206.W878   1993
305.4—dc20   92-23567
                                                CIP

Printed in the United States of America

WOMEN, RELATIONSHIPS, AND POWER: IMPLICATIONS FOR COUNSELING

Ellen Piel Cook, Editor
University of Cincinnati

AMERICAN
COUNSELING
ASSOCIATION

American Counseling Association
5999 Stevenson Avenue
Alexandria, VA 22304

Cover Design by Kay Bollen

Library of Congress Cataloging-in-Publication Data

Women, relationships, and power : implications for counseling / Ellen
Piel Cook, editor.
      p.   cm.
   Includes bibliographical references and index.
   ISBN 1-55620-100-1
   1. Women—Psychology.   2. Sex role.   3. Women—Counseling of.
I. Cook, Ellen Piel, 1952–
HQ1206.W878   1993
   305.4—dc20   92-23567
                                                       CIP

Printed in the United States of America

For our daughters

great deal of information and insight from the experts working with these disempowering issues.

This volume also reflects an awareness of diversity in relation to ethnicity, race, and socioeconomic background as well as sexual orientation. Dr. Cook and the contributors acknowledge the difficulty of describing issues for *all* women and the fact that, for many women, race or economic status may be more important than gender. Yet few would deny that many of the issues described, especially those of sexism, abuse, and violence, cut across racial, ethnic, and socioeconomic boundaries.

In addition, Dr. Cook points out the greater "convergence in women's and men's roles" today, the overlap between the sexes, and the danger of dichotomizing men and women into two cultures. She reminds us that the variability within the sexes may be greater than that between the sexes.

Perhaps one of this book's most important contributions to the thinking and experience of counselors and other helping professionals is to powerfully remind us of the cumulative power of gender on each of us. From a context of "the gendered nature of our lives," Dr. Cook provides a framework through which male and female counselors and those who train them can examine their assumptions, attitudes, practices, and interventions. Her discussion of the dangers of misuse of diagnosis and problem conceptualization should be extremely valuable to counseling practitioners.

Dr. Cook appropriately concludes the book with a chapter on "Helping Women Heal." That this is a volume written primarily *by* women (but not only *for* women) is evident in both the conceptual framework chosen—a more holistic view of women's lives, including the individual and the context—and the language used, as well as in the connectedness of the chapters through the rational theme.

This is an important book for both women and men and particularly for counselors and other helping professionals. As counselors strive to become more aware of the external and internal issues in women's development and to develop skills for empowering women, they will find this collection of snapshots at once painful and positive as well as critical to creating empowering interventions for their women clients.

Dr. Cook and the highly competent contributors she has selected to work with her have provided a real service to the counseling profession and to women, who comprise the largest segment of our clients. The authors deserve our thanks and appreciation. If there is any doubt among counselors that *gender* is a theme that shapes women's lives in both positive and negative ways, then this book will help dispel that doubt in ways that are empowering to counselors as well as to the women they serve.

This book will be one of the first publications of the American Counseling Association under our new professional name. I believe it should be read by every counselor and counselor educator in our profession and that it will be important for theory and practice in understanding gender issues in a new way. You will find it scholarly, clear, and compassionate.

Sunny Hansen, Ph.D.
AACD President, 1989–90
Professor, Educational Psychology
Director, BORN FREE, University of Minnesota
July 15, 1992

CONTRIBUTORS

Mary W. Armsworth, Ed.D., is an associate professor in the Department of Educational Psychology, University of Houston, and has a private practice.

Ellen Piel Cook, Ph.D., is an associate professor in the Counseling Program, Department of School Psychology and Counseling, University of Cincinnati.

Patricia A. Doherty, Ph.D., is a senior psychologist at the Counseling Center, University of Wisconsin-Stevens Point.

Paula Dupuy, Ed.D., is an assistant professor in the Department of Counselor Education and Human Services Education, University of Toledo.

Jean Egan, M.A., is an assistant professor of social science and management at Asnuntuck Community College, Enfield, Connecticut, and a doctoral candidate in adult and vocational education, University of Connecticut.

Suzanne Hedstrom, Ed.D., is an assistant professor in the Department of Counselor Education and Counseling Psychology, Western Michigan University.

Laurie B. Mintz, Ph.D., is an assistant professor of counseling psychology in the Psychology Department, University of Missouri-Columbia, and has a part-time private practice specializing in eating disorders and other women's issues.

James M. O'Neil, Ph.D., is a professor of family studies and educational psychology, University of Connecticut, and a licensed psychologist in private practice in South Windsor, Connecticut.

Laurie Anne Pearlman, Ph.D., is director of research at the Traumatic Stress Institute, South Windsor, Connecticut, an independent mental health facility providing clinical and educational services and research on trauma.

Diane Johnson Prosser, Ph.D., is an assistant professor in the Department of Counselor Education and Counseling Psychology, Western Michigan University.

Kathleen Y. Ritter, Ph.D., is coordinator of the counseling program and professor of counselor education, California State University-Bakersfield, and has a private practice at the Westchester Counseling Center.

Karen W. Saakvitne, Ph.D., is clinical director at the Traumatic Stress Institute, South Windsor, Connecticut, an independent mental health facility providing clinical and educational services and research on trauma.

Pamela Gulley Smith, Ed.D., is an assistant professor in the Department of Counselor Education and Human Services, University of Dayton.

Marian Stoltz-Loike, Ph.D., is President, Stoltz-Loike Associates, Flushing, New York, providing consultation on work-family issues.

Melanie A. Warnke, Ph.D., is an assistant professor in the Department of Counselor Education and Counseling Psychology, Western Michigan University.

Deborah M. Wright, M.A., is a counseling psychology doctoral candidate in the Psychology Department, University of Missouri-Columbia, and an intern at the Counseling Center.

INTRODUCTION

Ellen Piel Cook

One of the most fundamental and universal distinctions that humans use to describe each other is biological sex. Most people take it for granted that men and women differ from each other in many ways, although the explanations for the origins and significance of these differences vary widely. Only women can bear and nurse children. Beyond this essential biological difference are many other observable differences: in career choices and patterns over time, ways of behaving in social situations, clothing and color preferences, and so on. The term *gender* is commonly used to refer to the psychological, cultural, and social characteristics that distinguish the sexes.

We now recognize that our society itself is highly differentiated on the basis of gender. Every day men and women confront different expectations, opportunities, rewards, and resources on the basis of their biological sex. We perceive and respond to others in certain ways because of their biological sex, and how others respond to us in sex-differentiated ways shapes our own conceptions of ourselves as individuals.

The basic premise of this book is that gender continues to play a crucial role in shaping women's lives today. Recent decades have witnessed major changes in women's self-perceptions and choices. Some of the changes have resulted in a closer convergence of the sexes, for example, in increasing numbers of women developing professional careers and of men assuming a more active role in child-care and homemaking responsibilities. Yet, as the authors in this

1

book will argue, gender still does make a big difference in our lives. Recent research on gender has demonstrated that the commonalities between the sexes because of their shared humanity may be more numerous than previously assumed. In other respects, gender dynamics are probably more complicated and influential than appreciated before.

What is the source of these complex differences? Two types of popular explanations are useful for counselors to consider, because each perspective has different implications for how we work with women today. The two perspectives are the individualistic perspective and the contextual perspective. Each perspective has both its wisdom and its limitations.

THE INDIVIDUALISTIC PERSPECTIVE

The individualistic perspective sees gender as the property of the individual. That is, men and women behave the way that they do because either they were born that way or they learned to be that way from the earliest days of life. The focus is on what the individual woman or man is predisposed to do either because of biology or learning, rather than upon the context in which she or he behaves. Both versions of this perspective focus on the consistent and stable personality traits, attitudes, and behaviors that men and women typically bring to situations in order to explain gender differences in behavior.

Within a particular society, there is widespread agreement about what characteristics are generally associated with each sex, whether or not individuals agree that such distinctions are in fact desirable. Cook (1985) compiled a list of characteristics stereotypically associated with each sex:

> Men (Masculinity)—aggressive, independent, unemotional, objective, dominant, competitive, logical/rational, adventurous, decisive, self-confident, ambitious, worldly, acts as a leader, assertive, analytical, strong, sexual, knowledgeable, physical, successful, good in mathematics and science, and the reverse of the feminine characteristics listed below.

Women (Femininity)—emotional, sensitive, expressive, aware of others' feelings, tactful, gentle, security-oriented, quiet, nurturing, tender, cooperative, interested in pleasing others, interdependent, sympathetic, helpful, warm, interested in personal appearance and beauty in general, intuitive, focused upon home and family, sensual, good in art and literature, and the reverse of the masculine characteristics above. (p. 4)

The core of masculine characteristics involves assertive activity, goal orientation, self-development, and separations from others, often labeled as *instrumental* or *agentic* characteristics. The core of femininity involves emotionality, sensitivity, selflessness, and interrelationships, labeled as *expressive* or *communal* characteristics. These core descriptions were derived from the work of Parsons and Bales (1953) and Bakan (1966), respectively.

The characteristics listed in the femininity and masculinity dimensions above represent widely held beliefs about how men and women differ from each other. Research has demonstrated that men are likely to view the characteristics typically associated with men (masculine) as more descriptive of themselves than do women, whereas women tend to view feminine characteristics as more self-descriptive than do men (Bem, 1974; Spence, Helmreich, & Stapp, 1975). Researchers in the individualistic perspective have commonly assumed that variations in the extent to which individuals describe themselves as "masculine" or "feminine" can be reliably linked with behavioral differences across a variety of situations. That is, women describing themselves as highly feminine were expected to behave quite differently than women whose self-descriptions were not as emphatically feminine.

The individualistic perspective has been very popular among professionals and laypersons alike. Where do such differences in masculinity and femininity come from? A time-honored explanation attributes the many psychological and social differences we observe between the sexes to the fundamental biological makeup of the sexes. Thus, "girls will be girls" (and boys will be boys) because they were destined that way from conception. All of the manifold gender differences we observe are presumed to be as enduring and as dichotomous in nature as the biological dichotomy from which they apparently spring. In this explanation, the differences occurring within each sex (for example, among men in leadership abilities) are generally believed to be ones of degree, far eclipsed by the more essential differences *between* the sexes. Absence of a sex-typical characteristic is akin to a genetic abnormality—something missing in one's makeup as a woman or a man. For example, a woman who is not interested in bearing children is somehow not a "real" woman, according to this version.

Biological causes of psychological characteristics are, in general, extremely difficult to establish, because social learning begins at birth and continues throughout life. Thus, the relative contribution of nature and nurture to sex differences remains unclear. Research seems to suggest that relatively few sex differences are biological in origin (Maccoby, 1990; Maccoby & Jacklin, 1974; for recent critical reviews of sex difference research, see Hare-Mustin & Marecek, 1990b). At best, any biological factors are likely to serve as predispositions either elaborated or effaced by experiences after birth, rather than as firm determinants of behavior. It seems unlikely that biological explanations of gender will ever prove to be sufficient in themselves.

Most versions of the individualistic perspective adopted by professionals today elaborate how individual women and men learn to behave differently as the result of a complex individual socialization process initiated at birth. This socialization perspective recognizes that an individual's behavior is unique in many respects as a result of his or her unique learning history, but that in general, members of each sex develop certain personal characteristics in common. These personal characteristics are believed to be more extensive than the trait dichotomies embodied in the familiar masculinity/femininity dimensions described above, to include domains such as self-concept, attitudes, behavioral styles, and cognitive processing differences. Those personal characteristics generally shared by one sex, in turn, explain why men and women behave differently in various situations.

This socialization perspective has been extremely influential in recent years. O'Neil (1981) succinctly stated the implications of the gender socialization process: "men and women have each learned only about one-half of the attitudes, skills, and behaviors necessary to cope effectively in life" (p. 64). In today's rapidly changing world, counselors encounter an increasing number of individuals facing pain because their familiar, traditional roles have not prepared them to cope with new life options as a woman or man (Cook, 1985). Counselors have pondered how they can help clients escape their sex's gender-related conditioning of the past. Overcoming the socialization process through insight and practice can lead to new behavioral possibilities in the present.

The individualistic perspective in its varied forms focuses on gender as a property of the individual whether learned or inborn (or both). Today, counselors espousing this perspective typically focus on broad psychological differences between the sexes that cause them to behave quite differently in a variety of situations. A recent counterpoint to this emphasis is provided by a focus on the context in which individuals live their lives.

THE CONTEXTUAL PERSPECTIVE

The contextual perspective analyzes how gender differences occur within a broader context organized on the basis of sex. As Lott (1985) has stated, "it is not sex that matters but those life conditions that are systematically related to it by cultural prescription, regulation, or arrangement" (p. 162). Throughout life women and men are perceived and treated by others in certain unique ways because of their sex. This perspective emphasizes that our society prescribes and reinforces what personal characteristics, life roles, prerogatives, and responsibilities should belong to each sex on a *systemic* basis. This differentiation by sex is pervasive enough that in many respects, the sexes essentially live in different worlds (Cook, 1990, 1992).

Taken to its extreme, the individualistic perspective espouses a deterministic view of sex differences: Men and women can be reliably expected to behave differently because of their different natures. However, research has repeatedly pointed to the need to explain the variability in gender-related behavior. For example, members of one sex often behave differently from one another, while in many situations women and men behave similarly. Even members of the same sex classified as "feminine" or "masculine" to the same degree often do not behave in the same way (cf. Cook, 1985). An individual may behave consistently or inconsistently across situations for reasons that cannot be explained by personality traits or socialization. Gender-related behaviors are highly sensitive to changes in the social environment, and gender effects are often superseded by other variables such as social status (Lott, 1990). Other factors such as race or nationality often exert a profound impact on behaviors labeled as sex linked. Counselors are also aware that learning is a lifelong process. Early socialization may provide a template for subsequent learning throughout life, but later life learnings can also modify or replace such templates. For many reasons, an individual's inborn or learned characteristics represent only one part of the answer to the question of gender differences.

A fundamental assumption shared by many proponents of the contextual perspective is that the worlds occupied by the sexes are *not* separate but equal in influence and esteem. Instead, women are systematically devalued, restricted, and/or violated because of the greater power maintained for men as a group (see O'Neil and Egan's chapter). Epstein (1988) provocatively argues that the hierarchical segregation of the sexes—perpetuating a two-class system—is maintained by numerous forms of social control throughout society. Broad societal institutions shape even the individual choices we all make, so that certain choices consistent with the social ordering of the sexes are more likely than other choices. Women are systematically persuaded to assume positions of lesser power, while mechanisms of social control make sure that they do so. Traditional sex-based distinctions assign men responsibility for producing income (in the public sphere) and women for maintaining the family (in the private sphere). Thus men are in a position to attain cultural ideals of individuality, independence, and achievement, whereas women serve in invisible supportive roles (Hare-Mustin & Marecek, 1990a).

Analyses of gender-related power dynamics have been prominent in much of the literature on feminist therapy. For example, Gilbert (1980) described feminist therapy as emphasizing the relationship between women's personal experiences and broader social roles and norms maintained for women (see also Good, Gilbert, & Scher, 1990). Sociopolitical analysis of women's lives is central in the feminist therapy process, and social change is seen as essential to improve women's lot. Feminist therapy does also address a woman's personal life experiences, but it is unique among counseling approaches in how it views an individual against a broader backdrop of women's position within a sexist society.

Taken to its extreme, the contextual perspective would not elaborate upon how individuals respond to their social context on the basis of their unique makeup and experiences. Such an extreme might offer counselors a way to think about the broader social impact of gender, but little specific guidance in dealing with the gender-related problems presented by individual clients.

Counselors might argue that neither the individualistic nor the contextual perspective at its extreme is very helpful in counseling. Most experts within the helping professions recognize that both perspectives are needed to understand a client's life situation. In fact, in certain respects this distinction between perspectives is an artificial one. It might be impossible to separate out the effects of the person and the environment because of the constant, intimate interaction between them. This book adopts a third perspective on gender recognizing the reciprocal nature of this interaction.

THE RECIPROCAL PERSPECTIVE

The reciprocal perspective adopted here considers how individuals deal with their ever-developing selves as women or men and the demands placed on them by their own evolving life circumstances. Each of us has our own way of being a woman or a man who encounters potentially supportive or challenging situations on a daily basis. The gender-related factors influencing this interaction are complex: the predispositions, expectations, attitudes, and behaviors individuals bring to their daily life situations; such personal characteristics brought by others; and transient and enduring features of the environment, encompassing both characteristics of the immediate setting (e.g., a work setting) and those of society at large (cf. Deaux

& Major, 1987). Individuals actively attempt to select and influence their own environments (e.g., Unger, 1989) while others are attempting to do the same. All of our interpersonal interactions also occur within a broader sociocultural context, shaped by the economics, politics, and norms of our historical time.

Ideally, who we are as a woman or a man is valued by others, and our efforts to develop a personally meaningful place for ourselves in the world as we experience it meet with support. Personal empowerment can be the result: a commitment and ability to pursue personally meaningful relationships and individual achievements, with dignity and respect for self and others. Yet this process can be extraordinarily difficult and painful as well, in numerous ways understandable in terms of gender. For example, others or we ourselves may dismiss certain valuable possibilities simply because of gender (e.g., full-time homemaking for a man). Other possibilities may be viable but repudiated by others and may feel shameful to ourselves (e.g., a woman giving custody of her child to her former partner). Depending on perceptions of the "gender correctness" of a life option, certain possibilities may be celebrated, scarcely tolerated, punished, or simply unimaginable to an individual and others in her or his life. Abuse that we may suffer because of gender may also wound us to the point that we cannot see our lives as having any value or promise.

The reciprocal perspective proposes that to see what it means to be a woman or a man in today's society, we need to adjust our lens to focus variously on the gender learnings and preferences of individuals; the gender-relevant features of the environment, including those presented by other individuals and by the broader sociocultural context; and the interaction between them.

IMPLICATIONS FOR COUNSELING WOMEN

Counselors today generally agree that many issues brought by clients into counseling are gender related (Cook, 1990). For example, clients may restrict certain career interests and preferences because of occupational sex typing, and eating disorders and depression are more common among women than men. To understand the role of gender in women clients' problems, counselors need to be aware of how personal characteristics can affect what problems individual women develop and how these women respond to their problems. Counselors also need to consider how gender may shape the sociocultural context in which their clients live, affecting the interactions they have with others on a daily basis and the range of experiences open to them. Adopting this broad view of gender substantially extends counselors' range of options for helping women to cope constructively with their own issues.

How counselors see gender issues operating within their clients' lives will have an impact on what goals and strategies seem appropriate in counseling. Counselors focusing exclusively on a woman's personal characteristics are likely to ask: "What gender-socialized characteristics does this woman possess that are contributing to her problems?" This focus on "deficiencies" would prompt counselors to design remedial strategies to overcome them, such as teaching new behaviors (e.g., assertion skills) or helping a client to expand her range of appropriate life roles (e.g., being career oriented as well as a homemaker).

In contrast, counselors recognizing the more pervasive impact of gender would ask a broader range of questions to understand how gender operates within the client's environment as well. For example, counselors might ask questions such as: "How are others responding to this client as a woman? How would this change if she changed? Might the client be struggling with contradictory or restrictive messages about how she should behave?" Rather than focusing primarily on the client's deficiencies, the counselor may discuss with the client how to cope with discrimination by others against her, or with society's messages about what women "should" be doing today.

For some clients, the choice of perspectives can have radical consequences for how they come to see their problems. For example, in the case of a battered woman, a counselor focusing exclusively on her gender-related individual characteristics may concentrate on how her (feminine) passivity and dependence prevent her from leaving the situation. A counselor with a broader perspective on gender issues may well consider such factors, but might also consider how men are often socialized to use aggression as a form of interpersonal control (Ptacek, 1988) and how many women lack economic resources and community support to leave such a situation. There are no simple answers for counselors seeking to explain why such complex and serious problems occur in women's lives. The richer counselors' understanding is, the more opportunities they have to determine which perspectives will ultimately be the most empowering for their individual clients.

OVERVIEW OF THE BOOK

This book is intended to provide such a rich understanding of gender issues in women's lives. The overall conceptualization uniting this book invites counselors to see women as individuals negotiating a life course according to their own psychological makeup, their interactions with others, and their existence within a broad sociocultural context.

The two chapters immediately following this introduction complete a detailed conceptualization on gender and women's issues that is essential to read before the chapters covering specific issues. Each of these conceptualization chapters covers a topic of prominence in the women's literature today: the centrality of relationships in women's lives, and gender-related power dynamics endemic to our society. As suggested by the title of the book, these two topics are discussed in various ways throughout the book. In "No Woman Is an Island: Women and Relationships," Doherty and Cook discuss recent theoretical perspectives on the importance of relationships in women's lives. Experts on women's issues generally agree today that relationships are central to women's individual identities and psychological development, life choices, and values and priorities. Although individual women may report being relationship oriented out of personal nature and/or choice, such an orientation is, in fact, expected and repeatedly reinforced for women throughout their lives. Understanding the importance to women of relationship in its many forms is basic to understanding women's life patterns and problems.

The next chapter on women and power by O'Neil and Egan analyzes the pervasive differences in power between the sexes in our society. A systems view of gender and power illuminates how gender inequities develop and are sustained even without the conscious awareness of individuals. As O'Neil and Egan illustrate, power issues influence how women see themselves as individuals, how others treat them, and how women treat others in return. Such an analysis of power explains how the sexes, in some important respects, live in different worlds, and why gender dynamics are so ubiquitous, influential, and resistant to change.

The following chapters explore various issues that women commonly bring up in counseling, recognizing the interactive contribution of both women's individual characteristics and the gendered context of women's lives. Relationship issues and gender/power issues are recurrent themes. The topics selected for inclusion are quite complex, and in some cases counselors may need specialized training and supervision to develop expertise in working with them (e.g., eating disorders). These chapters specifically address how gender analysis can illuminate counselors' understanding of these complex issues. Other problems experienced by women were omitted (e.g., grief reactions) not because they are unimportant, but because at the present time gender analysis does not add substantially to our understanding of the problems.

Although the topic of relationships is a subtext throughout the chapters, two chapters explicitly focus on common relationship issues for women. Dupuy describes the experience of intimacy for women by contrasting two different orientations by which men and women relate to one another and by analyzing how these orientations are played out in various relationships. She emphasizes that although each orientation is generally more common in one sex than the other, both orientations cross gender lines. Stoltz-Loike draws upon women's relational orientation, career patterns, and partner issues to portray the dimensions of the juggling act many women perform to balance work and relationship priorities.

Depression is, unfortunately, a pervasive feature of women's emotional lives. Ritter extensively discusses the role of four factors in women's depression: the importance of relationships, women's cognitive and behavioral styles, unique societal and socioeconomic stressors in women's lives, and the oppressive conditions under which many women live. Her discussion of depression in ethnic minority and lesbian women is unusually detailed.

Two chapters focus on topics that are intimately related to women's physical health. Even "natural" biological functions characterizing women's reproductive life cycle (e.g., childbearing, menopause) are influenced by gender dynamics. Warnke and a number of colleagues discuss the gender-based reasons these issues are such complex ones for women. Then, in a richly detailed chapter, Mintz and Wright analyze the contributions of sociocultural, personal (including biological), and relational factors to women's eating disorders and addictions.

The next chapter complements ideas introduced in the conceptualization chapter on power to discuss the prevalence and impact of sexual violence on women. Saakvitne and Pearlman's description of "internalized misogyny" elegantly exemplifies how internal psychological processes are shaped by the gendered sociocultural context in which women live, and how both help to maintain the cycle of shame and hatred of women. At the book's close, I will highlight some recurring themes and issues important in working with women today.

The focus of the book is on issues faced by adult women, although in some cases the effect of certain childhood experiences (e.g., incest) on adult life is acknowledged. The reader will notice that there are no special chapters devoted to issues experienced by lesbian or bisexual women or by women of color. Certainly, sexual orientation and cultural/ethnic background have a profound impact on every woman's life experiences and perceptions, including those of women from dominant groups in our society (white, heterosexual). Authors of every chapter were instructed to include these factors as important individual, relationship, and/or contextual factors in their analysis. This approach reflects the belief that sexual orientation and cultural/ethnic identification are not "problems" or "special group topics," but instead fundamental aspects of every woman's life that counselors routinely need to consider. Gaps in our understanding about how these factors influence gender analysis of the issues covered in this book will be noted in the final summary chapter.

Finally, a word about terminology: Practitioners from a variety of helping professions address these issues in counseling and are likely to find this book helpful in their efforts to understand women today. For simplicity's sake, I have chosen to use the terms *counselor* and *counseling* to refer generically to helping professionals and the processes they use to assist clients. Regardless of their backgrounds, practitioners wishing to help women with many of these issues will need to obtain specialized training and supervision to prepare them for this work. This book amply illustrates the complexity of these issues in women's lives today.

REFERENCES

Bakan, D. (1966). *The duality of human existence.* Chicago: Rand McNally.

Bem, S. L. (1974). The measurement of psychological androgyny. *Journal of Consulting and Clinical Psychology, 31,* 155–162.

Cook, E. P. (1985). *Psychological androgyny.* Elmsford, NY: Pergamon.

Cook, E. P. (1990). Gender and psychological distress. *Journal of Counseling and Development, 68,* 371–375.

Cook, E. P. (1992). Empowering women: Gender issues in adulthood. In J. A. Lewis, B. Hayes, & L. Bradley (Eds.), *Counseling women over the lifespan* (pp. 135–154). Denver: Love.

Deaux, K., & Major, B. (1987). Putting gender into context: An interactive model of gender-related behavior. *Psychological Review, 94,* 369–389.

Epstein, C. F. (1988). *Deceptive distinctions: Sex, gender, and the social order.* New Haven: Yale University Press.

Gilbert, L. A. (1980). Feminist therapy. In A. M. Brodsky & R. T. Hare-Mustin (Eds.), *Women and psychotherapy* (pp. 245–265). New York: Guilford.

Good, G. E., Gilbert, L. A., & Scher, M. (1990). Gender aware therapy: A synthesis of feminist therapy and knowledge about gender. *Journal of Counseling and Development, 68,* 381–387.

Hare-Mustin, R. T., & Marecek, J. (1990a). Beyond difference. In R. T. Hare-Mustin & J. Marecek (Eds.), *Making a difference: Psychology and the construction of gender* (pp. 184–201). New Haven: Yale University Press.

Hare-Mustin, R. T., & Marecek, J. (Eds.) (1990b). *Making a difference: Psychology and the construction of gender.* New Haven: Yale University Press.

Lott, B. (1985). The potential enrichment of social/personality psychology through feminist research and vice versa. *American Psychologist,* 40, 155–164.

Lott, B. (1990). Dual natures or learned behavior: The challenge to feminist psychology. In R. T. Hare-Mustin & J. Marecek (Eds.), *Making a difference: Psychology and the construction of gender* (pp. 65–101). New Haven: Yale University Press.

Maccoby, E. E. (1990). Gender and relationships: A developmental account. *American Psychologist,* 45, 513–520.

Maccoby, E. E., & Jacklin, C. N. (1974). *The psychology of sex differences.* Stanford, CA: Stanford University Press.

O'Neil, J. M. (1981). Male sex role conflicts, sexism, and masculinity: Psychological implications for men, women, and the counseling psychologist. *The Counseling Psychologist,* 9, 61–80.

Parsons, T., & Bales, R. F. (1953). *Family, socialization, and interaction process.* New York: Free Press.

Ptacek, J. (1988). Why do men batter their wives? In K. Yllo & M. Bograd (Eds.), *Feminist perspectives on wife abuse* (pp. 133–157). Newbury Park, CA: Sage.

Spence, J. T., Helmreich, R., & Stapp, J. (1975). Ratings of self and peers on sex role attributes and their relation to self-esteem and conceptions of masculinity and femininity. *Journal of Personality and Social Psychology,* 32, 29–39.

Unger, R. (1989). Sex, gender, and epistemology. In M. Crawford & M. Gentry (Eds.), *Gender and thought: Psychological perspectives* (pp. 17–35). New York: Springer-Verlag.

No Woman Is an Island: Women and Relationships

Patricia A. Doherty and Ellen Piel Cook

Gender is one of the most important factors shaping a woman's existence from the moment of conception throughout her entire life. An individual female's possibilities and limits are largely defined by a combination of gender-related personal and societal factors that provide the context of her life. A major theme that emerges from the context of what it means to be female is caring for others and being connected in intimate interpersonal relationships (Chodorow, 1978; Gilligan, 1982; Miller, 1976, 1984/1991; Surrey, 1984/1991). A community orientation seems to permeate many aspects of women's lives and to influence behavior in powerful ways.

This chapter presents a way of understanding women that is grounded in theory and counseling observations about relationships in women's lives. The most influential contribution to this perspective in terms of counseling practice is generally labeled *self-in-relation theory* (Jordan, Kaplan, Miller, Stiver, & Surrey, 1991). Other experts with related ideas have also had a marked impact on thinking about women today (e.g., Belenky, Clinchy, Goldberger, & Tarule, 1986; Gilligan, 1982). This chapter's synthesis of recent perspectives on the importance of relationships in women's lives represents our understanding of this body of work and is called the *relational perspective*.

WOMEN'S RELATIONAL SELF

The centrality of relationships as a positive theme in women's lives has received growing attention in the literature in recent years. There are two fundamental themes in the relational perspective: (1) a focus on relationships as a counterpoint to the autonomous, separate view of the self implicitly accepted by counselors and our society at large; and (2) a valuing of women's typical characteristics as representing unappreciated strengths rather than liabilities.

Relationships and the Self

Our society values independent, goal-directed activity as essential to one's psychological health and social standing (e.g., Spence, 1985). Core characteristics include making it on one's own, setting and reaching personal goals, and using individual occupational achievements as an index of one's personal identity and importance. This individualistic view has been embodied in our psychological theories in such concepts as separation and individuation through development, and self-actualization. Experts are apt to explain an individual's behavior in terms of a "self" likely to be influenced by others, but defined as an integrated entity with its own characteristics clearly discriminable from others. Independent, goal-directed activity is the pathway to full realization of this self (see Enns, 1991; Gallos, 1989).

In an extremely influential book, Miller (1976) suggested that previous models of mature development emphasizing separation and autonomy were based on males and failed to take into account women's experience. Men's maturing is commonly described as an individuation process, establishing separateness defined by clear emotional boundaries. According to Miller, women grow to maturity through a different process, which involves developing and maintaining connections with others throughout life. This process, termed *relationship-differentiation,* stands in contrast to separation-individuation by emphasizing elaboration and articulation of connections with others rather than moving away from others (Surrey, 1984/1991). This perspective thus proposes an alternative pathway to psychological development. In recent years the female orientation toward connection has been recognized and elaborated upon extensively in the literature (Chodorow, 1978; Gilligan, 1982; Gilligan, Lyons, & Hamner, 1990; Josselson, 1987; Kaplan, Klein, & Gleason, 1985/1991; Surrey, 1984/1991; Tannen, 1990).

Surrey (1984/1991) referred to women's relational nature as a self-in-relation. The term suggests that for women the self exists in a relational context that is necessary to define identity. Thus, who an individual woman is and perceives herself to be is intimately intertwined with who she is to significant people in her life. The woman's desire to maintain these connections that are so important to self-definition will then have a powerful influence on who she may become. In this light self-growth and relational growth go hand in hand. In Miller's (1984/1991) words, women have a basic desire to develop all of themselves in increasingly complex ways, in increasingly complex relationships. This desire provides the impetus for growth throughout life. Psychological development is a process of evolving increasingly sophisticated abilities to perceive and respond to the feelings and experiences of others, while being able to use one's own feelings and experiences to enlarge the relationship for oneself and others. This capacity is developed only through participating in relationships with others.

It is important to emphasize that this focus on relationship in psychological development says more than that relationships are what women *do* well; it says that relationships are what women *are*. Self-in-relation theory (e.g., Surrey, 1984/1991) argues that relationships are such an integral part of women's psychological functioning that it is inaccurate to define women's selves as somehow autonomous and separate from others. The term self-in-relation portrays one's experience of oneself in connection with others as fundamental to one's experience of oneself as a living being. Other aspects of development (e.g., achievement competence) for women occur within healthy relationships.

Women experience a sense of empowerment or "zest" that derives from relational connections and provides energy to act in the world (Miller, 1986). Relationships with mutuality are characterized by an active interest in and responsiveness to the subjective experience of the other, with each person appreciating the uniqueness of the other (Jordan, 1986/1991). The essence of such growth-producing relationships is an empathic interplay in which each participant expresses thoughts and feelings and responds to those of the other empathically, also sharing thoughts and feelings that arise in response to the other. Each participant is thus attuned to the other, and each experiences a fuller recognition and expression of thoughts and feelings arising within the interaction. Miller (1986) describes such consequences of emotional connections as essential to psychological development.

Counselors adopting the relational perspective need to affirm women's relationship orientation as crucial to their psychological development and recognize it as a strength that helps women cope effectively with reality. It can also be a liability that leads to special vulnerabilities in a society where individual achievement and competition are rewarded and emotional isolation is too readily encouraged.

Valuing of Women's Qualities

A second major assumption in the relational perspective is that women's relational qualities are valuable. Men's traditional gender-socialized characteristics mirror those valued in society: autonomous, goal-directed activity, assertion, dominance, competition (see the introduction). In Jordan's (1991) words, "Living in a world which cannot clearly acknowledge the important contribution of emotional reaction and interpersonal sensitivity to thinking, to work, to all aspects of life" (p. 284) causes problems for many women. There is ample evidence that qualities traditionally labeled as the domain of women are devalued relative to masculine qualities (Cook, 1985). Miller (1976) extensively discussed how in a society that does not value the importance of relationships, relationships are relegated to women, who as a group are seen as subordinate to men. Women's differences from men have been viewed as deficiencies and cast in terms such as passivity, dependency, and overemotionality while more positive aspects such as receptivity, concern for others, emotional expressiveness, and capacity for empathy have been ignored. Gilligan (1982) has argued that qualities often perceived as women's weaknesses, including oversensitivity, susceptibility to influence, and indecisiveness, are also in fact the strengths that allow women to arrive at well-informed conclusions by looking at a situation from many angles and understanding its complexity. The relational perspective encourages counselors to consider carefully whether certain feminine characteristics are weaknesses warranting replacement, or strengths deserving buttressing.

MOTHER-DAUGHTER RELATIONSHIPS

Self-in-relation theory was originally formulated as a reaction to views of women commonly advanced by psychoanalytic and object relation approaches to counseling and psychotherapy (cf. Stiver, 1986/1991). Self-in-relation theory has retained emphasis on using self-structure as an important explanatory construct, and on the importance of early childhood experiences, particularly parent-child relationships, in shaping later development. In self-in-relation theory, mother-daughter relationships assume central importance: in forming the early sense of self-in-relation, and in serving as a prototype and foundation of relationships later in life.

Relationships between mothers and daughters are among the most complex and significant of all human relationships. Normal early emotional bonding between mother and infant is a powerful tie. Mothers and daughters seem to connect in especially intricate relationships that usually continue to be mutually important as both individuals grow and change throughout life (Baruch, Barnett, & Rivers, 1983; Chodorow, 1978; Josselson, 1987; Kaplan, Klein, & Gleason, 1985/1991; Surrey, 1984/1991).

Chodorow (1978) suggested that the mother's role as the primary caretaker of infants and young children is an influential model for her daughter. Despite recent social changes toward more sharing of parenting responsibilities, mothers still typically respond to most of the infant's early needs and provide the first strong emotional attachment. For daughters the mother's powerful role as caretaker is complemented by her modeling of what it means to be female. As the young daughter grows up watching her mother go about the business of living her daily life, what she is likely to observe is a woman who devotes time and energy to caring for children, husband or partner, extended family, and often a host of friends and community members. So it is that daughters typically learn to value and identify with nurturing as naturally as they learn to walk and talk.

Surrey (1984/1991) described the mother-daughter relationship as the basis for women's sense of self as a self-in-relation. Emotional bonding and mutual empathy develop between the mother and her infant daughter as a natural consequence of mutual attending. The exchange of feelings within the context of emotional attachment gives both mother and daughter a sense of personal power to influence the other and the relationship between them.

As the infant daughter grows into a young child and eventually becomes an adult woman, her initial dependency and attachment to her mother are refined, elaborated, and transformed as she learns about herself within the context of her relationship with mother. According to Surrey (1984/1991), the woman's very sense of personal identity is developed through the relationship, hence the term self-in-relation. Thus the daughter's task in growing to maturity is not to forge a separate identity from her mother but to develop her individuality within the context of this important emotional bond. As daughters develop in their own right they often discover that they are quite different from mother, and mother-daughter conflicts are common as differences are experienced and expressed.

The mother-daughter relationship is likely to be an important one for a woman throughout her life. The relationship also develops a sense of self-in-relation that will be elaborated throughout life, and it teaches women how to relate to others. Surrey (1984/1991) has argued for the importance of a woman becoming her own mother as part of her psychological maturing: internalizing this special empathic relationship as a way of recognizing her own experiences and bringing them into her relationships with others. Women's relationships and conflicts with their mothers may affect their development throughout their lives (Mercer, Nichols, & Doyle, 1989). Difficulties in the mother-daughter relationship may be reflected throughout life in such diverse realms as achievement conflicts (Stiver, 1982/1991) and eating disorders (Surrey, 1983/1991).

Close relationships between mothers and adult daughters have often been criticized as reflecting inappropriate dependency. However, in the relational perspective, a lifelong connection between mother and daughter seems better understood as a normal phenomenon of female development. In some cases, too much emphasis on mother-daughter issues can lead to mother-blaming when things go awry (Lerner, 1988). Yet a reality-based approach to helping women must take into account the powerful nature of this relationship for both good and ill.

ADOLESCENCE

Adolescence is a crucial period in young women's development. Dramatic bodily changes heralding the beginning of sexual maturity are accompanied by dramatic changes in interpersonal relationships and living situations. Broader social norms concerning appropriate gender-related behavior for adult women are increasingly imposed. And, relationships between mothers and daughters are often especially turbulent.

Many of the changes and indicators of maturity suggest moving away psychologically from parents, as when a young woman moves out of the family home or establishes primary romantic relationships with others. Yet proponents of the relational perspective argue that these indices do not signify the same kind of separation and individuation process in adolescent females as that described in traditional theories based on male developmental patterns (Gilligan, Lyons, & Hamner, 1990; Kaplan, Klein, & Gleason, 1985/1991). Rather, as the young woman negotiates adolescence and makes many new discoveries about herself, she uses her previous experience of growing through connection to attempt to bring new ways of being an individual into her relationship with her mother. These changes often do not proceed smoothly and may be accompanied by disruptions in the mother-daughter relationship. Such disruptions may be very disturbing to the adolescent. Yet, mothers continue to be central persons in their lives. Kaplan, Klein, and Gleason (1985/1991) noted that adolescent women most successful in peer relationships were those who maintained strong connections with their families as they negotiated adolescence.

Adolescence is also a time when young women's self-esteem is especially vulnerable. Recent studies have noted a sharp decline in women's self-esteem in adolescence (American Association of University Women, 1991; Gilligan, Lyons, & Hamner, 1990). A recent special issue of *Women and Therapy* (Gilligan, Rogers, & Tolman, 1991) extensively discussed the relational crisis facing young women, who perceive that to maintain relationships in adulthood, they must disavow themselves as individuals. Yet in doing so they risk undermining genuine relationships so important to them, because such relationships require investment of their "true" selves. Typical adolescent sexual relationships represent one example of how adolescent women learn to stay in a relationship by denying their own needs (Jordan, 1987).

Academically oriented young women face a struggle between their peer group emphasis upon social success and academic/career potential, so highly valued in adult society. Those bright young women who have heretofore enjoyed being good at schoolwork may now be especially at risk for problems in self-esteem and signs of emotional distress. Giftedness in women is at best a mixed blessing, as being accomplished in academics is likely to cause them to feel isolated and at risk for rejection by peers (Kaplan, Klein, & Gleason, 1985/1991; Noble, 1987). Academic settings stressing competitive achievement may minimize women's opportunities for growth, causing low self-esteem and feelings of being personally invalidated even in the face of academic accomplishment (Kaplan, Klein, & Gleason, 1985/1991).

Young women may also hide their intelligence and their competence even from themselves lest they jeopardize their current or possible future relationships. For these young women their highest priority is to establish connection with others, and being too different is risky business (Gilligan, Lyons, & Hamner, 1990; Tannen, 1990). It is still expected that women will be less intelligent, have less education, and be less committed to a career than their male partners

(Noble, 1987). No wonder self-esteem is so vulnerable when being successful in relationships, which is so crucial to feminine identity, seems to be in conflict with being successful in the world at large.

RELATIONSHIPS AND ADULT WOMEN

The relationship orientation developed in childhood comes to full flower in adulthood. Ideally, women participate in increasingly differentiated, complex relationships that continue the psychological development of themselves and others.

In adulthood, women fully encounter social expectations that they will nurture others as the fundamental activity of their life roles. Ideally, adult roles and responsibilities join with a woman's relational orientation and personal preferences to form a richly satisfying life. There are many viable avenues for establishing meaningful human connections that include personal sharing, mutual caring, and mutual benefit. Research has indicated that these connections are a central component of women's lives, offering stresses as well as joys (e.g., Belle, 1987; Wethington, McLeod, & Kessler, 1987).

Women's Relationship Networks

Consistent with social expectations for women, relationships with husbands are commonly the primary relationships in adulthood. Lesbian women also frequently form similarly committed, long-term partnerships, although society is not ready to recognize these as marriages in the legal sense. Living together over a long period of time provides a ready context for shared experiences and mutual acts of nurturing and caring. In addition to emotional intimacy, sexual satisfaction and economic security are highly rewarding aspects of the relationship (e.g., Baruch, Barnett, & Rivers, 1983).

For many women, relationships with children are very important to their satisfaction in life. The quality of these relationships is a significant component of well-being, particularly for mothers who are divorced (Baruch, Barnett, & Rivers, 1983). It seems that divorced mothers may derive a special sense of fulfillment from good relationships with their children and experience a concomitant special sense of failure when there are problems in those relationships. Yet, regardless of marital status, a woman may feel that the demands of motherhood are also burdensome (Barnett & Baruch, 1987) and add significantly to role overload (McBride, 1990).

Intimate friendships with other women, involving sharing feelings and personal details of their lives, are very important to many women (Aries, 1987; Baruch, Barnett, & Rivers, 1983; Josselson, 1987; Vaux, 1985). Worell (1988) described such relationships as self-expressive and disclosing, concerned with each other, and relatively equal in power and sharing of resources. From childhood on, females tend to engage each other in conversations about themselves, each other, and important relationships in their lives (Tannen, 1990). Women's relationships with other women tend to be emotionally closer than men's same-sex relationships (Worell, 1988).

Josselson (1987) suggests that mutually supportive, empowering friendships may serve as anchoring relationships, like a touchstone for staying in touch with oneself. Intimate friendships buffer much of life's stress, including illness, problems in family relationships, and difficult situations in school or on the job.

Female friends are especially important for single women who may live alone and lack the built-in avenues of intimacy that come with having a partner and/or children (Baruch, Barnett, & Rivers, 1983). However, the sustaining support of a close female confidante or two and a network of women friends is likely to be a valuable asset to any woman, whether married or single, employed outside the home or not.

Other relationships such as those with parents, siblings, and extended family as well as co-workers are important to many women. Women generally take major responsibility for caring for parents and in-laws (McBride, 1990) and provide emotional support to many within their relationship network. Women are also likely to seek social support from others more often than men do, and to use a variety of sources of support (Belle, 1987; Worell, 1988). It seems beneficial for women to develop a diverse relational network.

Ideally, women can craft a network of relationships that offer them rich opportunities for mutual empathy, development, and delight with others. Broader social attitudes help to make this undertaking a very challenging one for women. Three attitudes that influence adult women's relationships are (1) traditional social expectations about women's roles; (2) devaluation of women's nurturing activities; and (3) devaluation of relational qualities in the workplace.

Expectations About Women's Roles

So far this chapter has focused mainly on internal and developmental factors that bring relationships into focus as a central issue in women's lives. It is equally important to consider how the social context in which women live out their daily existence is structured to create and reinforce this orientation (Baruch, Barnett, & Rivers, 1983; Deaux & Major, 1987).

Although little girls demonstrate concern about connecting with others and cooperation in their childhood games (Lever, 1976) and even in their use of language (Tannen, 1990), from adolescence on women experience increased social pressures to devote attention to relationships. Being viewed as a successful adult woman in our society is related to meeting rigid standards of physical attractiveness, being involved with a high-status partner, providing support for a network of friends and family, and fulfilling the traditional female roles of wife, mother, and nurturing person.

Gender role expectations have loosened somewhat over the past decade, and large numbers of women are very involved in full- or part-time jobs or careers, whether from economic necessity or to fulfill personal aspirations. However, the rather massive exodus of women from strictly homemaking roles into the workplace has not changed the expectation that women take care of most household and family responsibilities nor has it altered the reality that they do (Baruch, Barnett, & Rivers, 1983; Gilbert & Rachlin, 1987). As Josselson (1987) has noted, success in a job or career is just one more expectation that has been added to our definition of ideal womanhood.

The very act of juggling multiple role expectations can cause women distress from too much responsibility and too little time (McBride, 1990) and from the relationship stresses arising from efforts to negotiate a less stereotypic division of labor at home.

Changes in women's life patterns in recent years mean that less time is available for roles previously defined as full-time responsibilities for women (e.g., taking care of young children, homemaking). While women often find this modern reallocation of time and energies to be crucial to their life satisfaction and self-esteem (Baruch, Biener, & Barnett, 1987), women can also feel guilty about not being "good enough" nurturers of their home and family. For some women, on-the-job behavior that is interpreted as indicating lack of ambition or knowledge about how to compete successfully may actually be an effort to balance home and career priorities. Any new task, however large or small, may threaten this "precarious balance" (Stiver, 1982/1991, p. 228) and cause feelings of anxiety and lack of control.

Women may also not conform to the expected role configuration of wife/mother/homemaker (and increasingly today, paid worker) for a variety of reasons: career commitment, sexual orientation, lack of a suitable partner, infertility, and a host of other personal factors that may or may not be of their choosing. While intimate relationships do contribute significantly to well-being, they do not necessarily have to come in the form of husband or children. Yet women who deviate from social role expectations for their gender can experience negative reactions from others, ranging from unspoken disapproval to forms of interpersonal violence. They may also devalue themselves for not being "real women" (see the next chapter for a complete discussion of such reactions from self and others).

Society's Devaluation of a Relational Orientation

Paradoxically, women who do carry out traditional feminine role responsibilities as expected also frequently experience devaluation of themselves and low self-esteem. While women are expected to be caretakers and keepers of the sacred fires of home and family, these activities are devalued by a society in which competition and individual achievement are the hallmarks of success (Voydanoff, 1988). Keeping a household running smoothly and providing for the multitude of practical and emotional needs of family members is very demanding work. Yet there is no economic compensation for these contributions and often very little recognition or even an expression of appreciation, which can be a significant reward. Nurturing is often taken for granted.

So a woman who devotes enormous time and energy to the very matters society has defined as important to fulfill her feminine role seems to have good reason to feel her contributions are discounted in the social order. For women who have chosen to invest heavily or exclusively in home and family roles, midlife may be a time of significant stress because of the loss of the mother role (Raup & Myers, 1989) or if divorce suddenly forces a new career choice upon them. Women clients at midlife can feel lost and cheated by a reward system that fails to recognize the value of what they have given.

While the career arena presents opportunities for women to gain both economic and personal rewards that contribute significantly to overall well-being (Baruch, Barnett, & Rivers, 1983; Josselson, 1987), the nature of certain work settings and activities can devalue women's relational orientation. Particularly in male-dominated positions, success in the workplace often hinges on individual efforts, instrumental and aggressive behaviors, and the desire to gain a competitive edge. The image of the hard-driving businessman immediately comes to mind. Most work environments are structured on a hierarchical, dominance model, in which status and economic rewards depend on competing successfully with others (Ragins & Sundstrom, 1989). Such a power-and-control-oriented system fosters emotional isolation as it is critical to guard against vulnerability on every front. Operative methods of achieving success in many work settings are inconsistent with establishing connections with others and developing cooperation among members of the community. Women are presented with the dilemma that doing well on the job requires setting aside nurturing and concern for others, values so at the heart of a self-in-relation orientation. When coupled with the subtle and overt discrimination against women still present in many workplaces (e.g., Ragins & Sundstrom, 1989), such circumstances make it unlikely that women's achievement and competence will flourish.

This devaluing of women in the workplace puts many women in a double-bind situation. As members of our society, many women have internalized to some extent the value placed on autonomous, competitive achievement. In particular, professional women are commonly reinforced for vigorously pursuing these values as part of their professional socialization. If they do so, they run the risk of compromising relationships. Self-in-relation theory points out that compromising relationships can feel to women like a violation of their very nature. Yet, choosing to prioritize one's relationships can also result in feeling devalued—by oneself and others. Choosing occupations that directly involve caring for others (e.g., social service) can be a solution for some women, but such occupations also tend to be lower paying and lower status than other occupations promising economic security and advancement (Voydanoff, 1988). There are no easy solutions to such dilemmas, since they reside within a woman's own perceptions of herself and her possibilities in the world.

When women do engage in the dominant and aggressive styles that are the norm for those in leadership roles, they run the risk of being perceived as pushy and bitchy (Tannen, 1990). The term *queen bee* has been used to refer negatively to women who achieve status by competitive behavior. To avoid such labels, some women may withdraw from active competition altogether. Other women may experience competitive behavior as alien to their relational orientation. Stiver (1982/1991) has noted that "when a woman is openly competitive, she frequently experiences herself as aggressive and destructive.... Women are trained to be concerned about other people and to be empathic, so that it is very hard to enjoy vanquishing a rival if one is at the same time empathic with that rival" (p. 230).

Over the past 20 years, many experts (e.g., Horner, 1972) have argued that women also withdraw from competition at school and at work because of a fear of success, an anxiety reflecting the belief that success will have negative consequences for them (Mednick, 1989a). Research on the topic has yielded mixed results (e.g., Henley, 1985; Mednick, 1989a,b), although many practitioners have continued to discuss it as an issue in women's lives (e.g., Stiver, 1982/1991). It does appear that although fear of success is certainly not universally experienced by women, in some situations women may fear that personal achievements will threaten their ability to form or maintain satisfying relationships.

It appears that many women experience a basic incompatibility between their work roles and their relational orientation. Consequently, some women may withdraw from the competitiveness of the work environment to seek greater involvement with home, family, and friends (Josselson, 1987). This incompatibility can be bridged in some respects, however. Recent literature recognizes that some women infuse a commitment to maintaining relationships into their work roles, for example, in how they define their work or relate to colleagues and subordinates (e.g., Grossman & Chester, 1990). Women can also distribute their time and energies in their present careers and over time in ways that combine their priorities for achievement and nurturance (Gallos, 1989). Workplace changes such as work-site child care, improved family leave policies, and flexible work schedules would add greatly to women's comfort and ability to succeed in the job arena by making it more compatible with family and relationship priorities. In the meantime, many women will continue to experience conflict between the demands of a competitive, impersonal work world and fulfilling personal and social gender expectations. Effective counseling must take into account the host of factors that contribute to this dilemma and limit opportunities for equality and satisfaction at work. Counselors can help women to recognize and explore the culturally defined contradictions between a relational orientation and common views about success, and to find personally satisfying ways to affirm what is important to them.

As discussed here, the relational perspective on women's lives asserts that the values and attitudes inherent in the broader sociocultural context do not recognize or validate women's relational orientation. The presence of this context, coupled with the prevalence of dissatisfying relationships in women's lives and a core sense of self in which disappointments in relationships are profoundly invalidating to women, means that relationship difficulties are at the heart of much emotional distress suffered by women.

RELATIONSHIP DIFFICULTIES AND
PSYCHOLOGICAL DISTRESS

The relational perspective places relationships at the heart of women's life roles and responsibilities, so it is not surprising that the sheer stress and strain involved in managing relationships can cause problems for women. Researchers have noted that women are more likely than men to be involved in a broader, emotionally intense relationship network, and to be more emotionally affected by events happening to others (Wethington, McLeod, & Kessler, 1987). Women are likely to be called upon by others in times of crisis and to experience a support gap in which they give more support to others than they receive in return (Belle, 1987). As counselors know well, a similar energy drain contributes to burnout in the helping professions.

Self-in-relation theory would argue, however, that while such demands are certainly stressful to women, they are not necessarily destructive to women's psychological integrity. It is the absence of relationships characterized by true emotional connection or the presence of emotionally disconnected relationships that threatens women's psychological health. Women are disempowered by difficulties they encounter in creating and nurturing a healthy relational context (Miller, 1984/1991; Surrey, 1987/1991).

There are a variety of reasons for relational difficulties, according to Jordan (1986/1991). To attain the empathic mutuality fundamental to psychologically healthy relationships, the commitment and full participation of both partners is required. Problems with empathic relating are complex, involving flexibility of self-boundaries and responsiveness to various affective experiences (Jordan, 1986/1991). Certainly, either partner may suffer from emotional problems, making it difficult to engage in the intimate give-and-take required for genuine mutuality.

Two commonly reported problems more directly address male-female differences. Women clients often report that men do not freely share their own feelings or respond to the feelings of their partners. Also, women are likely to develop a pattern of relating to men in which they do most of the accommodating and nurturing and feel more and more resentful and devalued. Jordan (1986/1991) noted that although practitioners are quick to blame women for developing this pattern, clearly both partners contribute to it.

Such patterns are familiar to many counselors, particularly those engaged in marital or family counseling. What self-in-relation theory emphasizes, however, is that relationships lacking mutuality have emotional consequences for women that extend far beyond disappointment and anger. Because the sense of oneself as a being who facilitates and thrives within deep connections with others is central to women, such nonmutual relationships "can leave women in a constant state of felt loss...the loss of confirmation of their core self-structure as one that can facilitate reciprocity and affective connection in relationships" (Kaplan, 1984/1991, p. 211). According to self-in-relation theory, disconnections from others, whatever their cause, can result in women feeling depressed, inadequate, guilty, and ashamed. Such feelings can arise from specific relationship issues (e.g., a divorce), or a buildup of more subtle disconnections within or across relationships over time. The pain is greatly magnified when others do not recognize the occurrence and consequences of these disconnections (Stiver & Miller, 1988).

Most women will go to great lengths to avoid losing a relationship in which they have invested emotionally. Such a loss is equated with a failure of the self and is often accompanied by severe emotional distress (Kaplan, 1984/1991). Women tend to blame themselves for relationship difficulties, whatever their cause. Some clients cling with great emotional tenacity to relationships that seem to have little purpose other than to make them miserable, and counselors may be prone to label such clients as suffering from unhealthy dependency. However, when understood in the context of the self-in-relation (Surrey, 1984/1991), a client's attempts to preserve these relationships at great cost take on meaning as attempts to hold onto or embellish her own sense of identity. While it may be an ultimate truth that not every relationship can or should be maintained, counselors must take great care to understand the meaning of the client's behavior in the context of her life and to respect her own views of her needs.

The imperative for women to take care of relationships coupled with society's devaluation of women has pervasive consequences for their psychological development. Self-in-relation theory discusses how a woman's early sense of self as a being-in-relation is forever affected by messages that she must defer to others' needs and desires (Miller, 1984/1991; 1991). She is taught that expressing and acting upon her own feelings and needs is destructive to relationships. Such actions can also feel *self*-destructive because of the importance of relationships to her sense of herself. The consequence of this directive is "the loss of the inner voice, of the awareness of one's own needs, desires, or interests in the effort to respond to external expectations" (Surrey, 1983/1991, p. 244). This dynamic is central to women's experience of depression, according to Kaplan (1984/1991). The denial of women's right to act upon their own feelings and desires is fundamental to women's difficulties in expressing anger, in that any expression of anger is seen as too much (Miller, 1983/1991).

Unfortunately, this cycle is self-perpetuating for many women. Self-in-relation theory suggests that women may be able to maintain relationships in a variety of settings and over time through self-inhibition and sacrifice. Such relationships, however, are likely to be further alienating and destructive to women, thus further threatening their core sense of themselves. The only solution for women is to strive for truly mutual, growth-enhancing relationships in which they can value and invest the full range of their perceptions, thoughts, and feelings in reciprocity with another. This process requires self-healing, support, and courage, to be gained only through deeply validating relationships, such as those ideally found in counseling.

IMPLICATIONS FOR COUNSELING WOMEN

The relational perspective on women's lives recognizes mutually empathic, supportive relationships as fundamental to mental health and psychological development throughout life. As already discussed, such growth-producing relationships are possible with a variety of individuals: family of origin, partners and children, friends, and acquaintances. Yet many women clients report feeling anxious and depressed, alienated from others and lonely, unsure about their own identities and unappreciated by others, convinced of their lack of self-worth. Self-in-relation theory explicitly links such commonly reported problems to difficulties in establishing and maintaining mutually empathic, validating relationships with others. Such difficulties may have little to do with a woman's interest in and ability to relate in such an intimate way. For whatever reasons they occur, relationship difficulties are likely to have a profound effect upon a woman's identity and sense of self-worth.

In this section, counseling goals based on these ideas, the nature of the counselor/client relationship, and a brief assessment of the value of this model in counseling women will be discussed.

Counseling Goals

Earlier in this chapter, some common elements in women's psychological problems in their varied forms were noted. First, our society at large has an individualistic bias in that autonomous, goal-directed activity, competitive strivings, and success earned through one's own efforts are prized. In this perspective, relationships with others belong to the "private world" and are not considered important in defining one's self. Second, in our society, women are given the responsibility for nurturing relationships both within and outside of the home. This responsibility tends to be devalued as less important than individual achievement strivings that serve as the focus for men's roles. Third, because women's priorities and experiences are devalued, women feel devalued as individuals as well. Women are aware that what they do well is not very important in a society that rewards individualistic success. Fourth, psychologically healthy relationships require commitment and participation by both partners. These qualities are often lacking in interpersonal relationships, particularly those between men and women. Yet women tend to blame themselves for relationship difficulties regardless of the reasons for the problems. Finally, relationship difficulties can profoundly threaten a woman's core sense of herself, because she tends to experience herself as a being-in-relation *with* others rather than a self-contained person *separate from* others. In an effort to salvage important relationships, many women learn to lose touch with their own perceptions, needs, and feelings. Thus women often enter counseling with low self-esteem and alienated from themselves.

In this perspective, a major theme in counseling is what has happened to a woman's being-in-relationship within a society that expects but does not facilitate or value her commitment to relationships with others. This approach is typically phenomenological in nature, focusing on how the client experiences and understands her world. In particular, this approach explicitly acknowledges relationships as an inseparable part of how she experiences herself as a person.

Jordan (1991) provides a succinct description of the purpose of counseling/therapy consistent with this orientation:

> Concerns about relationships lead many people, particularly women, into therapy in which a primary goal is to expand the experience of what might be called the sense of "real self," particularly in ongoing relationships....In its broadest sense, therapy offers an opportunity to expand relational presence, providing a sense of realness and contact with one's own inner experience and with the other's subjective experience. The route to this change is through the enhancement of empathy, both for other and for self....The goal in therapy is...to provide an opportunity to develop a new integration of self-other experience in which the validity of one's own experience as well as the other's gets acknowledged. This occurs in current real relationship and in memory organization of relationships. (pp. 283–284)

The context of counseling in this perspective is always the same: The ultimate goal is to enhance women's ability to function in relationships where they experience a sense of mutuality and wholeness. The focus for an individual client is diverse, to address her own experiences and skills in relationships. Some examples include—

- the impact of abusive relationships (past and present) on how she experiences self and others in relationship

- the degree of alienation she experiences from her own thoughts and feelings

- her willingness and ability to bring such self-experiences into relationships, and the reactions she anticipates from others if she were to do so
- disappointments in relationships she has suffered because of others' inability to relate fully to her
- conflicts she experiences in her life between her relational priorities and achievement strivings (e.g., on the job or in school)
- struggles between efforts to develop herself as a unique person while remaining in relationship with others (e.g., with parents or partner)
- grief over relationship losses, especially those that others have not validated for her (e.g., miscarriage; alienation of a best friend)

Women seek professional help for a variety of reasons. However, implicit in each client's situation is some deficiency in the relational context that inhibits effective functioning and/or further development. A good counseling relationship provides the empathic relational context in which she can explore, grieve, validate, and ultimately enhance her experiences of self as a relational being.

The Counseling Process

Carl Rogers (1951) suggested four decades ago that a facilitative human relationship between counselor and client is the central condition for therapeutic change. This potent interpersonal connection is a source of strength and stability, and it empowers the client to explore and move in the direction of growth. The relationship is a safe context in which to try out new ways of being. This is particularly crucial for women, whose independence, self-confidence, and differentiation develop within the context of attachment.

Self-in-relation theory was developed to ameliorate the biases associated with traditional psychoanalytic and object relations approaches, which were dominant theories of the time. In these approaches, counselors' emotional reactions are interpreted as countertransference, which is believed to interfere with the helping process because of the counselor's own emotional vulnerabilities.

While there has been enormous evolution in the theory and practice of counseling and psychotherapy since the early analysts began their work, the concepts of therapeutic distance and objectivity have endured in many professionals' minds as core conditions of effective helping (Stiver, 1985/1991).

Much of the discussion on the counseling/therapy process within the self-in-relation literature is aimed at refuting the idea that these conditions are necessary or even very helpful to women clients. Many counselors will find the ideas on process presented here to be second nature to them already, although for others these ideas might propose a "re-vision" of the interaction between counselor and client.

Caring

To foster women's development, what is most important is a relationship characterized by caring that is both felt and communicated. Strong professional prohibitions against overinvolvement with clients can keep counselors from freely offering the caring human connection that is lacking in women's lives and needed to empower their growth (Stiver, 1985/1991). This lack perpetuates low self-esteem as women continue to search for what they intuitively know they need but that is apparently not available to them. A client who finds her desperate search for interpersonal validation once again frustrated in the counseling relationship may be thrown into a crisis that could have been avoided by giving more careful attention to her needs.

Women clients benefit from a caring relationship characterized by what Rogers (1951) called warmth. They need to know that the counselor is there for them and involved, caring for and accepting their uniqueness. Stiver (1985/1991) makes an important distinction between this kind of caring and caretaking, the latter being a hyper-responsible stance akin to that of an overprotective parent.

It is also important that counselors be able to accept reciprocal caring from women clients, who are often seeking confirmation that they are giving as well as receiving something of value. The role distinction between counselor and client may cause counselors to be uncomfortable with or reject clients' expressions of genuine concern and warmth, causing a blow to clients' self-esteem. Counselors need to admit that their professional relationships are empowering for themselves as well. This recognition is consistent with a more egalitarian counselor-client relationship, which has long been advocated by proponents of gender-sensitive counseling for women (e.g., Gilbert, 1980; Good, Gilbert, & Scher, 1990; Rawlings & Carter, 1977). However, counselors must maintain responsibility for keeping appropriate professional boundaries in relationships with clients, to avoid exploiting clients to meet their own sexual and emotional needs.

Empathy and Genuineness

Empathy is a key factor in working with women clients. As Rogers (1951) suggested, in order to be helpful to the client, a counselor must be able to grasp her view of the world as if it were the counselor's own and communicate this understanding effectively. The role of empathy in women's development of a self-in-relation is crucial (Jordan, 1984/1991; Surrey, 1984/1991). A good therapeutic connection is based on the counselor's capacity to empathize with the client.

The as-if quality of empathy is very important, since clearly counselors often discover that many clients see the world very differently. To help the client, counselors need to assume that her view of the world has a legitimate basis from her own experience, and counselors need to understand what that experience has been. For example, a very high proportion of female clients have been victims of childhood incest or other sexual abuse (Courtois, 1988). This experience of being betrayed by people who seemed to offer warmth and should have been most nurturing and trustworthy seems logically to lead the client to view the world as an unpredictable and dangerous place. Women who have been so victimized often find it very difficult to trust in the counseling relationship, which is entirely understandable in light of their experience.

To build an alliance with such a client, counselors need to understand what has happened to her and communicate acceptance of her view as legitimate and self-protective on the basis of her experience. This affirmation is very empowering to the client, and in some cases it may be the first time she can remember being so validated. Thus empathy is healing, as the client feels understood and accepted for being as she is and can then understand and trust herself as she risks making personal changes.

Women clients can also especially benefit from a counseling relationship in which the counselor shares his or her own real self. Women clients generally respond positively to the power-equalizing aspects of counselor genuineness. Women experience disempowerment in so many ways in our society (see O'Neil and Egan's chapter). The counseling relationship is by its very nature unequal in the power each participant has to define the relationship and its parameters. Women clients may be especially likely to feel disempowered in a therapeutic dyad where the counselor is male, because this situation replicates the power difference they experience in other areas of life. However, female-female counseling dyads also have potential to exaggerate the client's sense of powerlessness. Counselor genuineness that reflects the counselor's humanness and vulnerability is powerful in establishing the kind of connection women clients seek to further their development. Counselors can also model appropriate interpersonal behavior and self-acceptance of vulnerabilities and limitations.

This discussion indicates that for women clients the quality of the interpersonal connection with the counselor is central to therapeutic change. This statement is a basic working assumption in many counseling approaches today. However, *why* this assumption has significance in self-in-relation theory is worth noting. Counseling relationships work not simply because they provide the medium for therapeutic change (via cognitive restructuring, behavioral rehearsal, and the like). They work because it is only through such relationships, characterized by deep trust, commitment to the relationship, and sharing and validation of each other's thoughts and feelings, that psychological development takes place. Effective counselors are able to use the immediate relationship to increase clients' ability to understand themselves as relational beings; to become aware of, to value, and to be able to invest their own selves in relationships with others; to engage in relationships that validate themselves as unique individuals while enhancing the uniqueness of others; to engage in interactions that serve to deepen the mutuality that each participant experiences within the relationship. To act as the midwife of a new relational reality for the client is indeed the art of counseling.

The counseling approach espoused here reinforces other conclusions about the counseling process made in recent years (e.g., Strupp, 1988). It is interesting to note that these views of what is therapeutic for women (and for men as well) hinge upon provision of a caring and nurturing context for growth—qualities our society associates with the feminine. Clearly, such qualities are not the exclusive domain of women, and professionals of both sexes may or may not be able to provide gender-sensitive counseling for women based upon their own personal characteristics, training, and experience. It certainly appears true that counselors' own comfort and ability to function within such relationships depends on their personal experiences with them. Is it also possible that the undervaluing of feminine strengths in our society has compromised counselors' ability to create a relationship with clients based on such qualities? Might counselors look for more definitive and measurable strategies of helping in part because the complexity of establishing and maintaining such relationships exhausts and eludes them as individuals? Proponents of self-in-relation theory would be likely to say yes.

REFLECTIONS ON THE RELATIONAL PERSPECTIVE

It would be difficult to overestimate the influence of this relational perspective on theory, research, and practice focused upon women today. These ideas are frequently discussed among women with a respect bordering on reverence. Such universal regard, however, also triggers an automatic skepticism in many counselors. Do these ideas merit such approbation?

As intuitively wise as the relational perspective seems to many counselors, it is not comprehensive in some important respects. While the mother-daughter relationship serves as a central theme, the literature is virtually silent on the father-daughter relationship, or on sibling or extended family relationships. A complete portrait of children's development within relationships today would need to place mother-daughter relationships within a context that recognizes other caretakers. Some experts (e.g., Lerner, 1988) have feared that the focus upon relationships with mother may perpetuate in a benign form the traditional attribution of sole responsibility for a child's early development to the mother. Mother glorification and mother blaming are flip sides of the same coin. Counselors need to give more attention to how the mother-child relationship occurs within the context of other relationships, which may enhance, challenge, or supplant it in importance within a child's life.

It is this lack of attention to contextual factors that has generated the most criticism for the relational perspective. Differences between the sexes are rooted within a sex-segregated society that treats the sexes differently throughout their lives (see Lott, 1985). Critics of the relational perspective have argued that it does not adequately recognize the impact of broader sociopolitical influences upon women's lives. Focusing upon women's relational issues may obscure the impact of factors such as economic dependency or legal restrictions upon women's lives (see Enns, 1991). The relational perspective certainly does not preclude consideration of such factors, but it might be easy for some counselors to overlook their importance if they focus exclusively upon an individual's relationship problems and relational solutions.

A major category of influences in women's lives that receives insufficient attention is the impact of racial/ethnic factors and class differences. Jordan, Kaplan, Miller, Stiver, and Surrey (1991) recognized in the introduction to their book that their ideas are clearly limited by their own life experiences, and that "we do not want to repeat the error of other theoreticians: speaking as if there is one voice, one reality for humans, for women, when in fact we recognize the exquisite contextuality of human life" (p. 7). How recognition of diversity might change the relational perspective on women has not been developed. Brown (1990) asserted that much feminist theory and research is based on central assumptions that are oriented toward white, Western, and middle- to upper class experiences (e.g., the nature of "usual" family structures). Gender may not be equally salient in the lives of women of color, poor women, and others. Counselors need to take seriously Brown's statement that an individual's internal reality may be influenced by a variety of external experiences and that women may or may not experience themselves in a similar way.

The issue of commonality across women's experiences—and differences from men—has provoked the largest controversy about the relational perspective. Portraits of women's relational nature versus men's individualistic nature ring true for many counselors based on their own experiences. Yet research on gender has repeatedly indicated the presence of extensive overlap between the sexes and variability within each sex on a wide range of variables (e.g., Cook, 1985). How likely is it that women as a group share a basic nature that is fundamentally different from that of men? Research within the relational perspective has often focused just upon women (e.g., Belenky, Clinchy, Goldberger, & Tarule, 1986), making comparisons with men difficult, or it has suggested that there may indeed be more overlap between the sexes than first thought (cf. Mednick, 1989b; Wallston, 1987).

Mednick (1989b) argued that recent theories about women's "differentness" from men have become immediately popular for a variety of reasons. It is very human to overemphasize personal (rather than situational) factors as causes of others' behavior and to believe our own experiences rather than scientific evidence. (Recent debates concerning the validity of standard empirical evidence are beyond the present discussion.) Such theories are consistent with perceptions about familiar gender stereotypes, albeit with different values about them. And, Mednick speculated, theories about the sexes' differentness mesh nicely with recent conservative political sentiment about women and the family. The relational perspective does *not* recommend traditional gender-role differentiation, but the relational perspective is certainly more palatable to proponents of traditional gender roles than views of gender differences as products of a repressive social structure. Regardless of why the relational perspective has been so attractive, Mednick feared that failure to recognize the role of sociopolitical factors in gender issues might focus too much on personal change and too little on the need to change society itself.

The relational perspective is open to critique and modification. Self-in-relation theorists have been careful to portray their work as works in progress, continually open to reexamination and revision. In particular, counselors should consider whether a dichotomization of the sexes' basic nature is indeed essential to the theory. For example, it is also possible that self-in-relation theory describes a way of being in the world that might be more typical of some groups of women for a variety of reasons, but that may be descriptive of many men as well (and not of some women). In this vein, Lawler (1990) described these ideas as proposing a different path of development available to all. The danger in both paths is one of excess, and she recommended a harmony within a person of separation and connection. Embracing a self-in-relation as a reality for men would mean that counselors would need to give much more attention to how such an orientation develops and operates in the world as diverse individuals experience it.

REFERENCES

American Association of University Women (1991). *Shortchanging girls: Shortchanging America*. Washington, DC: Author.

Aries, E. (1987). Gender and communication. In P. Shaver & C. Hendrick (Eds.), *Sex and gender* (pp. 149–176). Newbury Park, CA: Sage.

Barnett, R. C., & Baruch, G. K. (1987). Social roles, gender, and psychological distress. In R. C. Barnett, L. Biener, & G. K. Baruch (Eds.), *Gender and stress* (pp. 122–143). New York: The Free Press.

Baruch, G., Barnett, R., & Rivers, C. (1983). *Lifeprints.* New York: Signet.

Baruch, G. K., Biener, L., & Barnett, R. C. (1987). Women and gender in research on work and family stress. *American Psychologist, 42,* 130–136.

Belenky, M. F., Clinchy, B. M., Goldberger, N. R., & Tarule, J. M. (1986). *Women's ways of knowing.* New York: Basic Books.

Belle, D. (1987). Gender differences in the social moderators of stress. In R. C. Barnett, L. Biener, & G. K. Baruch (Eds.), *Gender and stress* (pp. 257–277). New York: The Free Press.

Brown, L. S. (1990). The meaning of a multicultural perspective for theory building in feminist therapy. *Women and Therapy, 9,* 1–21.

Chodorow, N. (1978). *The reproduction of mothering.* Berkeley: University of California Press.

Cook, E. P. (1985). *Psychological androgyny.* Elmsford, NY: Pergamon.

Courtois, C. (1988). *Healing the incest wound: Adult survivors in therapy.* New York: Norton.

Deaux, K., & Major, B. (1987). Putting gender in context: An interactive model of gender-related behavior. *Psychological Review, 94,* 369–389.

Enns, C. Z. (1991). The "new" relationship models of women's identity: A review and critique for counselors. *Journal of Counseling and Development, 69,* 209–217.

Gallos, J. V. (1989). Exploring women's development: Implications for career theory, practice, and research. In M. B. Arthur, D. T. Hall, & B. S. Lawrence (Eds.), *Handbook of career theory* (pp. 110–132). Cambridge, England: Cambridge University Press.

Gilbert, L. A. (1980). Feminist therapy. In A. N. Brodsky & R. Hare-Mustin (Eds.), *Women and psychotherapy: An assessment of research and practice* (pp. 245–265). New York: Guilford.

Gilbert, L. A., & Rachlin, V. (1987). Mental health and psychological functioning of dual career families. *The Counseling Psychologist, 15,* 7–49.

Gilligan, C. (1982). *In a different voice.* Cambridge, MA: Harvard University Press.

Gilligan, C., Lyons, N. P., & Hamner, T. J. (Eds.) (1990). *Making connections.* Cambridge, MA: Harvard University Press.

Gilligan, C., Rogers, A. G., & Tolman, D. L. (Eds.) (1991). Women, girls, and psychotherapy: Reframing resistance. *Women and Therapy, 11.*

Good, G. E., Gilbert, L. A., & Scher, M. (1990). Gender aware therapy: A synthesis of feminist therapy and knowledge about gender. *Journal of Counseling and Development, 68,* 376–380.

Grossman, H. Y., & Chester, N. L. (Eds.) (1990). *The experience and meaning of work in women's lives.* Hillsdale, NJ: Erlbaum.

Henley, N. (1985). Psychology and gender. *Signs: Journal of Women in Culture and Society, 11,* 104–119.

Horner, M. S. (1972). Toward an understanding of achievement related conflicts in women. *Journal of Social Issues, 28,* 157–175.

Jordan, J. V. (1984/1991). Empathy and self-boundaries. In J. V. Jordan, A. G. Kaplan, J. B. Miller, I. P. Stiver, & J. L. Surrey, *Women's growth in connection: Writings from the Stone Center* (Work in Progress No. 16) (pp. 67–80). New York: Guilford.

Jordan, J. V. (1986/1991). The meaning of mutuality. In J. V. Jordan, A. G. Kaplan, J. B. Miller, I. P. Stiver, & J. L. Surrey (Eds.), *Women's growth in connection: Writings from the Stone Center* (Work in Progress No. 23) (pp. 81–96). New York: Guilford.

Jordan, J. V. (1987). *Clarity in connection: Empathic knowing, desire, and sexuality* (Work in Progress No. 29). Wellesley, MA: Stone Center for Developmental Services and Studies.

Jordan, J. V. (1991). Empathy, mutuality and therapeutic change: Clinical implications of a relational model. In J. V. Jordan, A. G. Kaplan, J. B. Miller, I. P. Stiver, & J. L. Surrey (Eds.), *Women's growth in connection: Writings from the Stone Center* (pp. 283–289). New York: Guilford.

Jordan, J. V., Kaplan, A. G., Miller, J. B., Stiver, I. P., & Surrey, J. L. (Eds.) (1991). *Women's growth in connection: Writings from the Stone Center.* New York: Guilford.

Josselson, R. (1987). *Finding herself: Pathways to identity development in women.* San Francisco: Jossey-Bass.

Kaplan, A. (1984/1991). The "self-in-relation": Implications for depression in women. In J. V. Jordan, A. G. Kaplan, J. B. Miller, I. P. Stiver, & J. L. Surrey (Eds.) *Women's growth in connection: Writings from the Stone Center* (Work in Progress No. 14) (pp. 206–222). New York: Guilford.

Kaplan, A., Klein, R., & Gleason, N. (1985/1991). Women's self development in late adolescence. In J. V. Jordan, A. G. Kaplan, J. B. Miller, I. P. Stiver, & J. L. Surrey (Eds.), *Women's growth in connection: Writings from the Stone Center* (Work in Progress No.17) (pp. 122–140). New York: Guilford.

Lawler, A. C. (1990). The healthy self: Variations on a theme. *Journal of Counseling and Development, 68,* 652–654.

Lerner, H. G. (1988). *Women in therapy.* New York: Aronson.

Lever, J. (1976). Sex differences in the games children play. *Social Problems, 23,* 478–487.

Lott, B. (1985). The potential enrichment of social/personality psychology through feminist research and vice versa. *American Psychologist, 40,* 155–164.

McBride, A. B. (1990). Mental health effects of women's multiple roles. *American Psychologist, 45,* 381–384.

Mednick, M. T. (1989a). Fear of success. In H. Tierney (Ed.), *Women's studies encyclopedia, Vol. I* (pp. 132–133). New York: Greenwood Press.

Mednick, M. T. (1989b). On the politics of psychological constructs: Stop the bandwagon, I want to get off. *American Psychologist, 44,* 1118–1123.

Mercer, R. T., Nichols, E. G., & Doyle, G. C. (1989). *Transitions in a woman's life: Major life events in developmental context.* New York: Springer.

Miller, J. B. (1976). *Toward a new psychology of women.* Boston: Beacon Press.

Miller, J. B. (1983/1991). The construction of anger in women and men. In J. V. Jordan, A. G. Kaplan, J. B. Miller, I. P. Stiver, & J. L. Surrey (Eds.), *Women's growth in connection: Writings from the Stone Center* (Work in Progress No. 83–01) (pp. 181–196). New York: Guilford.

Miller, J. B. (1984/1991). The development of a woman's sense of self. In J. V. Jordan, A. G. Kaplan, J. B. Miller, I. P. Stiver, & J. L. Surrey, *Women's growth in connection: Writings from the Stone Center.* (Work in Progress No. 12) (pp. 11–26). New York: Guilford.

Miller, J. B. (1986). *What do we mean by relationships?* (Work in Progress No. 22). Wellesley, MA: Stone Center for Developmental Services and Studies.

Miller, J. B. (1991). Women and power. In J. V. Jordan, A. G. Kaplan, J. B. Miller, I. P. Stiver, & J. L. Surrey (Eds.), *Women's growth in connection: Writings from the Stone Center* (pp. 197–205). New York: Guilford.

Noble, K. D. (1987). The dilemma of the gifted woman. *Psychology of Women Quarterly, 11,* 367–378.

Ragins, B. R., & Sundstrom, E. (1989). Gender and power in organizations: A longitudinal perspective. *Psychological Bulletin, 105,* 51–88.

Raup, J. L., & Myers, J. E. (1989). The empty nest syndrome: Myth or reality? *Journal of Counseling and Development, 68,* 180–183.

Rawlings, E. I., & Carter, D. K. (Eds.) (1977). *Psychotherapy for women: Treatment towards equality.* Springfield, IL: Charles Thomas.

Rogers, C. (1951). *Client-centered therapy.* Boston: Houghton-Mifflin.

Spence, J. T. (1985). Achievement American style: The rewards and costs of individualism. *American Psychologist, 40,* 1285–1295.

Stiver, I. P. (1982/1991). Work inhibitions in women. In J. V. Jordan, A. G. Kaplan, J. B. Miller, I. P. Stiver, & J. L. Surrey (Eds.), *Women's growth in connection: Writings from the Stone Center* (Work in Progress No. 3) (pp. 223–236). New York: Guilford.

Stiver, I. P. (1985/1991). The meaning of care: Reframing treatment models. In J. V. Jordan, A. G. Kaplan, J. B. Miller, I. P. Stiver, & J. L. Surrey, *Women's growth in connection: Writings from the Stone Center* (Work in Progress No. 20) (pp. 250–267). New York: Guilford.

Stiver, I. P. (1986/1991). Beyond the Oedipus complex: Mothers and daughters. In J. V. Jordan, A. G. Kaplan, J. B. Miller, I. P. Stiver, & J. L. Surrey (Eds.), *Women's growth in connection: Writings from the Stone Center* (Work in Progress No. 26) (pp. 97–121). New York: Guilford.

Stiver, I. P., & Miller, J. B. (1988). *From depression to sadness in women's psychotherapy.* (Work in Progress No. 36). Wellesley, MA: Stone Center for Developmental Services and Studies.

Strupp, H. H. (1988). Commentary. *Psychotherapy, 25,* 182–184.

Surrey, J. L. (1983/1991). Eating patterns as a reflection of women's development. In J. V. Jordan, A. G. Kaplan, J. B. Miller, I. P. Stiver, & J. L. Surrey (Eds.), *Women's growth in connection: Writings from the Stone Center* (Work in Progress No. 9) (pp. 237–249). New York: Guilford.

Surrey, J. (1984/1991). The "self-in-relation": A theory of women's development. In J. V. Jordan, A. G. Kaplan, J. B. Miller, I. P. Stiver, & J. L. Surrey (Eds.), *Women's growth in connection: Writings from the Stone Center* (Work in Progress No. 13) (pp. 51–66). New York: Guilford.

Surrey, J. (1987/1991). Relationship and empowerment. In J. V. Jordan, A. G. Kaplan, J. B. Miller, I. P. Stiver, & J. L. Surrey (Eds.), *Women's growth in connection: Writings from the Stone Center* (Work in Progress No. 30) (pp. 162–180). New York: Guilford.

Tannen, D. T. (1990). *You just don't understand.* New York: William Morrow.

Vaux, A. (1985). Variations in social support associated with gender, ethnicity, and age. *Journal of Social Issues, 41,* 89–110.

Voydanoff, P. (1988). Women, work, and family: Bernard's perspective on the past, present, and future. *Psychology of Women Quarterly, 12,* 269–280.

Wallston, B. S. (1987). Social psychology of women and gender. *Journal of Applied Social Psychology, 17,* 1025–1050.

Wethington, E., McLeod, J. D., & Kessler, R. C. (1987). The importance of life events for explaining sex differences in psychological distress. In R. C. Barnett, L. Biener, & G. K. Baruch (Eds.), *Gender and stress* (pp. 144–156). New York: The Free Press.

Worell, J. (1988). Women's satisfaction in close relationships. *Clinical Psychology Review, 8,* 477–498.

Note: The dual reference notations for some material published in Jordan et al.'s book identify when the reprinted article was originally published, and the Work in Progress number is useful in ordering single copies of the original publication from the Stone Center for Developmental Services and Studies, Wellesley College, 106 Central St., Wellesley, MA 02181-8268.

Abuses of Power Against Women: Sexism, Gender Role Conflict, and Psychological Violence

James M. O'Neil and Jean Egan

Power, sexism, gender role conflict, and psychological violence are interrelated concepts that affect women's lives and deserve more attention by mental health practitioners. How power negatively affects women has received limited attention in the counseling and psychological literature. Women have gained power over the last few decades, but many still feel powerless because of personal and institutional sexism. There are numerous examples of alleged power imbalances and abuses directed at women. In 1991–1992 alone, the American public witnessed the William Kennedy Smith and Mike Tyson rape trials, the Clarence Thomas–Anita Hill Senate Hearings, and the endless debates over abortion. These media events again underscore the importance of understanding the complex relationship between women, power, and patriarchal sexism in our society.

Note: This chapter was supported by a grant from the Research Foundation of the University of Connecticut. Parts of this chapter were presented at the 99th and 100th annual conventions of the American Psychological Association in San Francisco, CA (August 1991) and Washington, DC (August 1992). We would like to express our appreciation to the three reviewers of this chapter and to Ellen Cook, who all provided helpful comments and critique. Ellen's ongoing critique was particularly helpful in resolving some of the conceptual dilemmas that we faced in explaining power abuses against women.

In the 1970s, conflicts between the sexes occurred because of changing gender roles and the influence of feminism. These changes in gender roles resulted in power losses to men and what Kahn (1984) describes as a "power war" between men and women. During the 1980s, questions were raised about men's use of power in work and interpersonal relationships. Feminists made critical analyses of how sexism and patriarchy are responsible for men's power over women. These analyses exposed male privilege and explained how women live in a sexist world that limits their power, roles, and human rights. Complicated power struggles between men and women often went unlabeled or were reduced to the axiom of the "battle of the sexes." Both women and men experienced difficulty adjusting to these interpersonal dynamics, and few models have evolved that demonstrate power sharing and equity between men and women.

What is needed in the 1990s is a more definitive vocabulary to allow dialogue about power issues in work and love. With rising levels of violence toward women and children in families, an understanding of power dynamics between the sexes is of critical importance. Few paradigms exist that help men and women communicate about power abuses and resolve their conflicts in nonviolent and equitable ways. Many couples "walk on the edges" of their power dynamics in their daily lives without facing the central themes that produce conflict. Women have legitimate anger about men's abuses of power and sexist control of their lives. Men who are unaware of sexism may wallow in denial and defensiveness or have polite exchanges that maintain the power patterns that subordinate women. Under these conditions, the truth about personal and institutional sexism as abuses of power never emerges. The outcomes of these sexist interactions are conflict, struggles, stress, and psychological pain.

Counselors can become experts in assessing the power dynamics in women's and men's lives. Many women express powerlessness and frustrations in their relationships with men. Furthermore, the despair that many women clients express is usually a result of these feelings of powerlessness. These women may not know how to obtain power, may not own or use the power they have, or may use power inappropriately in their relationships. Counselors can make more specific assessments of how power abuses are a destructive aspect of women's relationships. The goals of this chapter are (1) to explore how sexism and gender role socialization contribute to women's problems with power, and (2) to present a preliminary set of ideas that promote a more elaborate assessment of how abuses of power are expressed toward women.

There are several assumptions that parallel the different sections of the chapter. We specify 10 assumptions that provide a context for ideas about abuses of power against women:

1. How power is gained, lost, used, and abused is a complex issue.

2. Past definitions of power have not explained how sex and gender roles affect the exercise of power.

3. Patriarchy and sexism produce power conflicts and abuses of power between men and women.

4. Gender role socialization, power conflicts, and abuses between men and women are directly related.

5. Changing gender roles contribute to increased power conflicts between men and women.

6. Women experience gender role conflicts related to power because of their gender role socialization and the effects of patriarchal sexist structures.

7. When men's dominant position is used unfairly against women, abuses of power can occur.

8. Women can personally experience abuses of power as gender role devaluations, restrictions, and violations.

9. Power conflicts need to be assessed in a situational context in terms of power conflicts (1) caused by others, (2) within the woman, and (3) expressed toward others.

10. Psychological violence can occur between men and women, causing abuses of power against women.

In this chapter, we argue that patriarchy is one of the fundamental organizing principles of our society. Sexism maintains patriarchy by enforcing a primarily masculine worldview. Keeping women in less powerful positions through personal and institutional sexism maintains the patriarchal status quo and fosters women's powerlessness. In addition, the sexes are socialized to different processes with respect to personal power in families, in schools, and with peers. This socialization with respect to power makes the sexes potentially dysfunctional with each other.

Abuses of power against women in a patriarchal, sexist society are quite common. Women's assertion of their own power is often punished and considered inappropriate, while men's assertion of power is often expected and encouraged. Men can devalue, restrict, and violate women to maintain their sexist advantage. Women may also react to their own powerlessness by asserting their power in abusive ways or by devaluing, restricting, or violating themselves. The end result of these dysfunctional power dynamics is the disempowerment of women, whether caused by themselves or by others. Psychological as well as physical violence can be the consequence.

Through counseling, women can learn to understand the dynamics and consequences of gender-related power issues and to take responsibility for resolving conflicts that inhibit their own empowerment. To promote women's empowerment, counselors can more expertly assess women clients' conflicts with power. We make recommendations for counselors of women using the concepts in this chapter.

THE COMPLEXITY OF POWER: PATRIARCHY, SEXISM, GENDER ROLE SOCIALIZATION, GENDER ROLE CONFLICT, ABUSES OF POWER, AND PSYCHOLOGICAL VIOLENCE

Using the assumptions above, Figure 1 depicts the complexity of factors affecting the power and gender role dynamics in men's and women's lives. The relationships among these factors are discussed in the remainder of the chapter. Two triangular levels of analysis depict how power and gender roles interact at both a macro-societal and micro-interpersonal level. The macro-societal level is represented by the outer triangle. This level includes three factors: (1) patriarchal and sexist structures as organizers of society, (2) personal and institutional sexism against women, and (3) differential gender role socialization of the sexes that produces power differences. The bidirectional arrows for these three factors indicate that societal patriarchy, sexism, and gender role socialization are directly related to one another in complex ways. These three factors represent the political-social etiology of abuses of power against women.

The inner triangle depicts the micro-interpersonal expression of the macro-societal factors. These factors include (1) women's and men's gender role conflict, (2) power conflicts and abuses of power

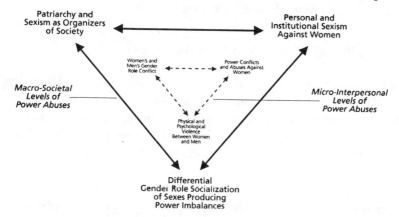

Figure 1. Factors explaining the macro-societal and micro-interpersonal levels of power abuses.

against women, and (3) physical and psychological violence between men and women. The bidirectional arrows indicate that power conflicts and abuses, gender role conflict, and psychological violence are related to one another in complex ways. Whether power abuses cause gender role conflict, or vice versa, is affected by the individual involved and the situational context. Likewise, whether power conflicts and gender role conflict cause psychological violence, or vice versa, also depends on the situation and the individuals involved. It is difficult to state categorically which of these factors causes the other because of the variability of situations and people's different gender role socialization experiences.

The question of how power abuses relate to men's and women's socialization and how they cause gender role conflict and psychological violence has gone unexplored. Power abuses, psychological violence, and gender role conflict are all complexly interrelated in ways that defy simple explanation. When men and women face this complexity, there may be difficulty in communicating and problem solving. Many times the complexity is reduced to anger, misunderstanding, and hopeless despair. What is rarely discussed, but usually clear, is that women's and men's lives are negatively affected by the relationship of power and gender roles. In the context of the model in Figure 1, the complexity of power and gender dynamics is discussed in the following sections.

Defining Power From a Gender Role Perspective

Power has many definitions and is a multifaceted concept (Boulding, 1989). Traditional definitions of power have referred to having the ability to mobilize others to accomplish things, having control over resources (DuBrin, 1990), and being able to get things done (Hunsaker & Hunsaker, 1986). Power refers to the capacity to influence the actions of others without undue coercion (Robbins, 1989). Power determines which goals are pursued and how resources are used. Power has also been described as the ability to compel obedience (Russell, 1969). French (1985) describes two types of power in our society: (1) "power to," which refers to capacity, ability, and implies freedom, and (2) "power over," which refers to domination of others. French argues that power over, or domination, is the goal of most institutions, including the military, businesses, churches, and the government. Individuals can also use power over others, leading to power conflicts in many interpersonal relationships.

Robbins (1989) makes a distinction between the sources of power and bases of power. *Bases of power* are the tools of using power and include coercion, reward, persuasion, and knowledge. *Sources of power* refers to where power emanates from and include position, expertise, information, and personal characteristics. From a different perspective, DuBrin (1990) distinguishes between position and personal power. *Position power* is defined by one's status or legally sanctioned role. In a sexist society, women's power is usually defined as less than men's in terms of position power. Women's position has been defined through their role in the home (see preceding chapter) and has long been devalued as unimportant in our masculine, male-dominated society. *Personal power* is defined by one's personality and ability to influence others. For women, personal power has been stereotypically attributed to feminine and physical characteristics such as beauty and charm. These characteristics are typically viewed as weak in the male-dominated world.

Past definitions of power have not focused on how gender roles mediate power relations. On the whole, the traditional definitions have not addressed how power affects relationships between men and women. For example, French and Raven (1959) do not discuss any sex differences with their sources of power. Frieze, Parsons, Johnson, Ruble, and Zellman (1978) give an informative analysis of women and power, but little mention of power dynamics between the sexes. In Boulding's (1989) excellent analysis of power, gender role and sex differences are unexplored. Miller (1986) has developed a new definition of power for women, but its implications for cross-sex relationships are not explored. Kahn's (1984) analysis of men's power loss does provide the integrative thought needed, explaining how gender roles and power issues interact in men's and women's lives. The recognition that sex and gender role stereotypes are critical parts of men's control and power over women has not been fully explored in feminist writings. New definitions of power are needed that incorporate the realities of sexism and the differing gender role socialization of men and women.

Through the gender role socialization process, men and women learn different perspectives on power that affect their interpersonal dynamics. Such perspectives are also supported by current sociopolitical realities of sex and gender role stereotypes.

For the purposes of this chapter, our definition of power focuses on how gender roles define men's and women's sources and bases of power. Power is operationally defined as the need to influence and control others to express personal gender role values and establish (or maintain) one's gender role identity. From this perspective, the use of power solidifies a person's self-identity and personal identity based on gender role values and attitudes. There are many demands on individuals to develop their self-identity through socially sanctioned, gender role attitudes and behaviors. Personal identity and self-identity, as they relate to one's gender role identity, are primary bases and sources of power for a person.

The nature of this definition does not always reflect a healthy notion of personal power. This definition of power relies exclusively on sexist stereotypes as a basis for personal and gender role identity. This focused definition of power does not exclude alternative motives for using power in relationships. For example, power may be positively used to ensure personal control, economic gain, status, self-esteem or identity. Exercising power to ensure these outcomes may or may not be relevant to a person's gender role identity.

Men's socialization conditions them to use power over women to validate their masculinity and to maintain their masculine self-identity. Many men struggle to retain their power and domination over women during life and family transitions. Men experience inevitable power losses (Kahn, 1984) over their life spans as they age and become less important to the capitalist system. When the "illusions of power" are confronted, many men may feel emasculated and lost.

In more extreme situations, men may use power against women and children to compensate for their lessening status in either career or family life. It is well known that when men lose their power, they are more likely to use abuse and violence (coercive power) to compensate for the loss (Kahn, 1984). In the case of intimate relationships, both psychological and physical violence can occur. (See Saakvitne and Pearlman's chapter for a discussion of men's efforts to reestablish their gender role identity.)

Other definitions used in this chapter follow from a gender role perspective. As noted in Robbins's definition, power bases are tools for using power. From a gender role perspective, *power bases* refer to the resources that people have, related to their gender role identity, that contribute to their ability to influence others. Men's and women's vastly different power bases develop from gender roles learned during gender role socialization. These roles are often stereotyped, and many are supported by sexist institutions and behaviors (see Figure 1).

Men are socialized to wield power in tangible ways in the world, with individuals and groups, and through institutions. Men are more comfortable with overt power because they have more practice and support in using it. Women are socialized to use power in more indirect and subtle ways. They learn to be powerful through their expressive, intuitive, and nurturant roles. Women have power in these roles, but it is quite different from men's social, political, and economic power.

From a gender role perspective, power is basically relational in nature. *Power dynamics* refers to the flow of power between individuals and, more specifically, to how gender roles affect *interpersonal* exchanges. *Power conflicts* occur when there are disagreements over goals or decisions, or when one person's increase of power might be perceived as decreasing the power of another person. Power conflicts and dynamics may also be experienced when the woman struggles internally with her own use of power. This is primarily an *intrapersonal* issue and will be discussed later in the chapter as power conflict within the woman. Power conflicts are inevitable in life and can be functional or dysfunctional. In functional power conflicts, power issues are discussed and aspects of compromise and conflict resolution are employed. In dysfunctional power conflicts, the power dynamics hinder the effective functioning of the individuals in the relationship. *Abuses of power* are situations in which power is used to devalue, restrict, or violate another person. In these cases, individuals' self-determination, freedom, and dignity are negatively affected by others' needs to validate themselves or have their own way. Psychological violence and manipulation may be employed during these dysfunctional power conflicts.

In the context of these definitions, the next sections describe the macro-societal factors depicted in Figure 1 that contribute to women's difficulties with power.

Patriarchal, Sexist, and Political Aspects of Power

Patriarchy and sexism are two political realities that have produced and continue to perpetuate women's and men's powerlessness and oppression. The emergence of patriarchal domination of women by men has a long history dating back to the fourth millennium B.C. (French, 1985). Patriarchy is classically defined as the supremacy of the father over his family members. More generally, patriarchy is the rule and domination of men over women and children in every aspect of life and culture. This domination is best represented in the economic oppression of women and overt discrimination of women in careers, religion, politics, families, and civic life. Doyle (1989) indicates that patriarchy "is in many ways one of the founding concepts of Western civilization and thus has influenced the lives of nearly every male and female in Western society for the last several thousand years" (pp. 26–27). Patriarchy oppresses women because it condones abuses of power toward women and permits violation of women's human rights. Men are also victims of sexism because of their gender role socialization and restricted ways of relating to the world (O'Neil, 1991). Patriarchy also violates men to the extent that men pay psychological costs for the oppression of others.

Sexism is the social, political, and personal expression of patriarchy in women's and men's lives. Sexism is any attitude, action, or institutional structure that devalues, restricts, or violates a person or group because of sex, gender role, or sexual orientation. Sexism maintains the patriarchal status quo by promoting power differences between men and women. This patriarchal value system makes sexism seem "natural," and only recently has sexism been identified as a form of psychopathology (Albee, 1981). Simply put, sexism is incongruent with democratic processes because it violates fundamental concepts of equality and human freedom.

Women in a sexist society have less power than men because of patriarchy and the insidious effects of sexism. Men's power over women is determined by sexist gender role stereotypes that imply the superiority of men and masculinity over women and femininity. Maintaining men's dominant gender role values in work and love is at the core of the battle between the sexes.

Power and Gender Role Socialization

In the context of the above political and economic realities, women and men are socialized to gender-specific role behaviors. As shown in Figure 1, the differential gender role socialization of the sexes produces power imbalances between men and women. Gender role socialization is the process by which children and adults acquire, internalize, and integrate the values, attitudes, and behaviors associated with femininity and masculinity (O'Neil, 1981a, 1982, 1990). Societal norms include expectations of logic, rationality, power, and control for men, and expectations of passivity, dependence, and submissiveness for women. These norms for women require yielding to external sources of power and authority. Women are often left feeling powerless in their relationships and in their own personal efficacy.

Societal institutions play an important part in enculturing men and women to sex-appropriate roles related to power. Messages from the family, media, schools, and the work environment perpetuate stereotyped images of men's and women's roles. The stereotypic role for women is to focus their lives on marriage, home, and children. There is a reliance on the male as provider for sustenance and status. The expectancy is that women will engage in nurturing and life-preserving activities through childbearing and caretaking behaviors. Additionally, there is an emphasis on personal appearance and a prohibition on direct expression of aggression, assertion, and striving for power (Keller, 1982).

The stereotypic role for men includes emphasizing physical strength and achievement, restricting emotionality (except for anger), avoiding emotional intimacy with same-sex peers, and providing sustenance and protection for women and children (Pleck, 1976). Clearly, these norms permit men to acquire and exercise instrumental power in society, while restricting women from, or sanctioning them for, engaging in stereotypical masculine behaviors. Socialization to power begins early and continues throughout adulthood. These socially defined roles are restrictive to both sexes and are currently being reexamined by both women and men.

Changing Gender Roles and Implications for Power

Traditionally, the macro-societal factors of patriarchy, personal and institutional sexism, and differential gender-role socialization have interacted to produce a power imbalance favoring men. The subtle and cumulative effects of gender role socialization to power have had a great impact on the roles of adult men and women. The socialization of the sexes in society (e.g., family and school) produces power inequities that can make the sexes dysfunctional with each other.

Recent changes in American society have produced shifts in the dynamics of traditional family roles and in the world of work. Therefore, power relationships between men and women have also been significantly altered. Dual-career couples, high divorce rates, and step-families are all examples of the changes occurring.

Such changes in gender roles, whether out of necessity or by choice, have produced dramatic shifts in power within relationships. These changes in power have produced stress and strain. Traditional gender role norms for men and women are currently being examined and debated. When women and men violate the traditional gender role norms, they experience gender role conflict (Good, Dell, & Mintz, 1989; O'Neil, Fishman, & Kinsella-Shaw, 1987; Pleck, 1981).

Changing gender roles prompt new power dynamics in relationships. Men and women struggle to negotiate new roles and shifting priorities in a changing world. Traditionally, men have power in the world of work, and women exercise power at home. This polarization of roles and realms can be dysfunctional, difficult, and resistant to change. Women who grow up taking care of the house and performing nurturing activities might fear losing power from these roles if they share them. Men who are socialized to work outside the home might be reluctant to perform housekeeping roles. They might view housework as women's work (i.e., feminine) and think performing such tasks will weaken their power base.

Ideally, men and women can resolve these stresses through communication and negotiation, thus affirming the freedom and dignity of everyone involved. In contrast, handling power in a dysfunctional manner can lead to power abuses.

POWER ABUSES, WOMEN'S POWERLESSNESS, AND GENDER ROLE CONFLICT

The effect of the macro-societal factors shown in the outer triangle of Figure 1 sets the stage for understanding the micro-interpersonal level of conflict between women and men shown in the inner triangle. In other words, the effects of patriarchy, sexism, and differential gender role socialization of the sexes become the foundation for men's and women's power and gender role conflicts. These power and gender role conflicts can cause abuses against women.

Gender role conflict occurs when rigid, sexist, or restrictive gender roles, learned during socialization, result in the personal restriction, devaluation, or violation of others or self (O'Neil, 1981a, 1981b, 1982, 1990). The ultimate outcome of this conflict is the restriction of the person's human potential or of someone else's potential. One reason that women experience gender role conflict is because personal and institutional sexism deprives them of personal and economic power.

Gender role conflict is related to power dynamics and requires consideration of (1) the personal experience, or the negative consequences of gender roles for an individual woman, and (2) the situational context, which describes how and from whom the conflict emerges for an individual women. Table 1 depicts three personal experiences of abuses of power and three situational contexts in which they occur.

The Personal Experience of Abuses of Power

When abuses of power occur, individuals attempt to validate themselves and maintain control of a situation at the expense of another person. Abuses of power against women can result in women's gender role devaluations, restrictions, and violations. *Gender role devaluations* are experienced when women either deviate from or conform to feminine gender role norms. This devaluation can occur because women actually exhibit power in stereotypically masculine ways or because they express powerlessness that is traditionally associated with the feminine stereotype. Others may punish a woman's nontraditional behavior, lessening her stature, status, and self-esteem. Women can also deny their power, begin to express it negatively, or use it in destructive ways. *Gender role restrictions* occur when women confine themselves or are confined by others to traditional gender role norms related to power. This confinement causes

Table 1

Diagnostic Schema to Assess Women's Power Conflicts Emanating From Abuses of Power

Situational Context of Power Conflicts

Personal experience of abuses of power	Power conflicts caused by others toward women D_1	Power conflicts within women D_2	Power conflicts expressed toward others by women D_3
D. Gender role devaluations	Devaluations of women's: • emotionality • accomplishments • intuition • attractiveness • work or career roles • intelligence • mothering • housekeeping abilities • competence • educational choices • friends	Self-devaluations: • lack of confidence • fear of failure • guilt • worries about success • worries about personal appearance • low expectancies for success • low self-esteem • inferiority • low self-efficacy	Devaluation of others': • life roles • values • emotionality • success and accomplishments • rationality • instrumentality • sexuality • friendships • hobbies • freedom
	R_1	R_2	R_3
R. Gender role restrictions	Restriction of women's: • work or career roles • emotional expression • friendship with others	Self-restrictions: • fear of success • non-competitiveness • passivity	Restriction of others': • thinking (through emotional manipulation) • friendships • accomplishments

Table 1 (cont'd)

Diagnostic Schema to Assess Women's Power Conflicts
Emanating From Abuses of Power

Situational Context of Power Conflicts

Personal experience of abuses of power	Power conflicts caused by others toward women	Power conflicts within women	Power conflicts expressed toward others by women
	R_1	R_2	R_3
R. Gender role restrictions, cont'd	• intimacy with others • reproductive rights • educational opportunities • sexual expression • economic or financial rights	• dependency • role conflict • lack of assertiveness • limited goal setting • homophobia • sexual dysfunction • helplessness • inadequate interpersonal skills • avoidance of risk	• communication with others • rights to see children after divorce • sexuality
	V_1	V_2	V_3
V. Gender role violations	Violation of women: • rape • sexual harassment • battering • psychological violence • emotional deprivation • physical deprivation (food, shelter, etc.) • poverty • sex discrimination • murder	Self-violations: • eating disorders • health care problems • addictions • depression • overwork • isolation • suicide	Violation of others through: • sexualized behavior • blackmail • unfair alimony settlements • physical assault • psychological violence • murder

violation of personal freedom and human rights. These restrictions may include situations in the family, at work, or in interpersonal relations. Restrictions limit options, deny needs, and often represent manipulative control and abusive uses of power. *Gender role violations* occur when women harm themselves, are harmed by others, or harm others because of destructive power dynamics. To be violated is to be abused, hurt, and victimized because of power and gender role conflict. These three negative experiences with power abuses define women's private pain and gender role conflict in three situational contexts.

Situational Context of Power Conflicts

As shown in Table 1, power conflicts can be (1) caused by others, (2) experienced within the woman, or (3) expressed toward others by the woman. Power conflicts *caused by others* are defined as thoughts, feelings, and behavioral patterns that produce negative emotions and consequences in a woman because of someone else's power conflicts. Other people's power conflicts or powerlessness can cause a woman to be devalued, restricted, and violated. Power conflicts *within the woman* are defined as thoughts, feelings, and behavioral patterns that produce negative emotions and consequences for the individual woman because of her own gender role and power conflicts. When a woman asserts her power with little positive result or when she feels powerless, she may experience specific outcomes of self-devaluation, self-restriction, and self-violation. Power conflicts *expressed toward others* are defined as a woman's thoughts, feelings, and behavioral patterns that produce negative emotions and consequences for others. A woman's power conflicts or powerlessness can cause her to devalue, restrict, and violate others.

The nine cells in Table 1 specify some of the gender role conflicts that women can experience related to power conflicts. The devaluations, restrictions, and violations of women caused by power conflicts from others are specified as D, R, and V. Each cell represents a personal experience and a situational context in which devaluations, restrictions, or violations can occur because of power abuses. Devaluation outcomes from power conflicts *caused by others* toward a woman are shown as D1. Devaluation outcomes from power conflicts *within self* are shown as D2. Power conflicts *expressed toward others* by a woman are shown by D3. The same categories of power conflict are shown for restrictions (R1, R2, R3) and violations (V1, V2, V3). Each of these cells is discussed below as a possible outcome of power conflicts women may experience in their lives.

For cell D1, power conflicts are a result of other people's devaluations of the woman's life, her gender role identity, or her personal situation. Those uncomfortable with the woman's expression of personal power or her deviation from traditional feminine stereotypes may devalue her personal characteristics. Her new roles and emerging power may produce irrational feelings that her power negates a man's power. For example, a man who feels his power is threatened by a woman's behavior may seek to reestablish his power base by devaluing the woman's emotionality, intuitive capacities, or attractiveness. If the woman has effectively entered a nontraditional career role or demonstrated success, these accomplishments may be devalued by other men and women. The woman's success may be experienced as a threat or met with jealousy. As the woman embraces more nontraditional roles, her reduced time for more traditional roles (i.e., housekeeping and mothering) may be criticized and devalued by others. She may be successful at work, but labeled a "bad" mother or spouse. Her new circle of friends and support network may also be devalued.

There are a number of psychological symptoms, problems, and outcomes that a woman may experience as a result of cell D2, which represents self-devaluations because of power conflicts within the woman. When the woman has been unable to solidify her personal power base, she feels unable to have an impact on others. In such situations, she may devalue her own abilities, potential, and worth rather than struggle with others to increase her power. Without a strong sense of self, she may experience low self-esteem, lack of confidence, inferiority, and fears of failure. Without ego strength, she may have worries about success or feel she is unattractive to others. If she has deviated from traditional gender role norms, she may feel guilt about violating the accepted roles for women rather than feeling confident about what is right for her. Under these unsettling emotional conditions, she may have very low self-efficacy, experience depression, and have either diffused or focused anger about her life situation.

Under the conditions described in cells D1 and D2, the woman may feel angry about how powerless she is. She may try to assert her power by devaluing other individuals' personality characteristics, life roles, activities, and hobbies (cell D3). When deviating from the feminine stereotypes has brought on devaluation from others, she may counterattack by devaluing both feminine and masculine stereotypes.

Restrictions caused by others (cell R1) occur when others are uncomfortable with the woman's changing or actual power base. In this case, there are actual attempts by others to restrict the woman's freedom and human rights. Men or other significant individuals (e.g., parents) may attempt to restrain the woman's growth because they fear or envy her new, nonstereotypic roles. They may be threatened by the woman's new sense of power or may not know how to relate to it in effective ways. There may be attempts to control the woman's career roles, educational opportunities, or reproductive rights. Others may attempt to control resources or relationships she needs (e.g., money, transportation, time, friendships) to ensure that she maintains stereotypical behaviors. Such attempts to control are a common feature of battering relationships. With increased interpersonal power, less restricted sexual behavior may occur, causing uncertainty with sexual partners.

For cell R2 (restriction because of power conflicts within the woman), a woman confines her behavior to traditional gender role norms. This self-restriction diminishes her personal power and is represented by a host of emotional and psychological problems. The lack of personal power may result in passivity, dependency, and inability to compete. The lack of assertiveness, limited goal-setting skills, and fears about taking risks keep the woman in a position of powerlessness. She may fear negative consequences of becoming successful (e.g., fear of success) or worry about role conflict with intimates or family members. If the self-imposed restrictions are due to underdeveloped interpersonal skills, the woman may fear making any changes in her life. She may fear that as she becomes less restricted (e.g., breaking the feminine stereotype), her relationships with others will negatively change. She may fear or become uncomfortable with her sexuality. Homophobia and sexual dysfunction may occur because her perspectives on power have changed her sexual dynamics with both men and women.

The woman may also restrict others (cell R3) in order to maintain her power or to decrease the possibility of being devalued or violated by others. She may believe that there is a limited amount of power to go around. Consequently, she may believe that for her power to increase, then other people's power has to decrease. This belief may result in attempts to restrict others' activities, successes, and relationships. She may try to control the communication process by restricting others' rights to expression. Threats, emotional manipulations, and sexual withdrawal may be used to gain control of the changing power dynamics.

Power conflicts from others that result in violations of women (cell V1) represent very serious issues. Emotional and physical deprivation can occur when a woman's increased power and control are feared. Sex discrimination in career and financial matters is a direct violation of women's rights under the law. When a woman's economic power is diminished through sex discrimination at work, or when she is deprived of economic support from men, poverty becomes a form of violation. Psychological violence against women (i.e., threats, humiliations, put-downs) can injure their spirit and determination to assume their rights and pursue new roles. The most serious abuses of power involve sexual harassment, rape, and partner battering. These kinds of power play are desperate attempts by men to keep women in a subordinate place by using force and violence. The threat of women's power is so great that men assault women to maintain male dominance and superiority.

Violations to self from power conflicts (cell V2) produce serious psychological outcomes for women. Self-violations occur when the anger and fear about powerlessness are turned back on oneself in destructive ways. Such women prefer to hurt themselves rather than directly confront their own powerlessness with others. Depression, addictions, overwork, and isolation from others can surface, and serious health disorders can occur under these conditions. Eating disorders may develop from a woman's attempt to maintain her traditional (feminine) source of power through her beauty and body shape. She maintains her illusions of power through attractiveness, but destroys her body in the process.

Women's violations of others because of their power conflicts (cell V3) are attempts to guard their power or to cope with their own powerlessness by striking out against others. These violations may also occur when women use power to obtain control over others or events. Sexualized or seductive behavior can be used against men to establish a position of power. Women can use psychological violence to victimize others and maintain their position of power. Unfair divorce and alimony settlements can be victimizing and abusing to others. Emotional blackmail reflects a woman's powerlessness and is a powerful strategy that can harm others.

Power Abuses and Psychological Violence

The effects of patriarchal sexist structures, power conflicts from sexist socialization experiences, and gender role conflict collectively represent the conditions for abuses of power against women. Abuses of power do more than simply maintain the gender role status quo. One way that the power conflicts and dynamics described in Table 1 occur and are maintained is through psychological violence.

Psychological violence exists when power is used by one person to dehumanize and treat another person as an object. Power is used to willfully destroy or impair a person's competence, respect, self-esteem, happiness, and dignity as a human being (O'Neil, 1991). Psychological violence can be conscious or unconscious, intentional or unintentional, overt or covert, continuous or sporadic.

It is not just the single act of psychological violence that has destructive outcomes, but rather the cumulative effects of these violations over time. There are no laws against acts of psychological violence as there are against sexual harassment, partner battering, and rape. Many people are victims of psychological violence but are unable to label the experience. They may internalize pain from such violations and suffer privately.

No developed vocabulary adequately describes how and why psychological violence occurs. The socialized and patriarchal role for women to be compliant, obedient, and submissive causes women to feel shame or conflict about fighting back or getting out of psychologically violent relationships. Confronting the violence deviates from feminine norms, and women may experience greater gender role conflict both as victims of psychological violence and in thinking about what to do about it.

The concept of psychological violence has emanated from the literature on abuse, neglect, and victimization. Psychological abuse, emotional maltreatment, and interpersonal violence are other terms used to describe psychological violence. Other authors have provided initial formulations of psychological violence (Burgess, Hartman, & Kelly, 1990; Degregoria, 1987; Garbarino & Gilliam, 1980; Lourie & Stefano, 1977; NiCarthy, 1986; Walker, 1979), but a full operational definition has not yet emerged.

Walker (1979) defined psychological or nonphysical abuse as coercive, manipulative, or other power-related behavior promoting one person's needs while neglecting the needs of others (Bruschi & Raymond, 1990; Degregoria, 1987). The essence of psychological violence is loss of control and powerlessness (Degregoria, 1987). Psychological violence involves active attempts to intimidate or diminish the well-being of an individual (Myers & Shelton, 1987) and provokes fears of violence or isolation (Giordano & Giordano, 1984). Walker (1979) delineated psychological abuse into distinct, although not mutually exclusive, categories, including (1) economic deprivation: the use of the husband's income as a coercive instrument; (2) social humiliation: the threat of public embarrassment through the use of aggressive or obnoxious behavior; (3) social isolation: the husband's determination of acceptable choices for his wife's associates and activities; and (4) verbal battering: threats, accusations, or name calling, all of which serve to undermine the woman's self-esteem. The most common form of psychological violence found in the literature was verbal abuse involving temper outbursts, sarcastic and critical exchanges, and recurrent bickering (Degregoria, 1987; Dobask & Dobask, 1977–1978; McClintock, 1978; Roy, 1977), as well as ridicule, excess criticism, and humiliation (Sugar, 1990).

Ronnau and Poertner (1989) indicated that the outcomes of emotional maltreatment are increased feelings of hostility and aggression, impaired self-esteem, emotional instability, unresponsiveness, and negativity. Those suffering from psychological violence tend to feel unloved, unwanted, inferior, inadequate, and unrelated to any social system. Sugar (1990) described verbal abuse as a type of psychological violence that included ridicule, excess criticism, and humiliation. The effects of verbal abuse can be long lasting and produce feelings of shame, worthlessness, confusion, incompetence, anger, mixed loyalty, and guilt.

Table 2 shows 18 specific dimensions of psychological violence that capture the previous definitions and our own clinical work with women and men. It is hypothesized that women may experience psychological violence through these 18 dimensions when abuses of power occur. The list in Table 2 is not exhaustive of the many dimensions of psychological violence, but it does translate the previous definitions into more concrete behaviors. The dimensions of psychological violence in Table 2 do not account for the physical victimization of individuals in the case of rape, partner battering, and physical-sexual child abuse. These acts are considered physical violence and are discussed later in the book. Yet acts of psychological violence can be precursors to physical assault, including rape, battering, and even murder.

Many acts of psychological violence are abuses of power in which one person attempts to devalue, restrict, or violate another person to maintain control, advantage, or position. The 18 dimensions in Table 2 can be categorized according to the three outcomes of gender role devaluations, restrictions, and violations defined in Table 1. Dimensions 1 through 5 are primarily related to devaluations. Dimensions 6 through 9 reflect attempts at personal restriction and dimensions 10 through 18 reflect violations of a person.

The power conflicts *caused by others* and *expressed toward others* (see D1, R1, V1 and D3, R3, and V3 in Table 1) are the primary situational

Table 2
Operational Dimensions and Definitions of Psychological Violence

Dimension	Definition
1. Put-downs	to disparage, belittle, criticize, disapprove of a person; to make that person ineffective.
2. Name calling	the use of offensive names to win an argument or to induce rejection or condemnation without objective consideration of the facts.
3. Humiliations	to reduce to a lower position in one's eyes or others' eyes; mortify, abuse; to be extremely destructive to one's self-respect or dignity.
4. Diminishing self-esteem	intentionally lowering another person's self-satisfaction and self-respect.
5. Gossip	rumor or report of an intimate nature; chatty talk that is destructive to a person.
6. Emotional and intellectual manipulations	to control or play upon by artful, unfair, or insidious means, especially to one's own advantage; to change by artful or unfair means so as to serve one's purpose.
7. Fear-inducing techniques	using an unpleasant, often strong emotion caused by anticipation or awareness of danger with a person.
8. Threats and intimidations	an expression of intention to inflict evil, injury, or damage on another person.
9. Coercion	to restrain or dominate another person; nullifying an individual's will; to compel to an act or choice; to enforce or bring about by force or threat (force).
10. Rejections	to refuse to accept or consider a person.
11. Scapegoating	when a person bears the blame for others.
12. Lying	marked by or given to falsehood; likely or calculated to mislead another person.
13. Dishonesty	lack of honesty or integrity; disposition to defraud or deceive; characterized by lack of truth, honesty, or trustworthiness with a person.
14. Personal neglect	to give little attention or respect; to disregard; to leave undone or unattended through carelessness.
15. Abandonment	desert, forsake, to give up completely; disinterest in the fate of another person.
16. Seductive behaviors	using sexual actions that have alluring or tempting qualities.
17. Harassment	to worry and impede another person by repeated raids; exhaust, fatigue; to annoy persistently another person (worry).
18. Sexual harassment	unwanted sexual overtures or actions that victimize a person.

contexts in which acts of psychological violence occur. Many times when women complain about power abuses from men, they describe interactions that include aspects of psychological violence as enumerated in D1, R1, and V1. Acts of psychological violence are usually desperate attempts by men or women to regain power that has been lost during power conflicts or previous abuses of power. Frequently the cumulative effect of unresolved psychological violence results in physical threats and actual assaults on women. Women may also commit acts of psychological violence in response to their feelings of powerlessness and frustration as enumerated in D3, R3, and V3. Since sexism is one way that power is abused, it follows that psychological violence would be directly related to the gender role devaluations, restrictions, and violations enumerated in Table 1.

Current Research on Psychological Violence

The dimensions of psychological violence in Table 2 were developed into a 48-item scale named the *Psychological Violence Scale* (O'Neil, Owen, Egan, Murry, Holmes, and Kunkler, 1992). Empirical research was conducted to determine more precisely whether there were any common factors across the dimensions in Table 2. The Psychological Violence Scale was administered to a sample of students and adults ($N = 500$). Thirty-seven of the orginal 48 items factored into four subscales: (1) overt anger, (2) emotional distance, (3) domination, and (4) distrust. Internal consistency estimates ranged from .73 through .87. This preliminary research provides some initial evidence for the concept of psychological violence, and further research is being conducted to refine the scale and the theory presented in this chapter.

IMPLICATIONS FOR COUNSELORS

Discussions about power have typically been taboo topics in work settings and intimate relationships. Power brokers at work may not want to discuss power dynamics inherent in their supervisory roles out of fear of losing their advantage. Likewise, in loving relationships, intimates may fear discussions of their power dynamics because the topic may threaten their romance or objectify their relationship in impersonal ways. Taboos against discussing power dynamics, conflicts, and abuses need to be overcome if men and women are to embrace the 1990s with honesty and build more effective lives together. This chapter's goal was to provide additional perspectives on power abuses against women and to diminish the taboos against discussing them more directly.

One of the limitations of the chapter is not enumerating power abuses directed against men by other men and by women. A similiar analysis of power abuses against men could be made using the macro-societal and micro-interpersonal factors depicted in Figure 1. Future analyses of abuses of power against men need to be generated if full comprehension is to be achieved of how gender and power interact in human relations. We hope that men who read this chapter will recognize that their masculine socialization is directly implicated in the power abuses against women suggested in Table 1. Furthermore, through this reading, we hope that both men and women will be motivated to analyze how men are also victims of sexism (O'Neil, 1991) from their sexist socialization.

The concepts presented in this chapter suggest that counselors of women need to become knowledgeable about power and its relationship to gender roles. Figure 1 provides both a societal and an interpersonal framework to understand how abuses of power occur against women. Knowledge about men's and women's differential gender role socialization to power is essential to understand how men and women are conflicted in their power dynamics.

To help women with power conflicts and abuses, counselors need to examine their own political perspectives on sexism and understand how the present political-economic system contributes to the oppression of women. Counselors need to evaluate how they see patriarchal and sexist structures that influence marital and familial relationships. Cultural and ethnic differences need to be analyzed to capture the multicultural implications of power abuses toward women. Political and psychological sensitivity to these issues may determine the depth of counselors' analyses and the degree to which they can intervene to liberate women from the bonds of male domination. Counselors are more likely to be helpful if they understand how their own personal relationships reflect the power abuses and imbalances inherent in a sexist society.

Table 1 provides an assessment paradigm for counselors to determine how a woman experiences personal devaluations, restrictions, and violations from power conflicts. When the client understands power conflicts within herself, from others, and directed toward others, she can take responsibility for resolving the conflicts that inhibit her empowerment. Once the types of power conflicts are understood, counseling goals can be specified and pursued.

Counselors can skillfully investigate women's previous power dynamics in primary families, in schools, and with peer relationships. Investigating past abuses may require deep probing and the stimulation of painful memories and past events. Exploring power relationships with parents and siblings may provide a useful historical context to understand a woman's present problems with power or powerlessness. Helping women put labels on their experiences may be the primary task in early stages of therapy. Helping a woman recognize how and why she feels devalued, restricted, and violated (using Table 1) can allow her to embrace unexpressed emotions and to confront dysfunctional power conflicts that inhibit growth.

The power conflicts within the woman (D2, R2, and V2) can provide interpersonal insights on the specific self-devaluations, restrictions, and violations. These insights can be used to conceptualize power conflicts caused by others (D1, R1, and V1) in specific situations. Counselors will need to use their clinical skill to work with the client's defense mechanisms (e.g., denial, projection, repression) that may prohibit self-analysis and corrective problem solving. Clients may need much support, assertiveness training, and risk-taking behaviors to change patterns of behavior that may have led them to be devalued, restricted, or violated. Likewise, the counselor may need to probe how the client participates in the devaluations, restrictions, and violations of others (D3, R3, and V3) to break the cycle of abuse. Table 1 can be used as a checklist for women to assess which devaluations, restrictions, and violations within a specific situational context are relevant to their power conflicts.

The operational definitions of psychological violence delineated in Table 2 can help women clients understand how power abuses are enmeshed in the complex power dynamics of any relationship. Helping clients link interpersonal exchanges with the specific dimensions of psychological violence (e.g., put-downs, humiliations, lying) may require in-depth probing and client self-monitoring over extended periods of time. Conversely, the sources and kinds of psychological violence may be very clear from the beginning, and the client may need to learn self-protective and assertive behaviors to extinguish the violence. Counselors can help clients analyze psychologically violent situations and help them develop strategies for problem solving.

In breaking with the traditional male definitions of power, Miller (1986) offers an alternative definition for women. She moves beyond the old definition of power over others and power for oneself. She describes power for women as the capacity to implement. This definition is useful for both women and men because it defines power as a tool for constructive purposes. From this perspective, expressing constructive power results not from personal control or domination, but rather from the empowerment of others through acts of liberation, transformation, and freedom. The use of power, as an act of empowerment, coincides exactly with the counseling profession's commitment to mobilizing people's potential for themselves and the betterment of society.

REFERENCES

Albee, G. W. (1981). The prevention of sexism. *Professional Psychology, 12,* 20–28.

Boulding, K. E. (1989). *Three faces of power.* Newbury Park, CA: Sage Publications.

Bruschi, I. G., & Raymond, B. (1990). What women think and what men think women think: Perceptions of abuse and kindness in dating relationships. *Psychological Reports, 67,* 115–118.

Burgess, A. W., Hartman, C. R., & Kelly, S. J. (1990). Assessing child abuse: The triads checklist. *Journal of Psychosocial Nursing, 28, 4,* 7–14.

Degregoria, B. (1987). Sex role attitude and perception of psychological abuse. *Sex Roles, 16 (5/6),* 227–235.

Dobask, R., & Dobask, R. (1977–1978). Wives. The appropriate victims of marital violence. *Victimology, 2,* 426–442.

Doyle, J. A. (1989). *The male experience* (2nd ed.) Dubuque, IA: William C. Brown Publishers.

DuBrin, A. J. (1990). *Essentials of management.* Cincinnati: South-Western Publishing Co.

French, J. R. P., & Raven, B. (1959). The bases of social power. In D. Cartwright (Ed.), *Studies in social power.* Ann Arbor, MI: Institute for Social Research.

French, M. (1985). *Beyond power: On women, men and morals.* New York: Ballantine.

Frieze, I. H., Parsons, J. E., Johnson, P. B., Ruble, D. N., & Zellman, G. L. (1978). *Women and sex roles: A social psychological perspective.* New York: W.W. Norton and Co.

Garbarino, J., & Gilliam, G. (1980). *Understanding abusive families.* Lexington, MA: Lexington Books.

Giordano, N. H., & Giordano, J. A. (1984). Elder abuse: A review of the literature. *Social Work, 29*(3), 232–236.

Good, G., Dell, D. M., & Mintz, L. B. (1989). Male roles and gender role conflict: Relationships to helpseeking in men. *Journal of Counseling Psychology, 3,* 295–300.

Hunsaker, J., & Hunsaker, P. (1986). *Strategies and skills for managerial women.* Cincinnati: South-Western Publishing Co.

Kahn, A. (1984). The power war: Male response to power loss under equality. *Psychology of Women Quarterly, 8 (3),* 234–247.

Keller, E. F. (1982). Feminism and science. *Signs, 7,* 589–602.

Lourie, I. R., & Stefano, O. (1977). On defining emotional abuse: Results of an NIMH/NCCAN workshop. In *Proceedings of the Second National Conference on Child Abuse and Neglect, Vol. 1* (pp. 201–208) (Publ. DHEW No. (OHDS) 78-30147). Washington, DC: National Center for Child Abuse and Neglect, Department of Health, Education, and Welfare.

McClintock, F. (1978). Criminological aspects of family violence. In J. Martin (Ed.), *Violence and the family.* New York: John Wiley & Sons.

Miller, J. (1986). *Toward a new psychology of women.* Boston: Beacon Press.

Myers, J. E., & Shelton, B. (1987). Abuse and older persons: Issues and implications for counselors. *Journal of Counseling and Development, 65,* 376.

NiCarthy, G. (1986). *Getting free: A handbook for women in abusive relationships.* Seattle, WA: The Seal Press.

O'Neil, J. M. (1981a). Male sex-role conflicts, sexism, and masculinity: Psychological implications for men, women, and the counseling psychologist. *The Counseling Psychologist, 9,* 61–80.

O'Neil, J. M. (1981b). Patterns of gender role conflict and strain: Sexism and fear of femininity in men's lives. *Personnel and Guidance Journal, 60,* 203–210.

O'Neil, J. M. (1982). Gender role conflict and strain in men's lives: Implications for psychiatrists, psychologists, and other human service providers. In K. Solomon & N. B. Levy (Eds.), *Men in Transitions: Changing male roles, theory, and therapy.* New York: Plenum Publishing Co.

O'Neil, J. M. (1990). Assessing men's gender role conflict. In D. Moore & F. Leafgren (Eds.), *Men in conflict: Problem solving strategies and interventions.* Alexandria, VA: American Association for Counseling and Development Press.

O'Neil, J. M. (1991 August). Men and women as victims of sexism: Metaphors for healing. Paper presented at the 99th annual convention of the American Psychological Association, San Francisco.

O'Neil, J. M., Fishman, D. M., & Kinsella-Shaw, M. (1987). Dual-career couples' career transitions and normative dilemmas: A preliminary assessment model. *The Counseling Psychologist, 15*(1), 50–96.

O'Neil, J. M., Owen, S., Egan, J., Murry, V., Holmes, S., & Kunkler, K. (1992). *The Psychological Violence Scale.* Unpublished measure, University of Connecticut, School of Family Studies.

Pleck, J., (1976). The male sex-role: Definitions, problems, and sources for change. *Journal of Social Issues, 32,* 15–164.

Pleck, J., (1981). *The myth of masculinity.* Cambridge, MA: MIT Press.

Robbins, S. P. (1989). *Organizational behavior: Concepts, controversies, and applications.* Englewood Cliffs, NJ: Prentice Hall.

Ronnau, J., & Poertner, J. (1989). Building consensus among child protection professionals. *Social Casework, 70*(7), 428–435.

Roy, M. (1977). A current survey of 150 cases. In M. Roy (Ed.), *Battered women.* New York: Van Nostrand Reinhold.

Russell, B. (1969). *Power: A new social analysis.* New York: Norton.

Sugar, M. (1990). Abuse and neglect in schools. *American Journal of Psychotherapy, 44*(4).

Walker, L. (1979). *The battered woman.* New York: Harper & Row.

WOMEN IN INTIMATE RELATIONSHIPS

Paula Dupuy

ntimacy is a much sought–after and yet elusive experience for most individuals in our society. Writers in the popular and professional realms tend to agree that defining intimacy is difficult and its existence in our current culture is rare. A range of reasons is theorized for the problems with intimate relationships in today's society, from individual characteristics (e.g., mental and personality disorders) to more global societal and cultural influences (e.g., economics and social norms). This range is well illustrated by the number of self-help books and professional publications coming from such perspectives as addiction and codependency (Beattie, 1987; Schaef, 1989), communication differences between men and women (Tannen, 1990), gender role socialization (Papp, 1988), and remediating individual characteristics (Morgan, 1985). The importance of this topic to individuals is documented by the large number of writings addressing this area, and it appears that Schaef (1989) may be correct when she writes, "What do we really know about intimacy in this culture? Not very much" (p. 123).

Although intimate relationships may take many forms, for the most part we talk about intimacy in the context of dyadic relationships. Lerner (1989) described an intimate relationship as one in which "we can be who we are in a relationship, and allow the other person to do the same" (p. 3). Intimacy is the experience of relationship that provides an environment in which both individuals can mutually share their essential, deepest selves.

The intimacy experience always lies in the context of some social system. Before discussing the nature of this experience for women, it is essential to identify the most salient factors of the societal and cultural environment in which intimacy occurs. Traditional writings in counseling and psychology have often assumed that most individuals share common basic developmental and psychological experiences. However, research has indicated that membership in certain groups often influences one's individual experience differently. Membership related to race, socioeconomic status, religion, sexual preference, and gender creates a context for understanding some of the differences in personal experience. As this chapter focuses on intimate relationships for women, gender becomes an important construct of analysis for placing this experience in a social context. Recent theoretical developments have suggested that men and women experience life events differently in many aspects of our culture.

Although intimate relationships have traditionally been seen as important to all human development, these relationships have been conceptualized within a model that describes human identity as basically autonomous and separate (Miller, 1976). Intimacy, in this context, has been seen as a relationship between two autonomous individuals who relate in relatively differentiated ways. In addition, although important to the individual, intimacy has been seen as basically separate from one's "healthy ego" and often irrelevant to one's sense of self. Finally, intimacy has usually been defined within the context of heterosexual, romantic, dyadic relationships, thus specifying traditional gender roles for both men and women. Recent critics of the autonomy model base their arguments against using this model for describing and evaluating human experience on the belief that the model may describe most men's experience in this culture, but not most women's. With the onset of recent research focused on women's lives, this traditional way of viewing intimacy appears to be severely deficient in describing intimacy for a majority of women (and most likely for some men, as well).

Because of these limitations, a brief review of the recent understandings related to women's experience is provided as a foundation to discussion of their intimate relationships. Acknowledging the dangers of assuming similarities among any group, this context will, nevertheless, be used for describing the common experiences and problems related to intimacy in women's lives.

IMPLICATIONS OF THE RELATIONAL MODEL FOR INTIMACY

Based on the evidence that gender is one aspect of human experience that defines the nature of reality for individuals, researchers have found that the traditional masculine way of looking at experience does not describe the reality of most women. As discussed earlier, the differences between women and men are commonly understood to occur through the process of gender role socialization and are unequally valued within our society.

Recent research in the area of women's experience has focused on the exploration of the relationship model in an attempt to name, describe, validate, and further understand women's realities. This exploration has direct importance for mental health professionals working with both women and men. If our traditional models for viewing human experience are biased, limited, or incomplete, as counselors we risk the possibility of misunderstanding, misdiagnosing, and mistreating our clients. It follows, then, that a discussion of women and intimacy must be placed within both relational and autonomy models.

Jordan (1986), adapting Miller's theoretical bases of self-in-relation, discusses the nature of relationship, particularly in dyadic love relationships, through the concept of *mutual intersubjectivity*. In mutual intersubjectivity the relationship is seen as reciprocal and characterized by intimacy. Mutuality involves an empathic valuing of the wholeness of the other person and a receptive, active initiation toward the other. Mutual empathy is seen as a flow between two individuals that generates a "holding" space in which similarities and differences may be experienced. In contrast to loss of self (the more traditional understanding), this experience of intense affiliation actually expands one's self-esteem through the "transcendence of the self, a sense of the self as part of a larger relational unit" (p. 2).

The nature of relating described by Jordan (1986) supports the idea that a woman's sense of identity may be derived within her intimate relationships. This idea is supported in a recent study by White, Houlihan, Costos, and Speisman (1990), who found that intimacy maturity (defined as a continuum from self-focused to role-focused to individuated-connected) is directly related to a woman's ego development: the higher the level of maturity, the higher the ego development. This finding contrasted with men's experience, which showed no relationship between intimacy maturity and ego development. This difference is intuitively understandable if women's sense of self is derived primarily from the experience of self-in-relation.

While intimacy may be a possible outgrowth or inherent aspect of the self-in-relation experience for women, to be an accepted aspect of identity it must be acknowledged and valued by the individual and society. The societal devaluing of connection and the internalization of that devaluing by individuals often leads to low self-esteem and difficulties in actually establishing and maintaining intimate relationships.

In this culture, intimacy is most commonly desired and expected in the context of a couple. However, intimacy in couple relationships is often absent, deficient, or difficult to maintain. Gender role socialization plays a major part in the experience of intimacy for women in both heterosexual and lesbian couple relationships. Both lesbian and heterosexual women have grown up in the same gender-defined culture that promotes strong implicit and explicit messages about their roles as women. Women's relational experience is believed to be generated from their gender role socialization, regardless of sexual orientation, although it may have some different implications for each lifestyle. In addition, common issues for lesbian and heterosexual couples (e.g., communication, closeness and separateness patterns, dependency, anger, and violence) are also influenced by relationship and autonomy orientations.

INTIMATE COUPLE RELATIONSHIPS

An intimate relationship, as Lerner (1989) suggests, can be conceptualized as a dance created by two partners. The rhythm, technique, and flow of the relationship's movement often are generated by attempts by both individuals to meet their own and each other's needs. Woititz (1985) emphasized the importance of each partner's needs when she described healthy intimate relationships in the context of an environment in which, "(a) I can be me. (b) You can be you. (c) We can be us. (d) I can grow. (e) You can grow. (f) We can grow" (p. 20). Because each partner's needs and ways of satisfying those needs will at times be in conflict, the couple is continually challenged to be open for negotiation and change. The tension in the dance, therefore, is one of holding similarities and differences, togetherness and separateness, at the same time. This tension is necessary for the process of intimacy to continue to evolve in the presence of changing individuals. How this tension is generated, nurtured, and cared for by the couple often is bound by socially prescribed gender roles.

Gender roles typically regulate the ways individuals think, feel, and act within intimate relationships. In fact, few if any alternative models exist for couples attempting to relate in non-gender-stereotypical ways. Couples dissatisfied with the traditional gender role model find themselves struggling to create their own model, often without markers, rituals, or ceremonies that serve to define and validate the relationship for the couple and society (Roth, 1989).

The traditional model for heterosexual couples is marriage, historically based on a division of labor in which social roles are used to provide the structure for intimacy to occur. In this model, one partner (usually the man) serves the function of provider and the other (usually the woman), that of the caregiver (Papp, 1988). This division of labor, in and of itself, is problematic because of the greater power attributed to men's roles in our society (see O'Neil and Egan's chapter) and the rigidity with which these roles are ascribed to men and women. Although inconsistent results have been found (see, e.g., Barnett & Baruch, 1987) regarding the specific effects of marriage on self-esteem, mental health, and life satisfaction for women and men, most scholars would agree that overall, marriage produces more psychological benefits for men than women (e.g., Avis, 1985; Baruch & Barnett, 1986). McGoldrick (1989) concludes her discussion on gender differences in marriage by stating that "in almost every way, marriage improves men's mental health, while mentally, physically, and even in crime statistics, single women are healthier than married women" (p. 211).

The provider/caregiver structure appears to be changing because of the numbers of women entering the work force over the last few decades, but in reality the change has been slight, as women continue to perform most caregiving and homemaking tasks (see Stoltz-Loike's chapter). In addition, men's earning potential and income are still significantly higher than women's (Faludi, 1991). The economic inequality found in most marriages is a salient factor in how relationships are perceived and experienced. As a specific example, wives' economic dependence on their husbands is a strong determiner of wives staying with or returning to abusive husbands (Aguirre, 1985). Although some couples have been able to form economically egalitarian relationships in which money is not an aspect of power or value within the relationship, this situation appears to be the exception, not the rule. In fact, Blumstein and Schwartz (1983) found that lesbian couples (as compared with heterosexual married or cohabiting couples) were the only group for whom money did not determine the power balance.

These socially and economically based gender roles have psychological consequences for how couples relate. The traditional gender-defined roles of husband and wife are embedded in our culture and are presented as the only model for relating as a couple. Although individual couples may create ways to transcend these roles, the roles' psychological aspects are inculcated in each of us, simply because we have grown up in this society. The ways in which these gender roles and responsibilities are translated into relationship behaviors can be described on two levels—as general orientation differences and as specific behavior patterns in relationships.

Autonomy and Relational Orientations in Intimate Relationships

Gender role socialization based on prescribed characteristics and roles for men and women generates two different orientations for relating to another in an intimate relationship: *autonomy* and *relational*. Both autonomy and relational orientations are likely found in all individuals but are usually thought of and experienced more typically by men and women, respectively. They are described here in their general form and coupled with their most common gender affiliation. This is not to imply that all women behave from a relational orientation and all men behave from an autonomy orientation, but that each pattern is generally more typical in one sex than the other. It appears that both modes are ways of structuring the dance in intimate relationships; however, each is given a different value and emphasis in our society.

Autonomy Orientation

The autonomy orientation is usually ascribed to and experienced by males and is generated from the integration of the masculine characteristics identified above. The foundation of this orientation is based on independence and autonomy, requiring an identity defined as separate. Relationships in this context are seen as a way to satisfy the individual's need for affiliation, while not disturbing the need for autonomy and independence. From this perspective, a partner is seen as an independent and separate person with needs and desires that must be balanced and negotiated with one's own. For example, when a man from the autonomy orientation wants to get to know another, it is usually to get the other to comply with the man's belief in what he wants or needs. The fulfillment of his affiliation needs is perceived as the result of his autonomous efforts and not as dependency. In this way intimacy can be experienced while independence can be maintained. In addition, he may expect the woman (in this case) to be coming from the same orientation and to approach him in the same manner. The dance would then be perceived as two partners negotiating their own independent needs and desires.

In some cases, independence can engender the need for control, in which one's autonomy and separateness are protected by controlling those who fulfill one's emotional needs. One way to do this would be to deny one's needs while finding a way to satisfy them. Often, this process is accomplished by devaluing or invalidating the actions of the person who is fulfilling one's needs. In describing the negative aspects of this orientation, which she calls the "objectivity-power-control mode," Jordan (1987) suggests that it can create a competitive, often hostile environment in which one's worth is determined by "being better than" one's partner. If both partners relate from this mode, the relationship can become one of severe competition, in which pride and arrogance can generate a strong defense against experiencing one's own needs, fears, and feelings of helplessness and isolation. Jordan (1987) suggests that in the extreme form, this mode of relating creates severe limits in all relationships and often leads to isolation and a profoundly fragile sense of self.

Men are often socialized, supported, and reinforced for the autonomy orientation in this culture by a sense of entitlement, a belief in one's right to independence and sometimes control. Although useful as a model, in isolation it seems to exclude some of the complexities inherent in intimate relationships. Other models for understanding intimate relationships are needed. The relational orientation described below is offered as an additional way to view human behavior in intimate relationships.

Relational Orientation

The relational orientation, thought to be basically a product of women's socialization, is derived from an identity of self-in-relation (Miller, 1976). In this orientation, mutuality is seen as one of the major characteristics of intimate relationships. Mutuality is sought through empathy, and the commonality and uniqueness of self and another are experienced through this process (Jordan, 1987). Jordan describes the empathetic process of the relational orientation as the "empathetic-love mode of relating" in which mutuality is seen as a source of empowerment for both partners. Joy is experienced with clarity through connection; joy and confidence in oneself and another are considered sources of good feelings about oneself. Surrey (1984) notes that in many intimate relationships between men and women, "taking care of the relationship" is seen by both partners as only the woman's responsibility, inherently upsetting the mutuality of the interaction.

Often women are socialized, supported, and reinforced to use this way of relating primarily to take care of others but not themselves. For some women the actual experience of communicating their own needs is seen as an expression of selfishness (Stiver, 1984) and creates extreme feelings of guilt. In an intimate relationship, a woman's focus on the relationship and her partner can lead to understanding and acting upon her partner's needs rather than her own. The lack of mutuality created by the imbalance in the relationship may be experienced as a loss of self, generating feelings of confusion, vagueness, emptiness, and low self-esteem. Jordan (1987) suggests that

> when people talk about merging or experiencing a "loss of self", they are likely talking about a decreasing clarity, distinctness, and focus about their experience: I cannot see myself clearly, my affect is not highly articulated or differentiated, intentions either become hazy or drop away altogether. (p. 4)

For many women, identity is embedded in the nature and mutuality of their intimate relationships. Specifically, when met with an empathetic, validating response from her partner, a woman senses her own experience coming into focus; without it she may find that her own reality and, in extreme cases, her sense of self will blur.

Aspects of these differing orientations are experienced (albeit in differing degrees) in most relationships. The specific sex or gender of the partners may be fairly predictable in some situations, but the orientations can, and often do, cross sex/gender lines. Orientation differences for individuals in intimate relationships often generate misunderstandings in communication (Tannen, 1990), differing ways of expressing anger (Miller, 1983), and differing ways of defining closeness, intimacy, and trust (e.g, Jordan, 1987; Levenson, 1984). Overall, both orientations serve a similar mission: to structure an individual's experience of reality, self, and relationship. The following sections describe some of the more common patterns created by these differing orientations that emerge within couple relationships.

Orientation Behavior Patterns in Intimate Relationships

Conversation and Interaction Styles

Communication is experienced differently by individuals operating out of the autonomy and relational orientations in regard to purpose, content, and actual style of expression. This difference is illustrated through patterns in conversations between men and women. In general, women's conversations tend to revolve around personal feelings and relationships, whereas men's usually focus on work, sports, and other issues external to the individual (Aries, 1987). Whereas women see conversation as a way of connecting and being intimate, often regardless of content, for men it seems to have another purpose. Tannen (1990) points out that men talk as a way to negotiate status and usually talk more in public situations with people they know less well. In this sense, men do not see conversation as a way to create intimacy, do not feel the need to negotiate their status at home, and actually tend to talk much less at home than women do. Men appear to see conversation as basically a way of sharing information.

Tannen (1990) uses the common example of "trouble talk" to illustrate how these gender differences are played out in couples. She describes a situation in which a woman presents a problem to her husband. For women, Tannen maintains, discussing troubles is the essence of connection. The woman in this situation might be attempting to relate intimately by sharing her feelings and experiences. The man in this scenario responds typically by giving advice, usually in the form of a solution to the problem. Tannen explains that the man's response comes out of his belief that talking about problems is wallowing and just makes him feel worse. In addition, trouble talk is often labeled as complaining, and the woman is perceived as not being willing to do anything to make the situation better. What seems to happen in this situation is that men and women misunderstand the intentions of each other's communication. The woman often feels unheard and devalued; the man, frustrated and helpless to solve his partner's problem.

These differences in communication patterns are further reflected in more general ways of interacting. Aries (1987) suggests that men's interactions are characterized as "more task oriented, dominant, directive, hierarchical"; women's are characterized as "more social-emotional, expressive, supportive, facilitative, cooperative, personal, and egalitarian" (p. 170). These ways of interacting are consistent with autonomy and relational orientations and influence the relationships between men and women, men and men, and women and women.

Caldwell and Peplau (1982) report that friendships between women are more emotionally intense and supportive than those among men. These characteristics of same-sex friendships for women are consistent also with interaction characteristics found in lesbian relationships (e.g., Elise, 1986; Pearlman, 1989; Vargo, 1987). What is interesting to note is that both men and women report more emotional support and intimacy with their friendships with women (e.g., Aukett, Ritchie, & Mill, 1988; Buhrke & Fuqua, 1987). Further, Williams (1985) found that both males and females who were high in levels of femininity (sharing characteristics with the relational orientation) reported higher levels of emotional intimacy in same-sex friendships than those who scored lower on the feminine scale.

Movement: Toward and Away

Movement in the dance of intimate relationships is traditionally experienced as a pattern of closeness and distance. The way this pattern is executed appears to be different for each orientation. For couples in which both orientations are operating (usually heterosexual couples), the difference generates a tension in which the man typically distances and the woman moves closer. This tension, then, generates an overall pattern of relating that holds both closeness and distance. Specifically, in the autonomy orientation, too much closeness needs to be balanced with distance to avoid the loss of self. From the relational orientation, loss of self is often experienced through the lack of closeness—too much distance (Jordan, 1987). Whereas many women can experience intimacy as holding both a sense of self and closeness, most men often experience closeness as different from an independent self. It follows that in heterosexual couples the classic pattern of "nagging" and "withdrawal" ("women cling, men distance" [Krestan & Bepko, 1980]; "pursuer-distancer syndrome" [Papp, 1988]) occurs. Although these words' connotations are judgmental and degrading (e.g., nagging), the actual pattern makes sense based on the individuals' major modes of relating. That is, women move toward their partners to connect, for both the togetherness and their sense of self, while men move toward their partners for togetherness and away (separateness) for their sense of self. By adapting traditional gender-defined roles and movement patterns, some lesbian couples experience this same pattern and report "long periods of extreme and unbreachable distance, in part a response to a fear of loss of self, or fusion" (Krestan & Bepko, cited in Roth, 1989, p. 288).

Papp (1988) describes two of the most common ways of intervening in this pattern in the therapeutic setting. One is to instruct the woman to pull back (assuming that the man will automatically move closer); the other is to urge the man to move closer and share his feelings (not acknowledging the vulnerability and loss of autonomy he might experience). These interventions do not take into account the social gender-defined model of reciprocity. What results is a devaluing of the woman's need for closeness, reinforcing her sense of isolation and, in extreme cases, "craziness." For men, the intervention demonstrates a disregard for the protective function of separating behaviors, often resulting in further distancing (Papp, 1988). It is important to reconceptualize and relabel both individuals' behaviors as different approaches to satisfying their needs for closeness and distance in the intimate relationship. This "reframing" values both modes and generates a base for interventions in which both partners can appreciate the complementary function that each provides the other.

For couples in which both partners are operating out of the relational orientation, the tension for togetherness and separateness is experienced differently. This dance is often labeled *merger* and is defined as "a psychological state in which there is a loss of a sense of oneself as independent and separate" (Pearlman, 1989, p. 78). Merger is a common experience, in different degrees, for all couples during the beginning stages and, at certain times, throughout romantic relationships (e.g., during sexual intimacy, joy, and passionate emotional intimacy). However, merger or fusion occurs with characteristic frequency in lesbian couple relationships (Elise, 1986; Pearlman, 1989; Vargo, 1987) and is often presented as a primary issue in clinical settings.

Merger in lesbian relationships can be seen as an outcome of women's socialization process and homophobic societal norms (Elise, 1986; Vargo, 1987). Pearlman (1989) defines three factors that influence the frequency of the occurrence of merger in lesbian relationships: (1) the intensity of the attunement and emotional connection in relationships between women, (2) the difficulties women have with physical and emotional distance in romantic relationships, and (3) the negations and disruptions most lesbian couples experience because of a homophobic environment.

Relational couples lack the complementary function of two orientations operating to create a balanced tension between closeness and distance. They need to learn the distinction between merger, in which both partners experience themselves as similar and different within the closeness, and the static state of merger, in which both partners lose their differences in the closeness. In the first, more desirable state of merger, both partners experience themselves as together and separate in a relational context. In the second, the togetherness is a static state in which the couple is not responsive to the changing feelings and perceptions and differences of both partners. A static state of merger effectively precludes the intersubjectivity necessary for true intimacy.

Models of intervention for the static state of merger in lesbian couples often emphasize the distinction between similarities and differences rather than between distance and closeness. Roth (1989) reviews different ways counselors attempt to help lesbian couples reach greater individual autonomy within their relationship by (1) encouraging both partners to make self-declaring and individuated statements; (2) teaching concepts such as boundaries, triangling, and fusion; and (3) reframing undifferentiated caretaking as disrespectful of one's partner and a demonstration of lack of care. For relational couples, interventions aimed at increasing "individual autonomy" would emphasize the development of an awareness of the similarities and differences of each partner. The exploration of differences would allow each partner to experience herself as unique, yet still connected in closeness. For these couples the more appropriate tension may be best described as one of similarity and difference in contrast to the closeness-distance dance of two-orientation couples.

Another way of intervening in lesbian relationships that are stuck in static merger addresses the couple's position in society. From this perspective, the couple's static merger can be seen to share characteristics similar to the family dynamic of enmeshment (Minuchin, 1974). Functioning as a closed system, the couple actually closes itself off from the rest of the world. Elise (1986) suggests that this process occurs in some lesbian couples as a response to the negative feedback from society to their relationship. The couple could be viewed as distancing from society and growing ever closer to each other. Intervention in this situation would focus on decreasing the distance between the couple and the outside world while maintaining their connection with each other.

The distinction between merger as a shared relational experience and merger as a static state needs to be further explored. The tension of closeness-distance and sameness-differentness is probably experienced differently among individuals relating from two different orientations and individuals relating from the same orientation. Therefore, interventions aimed at closeness-distance problems in intimate relationships should reflect the unique orientation configuration of each couple.

Affiliation Needs: Dependency

The need for affiliation, specifically the need for others, in a general sense is acknowledged and valued by most men and women. In the context of intimate relationships, the need for affiliation is often addressed by couples and professionals as dependency. However, dependency usually carries a negative, often pathological connotation in contrast to the basic universal need for depending on or needing another. It appears that although we assume that "healthy dependency" (the need for affiliation) is part of all human experience, the words and conceptualizations we use to describe the phenomenon are laden with "unhealthy" meaning. The distinction, then, between healthy and unhealthy dependency becomes blurred.

Dependency is a characteristic commonly ascribed to women and the relational orientation, usually connoting an unhealthy or pathological condition. For example, the diagnosis of Dependent Personality Disorder is disproportionately given to women clients (Landrine, 1989). From the autonomy orientation, dependency would suggest a lack of independence and, thus, would be avoided or denied at any cost (Stiver,

1984). The relational orientation, which is grounded in the mutual needs of both partners, would be seen from the autonomy orientation as a dependent way of being in the world. By defining dependency as a characteristic of women and the relational orientation, individuals operating out of the autonomy orientation can often get their dependency needs met while actually denying them and devaluing the dependent group (women) who are usually given the responsibility for meeting those needs. In a couple this situation can lead to a nonmutual way of relating that hinders intimacy.

For example, in heterosexual couples women often can describe the needs of their spouses, children, relatives, and neighbors but cannot define their own needs (Stiver, 1984). Many women, through the relational socialization process, have developed the very astute skill of perceiving another's need, often before the other individual does (Miller, 1976). This perception is often generated unconsciously through intuition, empathy, and without verbal communication. The woman cares for her partner's need as she perceives it (often appropriately), without clarifying the need with her partner, assessing her desire to meet the need, or acknowledging the act herself. The man, in turn, does not acknowledge or express his dependency needs, which makes it extremely difficult for him to accept another's needs. In addition, Papp (1988) reports that men often wait for the women in their lives to read their feelings rather than show any dependency; if these women fail to read them accurately, the man gets angry and they end up arguing over other superficial issues.

The woman in this scenario may see her behavior as a natural way of showing care and affection and expect the same care in return. Often the expected mutual commitment to this show of affection is not present. In the absence of perceived mutual affection, women often feel depressed, empty, and angry, and they often lose clarity regarding their own needs (Jordan, 1986). In extreme cases, the woman may adopt her partner's needs as her own and not be able to touch her "own voice." In addition, the devaluing of dependency by society's general autonomy orientation often is internalized by women, leaving them to feel ashamed of their basic universal dependency needs (Stiver, 1984).

The man in this example also pays a price. In this situation it is not necessary for him to acknowledge, express, or accept the dependency parts of himself. Extreme independence can lead to feelings of isolation, even in the context of another's care. The acknowledgement and fulfillment of dependency needs seems to be an important aspect of intimacy for both partners, regardless of orientation.

It seems important to distinguish unhealthy from healthy dependency within both modes of relating. In the relational orientation, healthy dependency would mean caring for one's own needs with the same value and energy as caring for one's partner's. In the autonomy orientation healthy dependency would mean acknowledging and accepting within oneself the need for another and valuing one's partner's efforts to meet those needs.

Affiliation Needs: Codependency

Historically, the concept of codependency was derived from the addiction field and used to describe persons in addictive relationships (e.g., spouses of alcoholics) (Morgan, 1991). Definitions of codependency abound in the self-help arena, but all appear to share common characteristics. Codependency appears to be very similar to dependency with the added dimension of control: "a codependent person is one who has let another person's behavior affect him or her, and who is obsessed with controlling that person's behavior" (Beattie, 1987, p. 31). Wegscheider-Cruse's definition of codependency directly relates it to dependency: "a specific condition that is characterized by preoccupation and extreme dependency (emotionally, socially, and sometimes physically) on a person or object..."(quoted in Morgan, 1991, p. 724).

As the concept of codependency has become popular in the self-help movement, mental health professionals have also been attempting to define and use the construct in clinical settings (Myer, Peterson, & Stoffel-Rosales, 1991). Cermak (1986) has suggested that codependency is a personality disorder and has provided criteria for possible inclusion in the *Diagnostic and Statistical Manual of Mental Disorders,* Fourth Edition (DSM-IV). Although some writers (Myer et al., 1991) have cautioned against the premature adoption of codependency as a pathology, the general public and many mental health professions have used the term to describe just about anyone who grew up in a dysfunctional family. In fact, because the concept is so ambiguous, some suggest that as much as 95 percent of the U.S. population can be considered codependent (Wegscheider-Cruse, cited in Myer, Peterson, & Stoffel-Rosales, 1991).

In addressing this ambiguity, Morgan (1991) points out that "the term 'codependency' has been used on each of three levels of meaning: as a didactic tool, psychological concept, and disease entity" (p.722). Similarly, Myer, Peterson, and Stoffel-Rosales (1991) analyzed the underlying assumptions of codependency and con-cluded that Cermak's assumption that codependency is a disease is premature. In fact, they suggest that the label "Self-Defeating Per-sonality Disorder" (and accompanying diagnostic criteria) presented in the DSM-III-R as a potential personality disorder needing further study "better characterizes and communicates the symptoms than does the label codependency" (p. 456).

Codependency in a couple relationship is experienced in much the same way as dependency (discussed above). However, the impact of the wide popularity of the codependency movement has generated discussions on a much more political level. These discussions usually focus on the codependent woman and provide some important considerations for counselors.

Tavris (1990a, 1990b) and Hagan (cited in Morgan, 1991) both suggest that codependency is another manifestation of the devaluing and oppression of women. Tavris (1990a) makes this point clearly when she says—

> In the 1970s, the problem was women's "fear of success." In 1981, it was the "Cinderella Complex—a hidden fear of inde-pendence." In 1985, it was the fact that women "love too much." Now we're told that women's problem is the "disease" of "codependency"—they are addicted to abusers, addicted to bad relationships, addicted to people with addictions. They are "enablers," the partners whose concern for their alcoholic or drug-abusing spouses allows addiction to continue. (p. 26)

Lerner (quoted in Tavris, 1990b) expands this notion of women as sick to the larger social context and maintains that this disease mentality serves an important function in the oppression of women in society. Specifically, "society is more comfortable with women who feel inadequate, self-doubting, guilty, sick and 'diseased' than with women who are angry or confronting" (Lerner, quoted in Tavris, 1990b, p. 43). In sum, as long as women internalize the negation and devaluation of their gender role characteristics, the oppressive structure of society will not change.

Landrine (1989) proposed a social-role hypothesis as a way of viewing personality disorders that provides a useful model for conceptualizing codependency. The social-role hypothesis states that "each personality disorder represents the roles/role-stereotype of the specific status group that tends to receive that diagnosis most often, such that the personality disorder categories as a whole represent the roles/role-stereotypes of both sexes" (p. 326). Landrine specifically investigated this hypothesis with the Self-Defeating Personality Disorder (SDPD), described by Myer et al. (1991) as characterizing the symptoms of codependency. Landrine found, as predicted, that all subjects perceived the description of SDPD as that of a woman. She concluded that personality disorders are political on three levels, one of which addresses the purposes of "masquerading gender roles with madness" (p. 332).

Although the codependency movement has generated many helpful recovery programs (e.g., 12-step programs: AlAnon, Codependents Anonymous, and Adult Children of Dysfunctional Families; "healing the inner child" books and groups), it also creates a fundamental concern regarding the relational orientation. That is, the overall connotation of codependency may be another way mental health professionals and society label the relational orientation as pathological. If the relational orientation is seen by society as less valuable or as a mental illness, both men and women may limit their ways of relating intimately. It appears that the ambiguity of the term *codependency* may blur the distinction between relating in a relational way versus losing sight of one's own needs or attempting to control another. Clarifying this distinction, especially in counseling situations, could engender an environment in which the relational orientation is acknowledged and valued and the useful aspects of codependency recovery programs could be applied. For example, instead of labeling behavior as "loving too much," the same behavior could be seen as a highly developed skill (and a potential source of self-esteem), and the focus in counseling may be placed on the lack of love for oneself. In this way, the highly developed skill of empathically loving another could be used as a foundation for the development of the empathic love of self.

Conflict: Anger

The open discussion of disagreement and conflict among couples is necessary for intimacy to occur. Anger is an emotion that tells us that something is wrong, something hurts, and something needs to be changed within the relationship (Miller, 1983). The emotion of anger serves as a powerful motivator to bring about immediate change. When anger is recognized and expressed, couples can negotiate the area of conflict and resolve the area of difference, and the anger will usually dissipate. In this process, individuals may experience the pain of becoming aware of their differences, but neither need be damaged.

Miller (1983) proposed that the actual model for the expression of anger in our culture is one in which we have come to know anger as an "aggressive, isolating, and destructive experience" (p. 7). Anger is viewed as a way to control others instead of as a signal for individuals to work through differences. In addition, Miller maintains that constraints are placed on the expression of anger in our society for all individuals. However, different types of constraints are placed for dominant and subordinate groups.

Anger as a legitimate emotion is reserved for those in the dominant position. For the subordinate group, the expression of anger is often seen as pathological. Usually, on the societal level, the dominant and subordinate groups are defined as male and female, respectively (Miller, 1983). Lerner (1985) maintains that women's anger could be an agent of personal and social change and would challenge the status quo. For this reason, Miller (1983) sees the suppression of women's anger on the societal level as being socially and psychologically reinforced. In couple relationships, Miller's analysis is helpful for conceptualizing the societal factors that influence both men's and women's ways of expressing anger. However, in couples, the partners' positions of dominance and subordinance may change based on the situation. In addition, the orientation of each partner affects the dance of conflict expression and resolution.

Strong social messages create constraints on the expression of anger for most women. As one woman client said, "I have been raised such that I continually live with a gag-order on anger." Psychologically, the suppression of anger by women is reinforced by (1) the threat of violence (rape, beatings, and other forms of brutality), (2) the message that they have no cause for anger (it is something wrong with them), and (3) the internalization of those beliefs (I am weak, I am unworthy, I have "no right" to be angry) (Miller, 1983). For women from a relational orientation, these factors, along with a model for the expression of anger that is based on control, can make anger incompatible with their orientation. For such women, anger often feels like a threat to their identity and to the valued relationship. Thus, in an intimate relationship, women are often afraid to feel even the smallest stirring of anger.

For women in intimate relationships, the denial of anger may take on two common patterns: symptoms or explosions. It is often easier for women and their partners to deal with sickness than anger (Lerner, 1985). For women, this sickness is often in the form of depression (Hafner, 1986; Miller, 1983) and is treated clinically as a personal pathology.

Explosions of anger occur through "spiraling phenomena" (Miller, 1983), in which unexpressed conflicts and emotions build to the point of consuming the individual. Women often report this process after an awareness of "feeling full of anger" (Miller, 1983, p. 3). When finally expressed, the anger is often too general, confused, and exaggerated to facilitate open dialogue regarding change. Often this anger is labeled as hysterical and the woman described as "castrating." In marital counseling, it is common for the therapist and the woman's partner to focus on her emotive style (often seen as the pathology) instead of the problem that caused her to emote (Papp, 1988).

Another pattern that often occurs in heterosexual couples is what Papp (1988) calls "emoting for two" (p. 211). In this dance, the man responds to the woman's anger by avoidance and withdrawal. From the autonomy orientation, "emotional scenes" are to be avoided, especially if his partner's affection might be withdrawn or, in some cases, his control compromised. If both partners, then, avoid open discussion or confrontation, the woman often feels even more frustration and rage and ends up emoting for both of them (Papp, 1988). The denial of anger by either partner has severe consequences for the couple. The very mechanism for monitoring differences is nonfunctional, and potential negotiation is aborted.

The subordinate/dominant analysis can also be useful in understanding the dance of conflict in intimate relationships. For individuals who find themselves in both subordinate and dominant positions in different areas of their lives, intimate partners are often the targets of misplaced anger. For example, in a heterosexual relationship, a man finds himself in a subordinate position at work with constraints placed on his expression of anger in that position. However, when he comes home, his position changes to one of dominance and the constraints loosen, allowing him to direct often- unrelated anger toward his partner (Papp, 1988; Miller, 1983).

Counseling interventions designed to change anger expression patterns need to focus on reframing anger as a useful emotion that sends information to the couple that something is wrong and hurtful. Then anger would not need to be seen as a negative emotion to be avoided, but as a crucial, powerful, and enhancing aspect of any intimate relationship. The couple could then negotiate the differentness within the mutual closeness of the relationship. Anger would be handled as an assertive attempt to generate togetherness rather than as a reactionary outcome of previously suppressed pain (Papp, 1988).

Conflict: Couple Violence

One way to view couple violence is as an extreme expression of anger for the purpose of controlling another. This view is illustrated in the actual definition of battering in intimate relationships. Although specifically presented for the context of lesbian relationships, Hart's (1986) definition of battering is appropriate for heterosexual couples as well. Battering is "that pattern of violent and coercive behaviors whereby a lesbian seeks to control the thoughts, beliefs, or conduct of her intimate partner or to punish the intimate for resisting the perpetrator's control over her" (p. 173). Although historically the focus was placed on the psychological characteristics of the victim, the current emphasis usually places responsibility for the abuse on the perpetrator (Papp, 1988). Often explained from a gender role analysis (e.g., Walker, 1981), the dynamics have traditionally been defined from heterosexual relationships. By looking at couple violence through the model of anger expression presented by Miller (1983), the dynamics of battering relationships can be expanded to include any couple in which anger in its extreme physical form is used to control one's partner. This perspective is consistent with the discussion of psychological violence earlier in this book.

The experience of violence in intimate relationships has been found to escalate in severity over time and follow a cycle defined by Walker (1984). The autonomous and relational orientations, in their extreme form, may provide one explanation for some of the patterns of behavior in this cycle. For example, consider a couple relating from two different orientations moving through Walker's (1984) three-phase cycle of violence. The first is the tension-building phase, characterized by stress, frustration, communication difficulties, and attempts by the victim to pacify the batterer. The batterer is relating from the autonomous orientation in its extreme form. Stress and frustration lead to conflict, and the batterer expresses anger in the attempt to control his or her partner. The partner, relating from a relational orientation, may use empathetic skills to try to determine the abuser's needs and fulfill them in an attempt to avoid the violence. Contrary to historical views that portray the victim as passive and even masochistic, battered persons usually attempt to contain the violence throughout the cycle (Caplan, 1985). Walker (1981) suggests that victims often try to protect the abuser from stress as a way to avoid the cycle and, in situations in which abuse is seen as inevitable, they might actually initiate the second phase, violence, as a way to control and contain the potential harm to themselves. In the third phase, the honeymoon phase, the batterer apologizes and attempts to convince the victim that the violence will never happen again. This behavior can also be viewed as a form of controlling one's partner, with the additional benefit of using the control as a way for the batterer to maintain a self-perception of independence while keeping the victim in the relationship.

The relational orientation may influence how a victim behaves with her partner but does not fully account for why she stays. Both lesbian and heterosexual battered women are often reluctant to seek help and leave abusive partners because of (1) economic dependency on the abuser, (2) the threat of more severe violence in the future, (3) isolation, (4) the belief that she is responsible, (5) the fear of confronting the ambivalence inherent in loving someone who is brutal toward her, and (6) a hope that things will get better in time (Mason & Blankenship, 1987; Morrow & Hawxhurst, 1989; Walker, 1984). In addition, Morrow and Hawxhurst suggest that a lesbian batterer may use homophobic controls, such as threatening to expose her partner's sexual orientation, convincing the victim that she will not get help because she is a lesbian (women's shelters are often nonaccepting of lesbian women), and telling her partner that she is not a "real lesbian."

From an orientation perspective, counseling interventions need to be aimed at building on the strengths of the relational and autonomy modes while diminishing the negative affects of their extreme forms. To do so would necessitate finding ways for autonomy-oriented batterers to experience autonomy and affiliation without having to control their partners. For relational-oriented partners in violent relationships, the lack of mutuality within the couple could be emphasized, along with support and direction for self-care and safety. New models for the expression and conceptualization of anger as a healthy, potentially growth-producing mechanism for change would help facilitate a decline in violence used to control intimate partners.

SOME CONCLUDING THOUGHTS

This chapter has been written in an attempt to provide a mind-set from which to conceptualize and treat women's concerns within intimate relationships. The purpose was to provide a framework that challenges and, it is hoped, expands our current understanding of models for "dancing" in intimate relationships. This is extremely necessary because of the lack of life-enhancing models for relating as couples.

In addition to women, other marginalized groups of people (e.g., minority and ethnic groups, gay males, single heads of households, poor and working-class poor families) have often had to come up with different models for relating intimately. To date, these groups are markedly absent from the popular and professional literature. Models of intimate relationships are desperately needed from these groups in our society. Often they have experienced most concretely the ill-fitting nature of our limited models for relating and have been challenged to create their own. We can all benefit from creative, life-enhancing ways of relating as couples. The ultimate vision is toward numerous models, valued equally, from which persons can relate.

THE EXAMPLE OF LISA AND BILL

Lisa entered counseling with vague symptoms of uneasiness, mild depression, and a gnawing sense of emptiness. She reported that she was satisfied with her career as a nurse, had a good network of friends, and was generally physically healthy. The "uneasiness" seemed to "creep up on her," growing continually worse over the last three months. She had put off seeking outside help hoping that she would be able to identify "the problem" and correct it on her own. Over the last few weeks, however, her husband had become very concerned with her unhappiness and encouraged her to seek counseling.

Lisa and Bill had been married for two years when Lisa presented for counseling. Lisa described herself and her husband as a typical dual-career couple planning to begin a family within the next few years after Bill's engineering career was more under way. Convinced that the problem was all hers, Lisa spoke glowingly about Bill as a husband and about their marriage. However, as we began to explore in greater detail, Lisa suggested that recently she was feeling that something was changing within their relationship. She identified that their communication had become less intimate, they were spending less time together, and their sexual relations had lost "a lot of passion." As we explored her experience further, it appeared that her relationship with Bill was of primary concern, and at least part of her uneasiness stemmed from the recent, often vague, feeling of "disconnection" in that relationship.

By the end of the first session, Lisa expressed grave concern that her current emotional state would damage her marriage and her goal for counseling was to "feel better" and thus protect the marriage. Because the marriage was a key focus of Lisa's concern, it appeared most beneficial to restructure future counseling sessions to include Bill. This decision served to reframe the presenting problem from a personal to an interpersonal one. Even though Lisa attributed the current dissatisfaction with her life and marriage to there being something wrong with her, she acknowledged the importance of the relational context of her experience. She felt that Bill would be open to involvement in the counseling process and would support her therapeutic work.

Bill was openly concerned about his wife and very committed to the marriage. He reported that he did not perceive any difficulties with their ways of relating but had noticed a shift in Lisa's satisfaction with him. He also noted the change in their sexual activity and "passion" and mentioned that he felt rather frustrated that he couldn't come up with ways to make Lisa "happy." While very concerned, both Lisa and Bill unquestioningly attributed the difficulties to Lisa's emotional problems.

In my experience, this is a common dynamic, and the first conceptual intervention was to change the focus of the problem from Lisa to the marital relationship. Often metaphors are quite helpful in this reframing process. With Lisa and Bill, the metaphor of their relationship as a dance proved helpful. Together, we discussed the dance of couples, predictable changes over time as a couple moves from courtship to partnership, and the give-and-take necessary for two individuals to create the emotional space to grow personally and as a couple. The identification and generation of a dance in which both Bill's and Lisa's needs could be met (individually and as a couple) became our common working objective. We approached this process by exploring some of the cultural, family-of-origin, and individual experiences Lisa and Bill brought to the marriage. Specifically, models of relating that both Lisa and Bill had known were identified, clarified, and explored.

Within a personal and cultural context, Lisa and Bill discussed their ideas regarding what it means to be a woman-wife and man-husband, respectively. They also shared their expectations for each other surrounding these roles. These expectations were often difficult to articulate, and at times both seemed surprised at the other's perception of themselves and of each other. Lisa's and Bill's expectations were usually very similar. For example, both wanted support, love, and loyalty, but the manners in which these qualities were requested and given were often very different. The differences then generated misunderstandings and misinterpretations of intent.

In most situations, Lisa operated from a relational orientation, while Bill related from an autonomy orientation. Typical patterns of this difference of relating were evident in Lisa's attempts to move closer and connect and Bill's emotional distancing. The expression of anger was difficult for both. Bill would often have outbursts of anger followed by withdrawal. Lisa, believing that her anger would lead to disconnection, avoided any expression of anger, creating periods of vague tension in the relationship. We explored these patterns through the conceptual framework of relational and autonomous orientations, culturally defined gender roles, and family-of-origin behaviors.

Uncovering these patterns was freeing to both in at least two ways. First, it dissipated some of the tension and blame by providing a contextual understanding of each partner's behavior and experience. Second, it allowed Lisa and Bill to look at their modes of relating in a new way. As the relationship patterns were made explicit and conscious, the couple could make decisions regarding which aspects of relating they wanted to retain and which they wanted to work on changing.

As counseling progressed, it became clear that Lisa's feelings of disconnection were strongly connected with her general well-being and self-esteem. Bill was able to hear and respect the importance Lisa placed on their marriage and how integral the relationship was to Lisa's quality of life. The couple was able to acknowledge Bill's feelings of responsibility and frustration at often not being able to "fix" things within the relationship. Both Lisa and Bill continued to frame their concerns as couple issues instead of as Lisa's problem. As a couple, Lisa and Bill identified the need to continue to work on the open expression of conflict and anger, as both had grown up in families where that was problematic. Lisa worked specifically on being able to express her needs, desires, and conflicts in ways that felt to her as promoting the relationship rather than damaging it. Bill worked on finding more effective ways to express his anger and to accept his frustration at not always solving their problems.

REFERENCES

Aguirre, B. (1985). Why do they return? Abused wives in shelters. *Social Work, 30*(3), 350–354.

Aries, E. (1987). Gender and communication. In P. C. Hendrick (Ed.), *Sex and gender* (pp. 149–176). Newbury Park, CA: Sage.

Aukett, R., Ritchie, J., & Mill, K. (1988). Gender differences in friendship patterns. *Sex Roles, 19,* 57–66.

Avis, J. (1985). The politics of functional family therapy: A feminist critique. *Journal of Marital and Family Therapy, 11,* 127–138.

Barnett, R., & Baruch, G. (1987). Social roles, gender, and psychological distress. In R. Barnett, L. Biener, & G. Baruch (Eds.), *Gender and Stress* (pp. 122–143). New York: The Free Press.

Baruch, G., & Barnett, R. (1986). Role quality, multiple role involvement, and psychological well-being in midlife women. *Journal of Personality and Social Psychology, 51,* 578–585.

Beattie, M. (1987). *Co-dependent no more.* New York: Hazelden.

Blumstein, P., & Schwartz, P. (1983). *American couples.* New York: William Morrow.

Buhrke, R. A., & Fuqua, D. R. (1987). Sex differences in same- and cross-sex supportive relationships. *Sex Roles, 17,* 339–352.

Caldwell, M., & Peplau, L. (1982). Sex differences in same-sex friendship. *Sex Roles, 8,* 721–732.

Caplan, P. J. (1985). *The myth of women's masochism.* New York: E. P. Dutton.

Cermak, T. L. (1986). *Diagnosing and treating co-dependence.* Minneapolis: Johnston Institute Books.

Elise, D. (1986). Lesbian couples: The implications of sex differences in separation-individuation. *Psychotherapy, 23,* 305–310.

Faludi, S. (1991). *Backlash: The undeclared war against American women.* New York: Crown.

Hafner, R. J. (1986). *Marriage and mental illness.* New York: Guilford Press.

Hart, B. J. (1986). Lesbian battering: An examination. In K. Lobel (Ed.), *Naming the violence: Speaking out about lesbian battering* (pp. 173–189). Seattle: Seal Press.

Jordan, J. (1986). *The meaning of mutuality* (Work in Progress No. 23). Stone Center Working Papers. Wellesley, MA: Stone Center for Developmental Services and Studies.

Jordan, J. (1987). *Clarity in connection: Empathic knowing, desire and sexuality.* (Work in Progress No. 29). Stone Center Working Papers. Wellesley, MA: Stone Center for Developmental Services and Studies.

Krestan, J., & Bepko, C. (1980). The problem of fusion in the lesbian relationship. *Family Process, 19,* 277–281.

Landrine, H. (1989). The politics of personality disorder. *Psychology of Women Quarterly, 13,* 325–339.

Lerner, H. G. (1985). *The dance of anger.* New York: Harper & Row.

Lerner, H. G. (1989). *The dance of intimacy: A woman's guide to courageous acts of change in key relationships.* New York: Harper & Row.

Levenson, R. (1984). Intimacy, autonomy and gender: Developmental differences and their reflection in adult relationships. *Journal of the American Academy of Psychoanalysis, 12*(4):529–544.

Mason, A., & Blankenship, V. (1987). Power and affiliation motivation, stress, and abuse in intimate relationships. *Journal of Personality and Social Psychology, 52,* 203–210.

McGoldrick, M. (1989). Women and the family life cycle. In B. Carter & M. McGoldrick (Eds.), *The changing family life cycle: A framework for family therapy* (2nd ed.) (pp. 29–68). Boston: Allyn and Bacon.

Miller, J. B. (1976). *Toward a new psychology of women*. New York: Beacon Press.

Miller, J. B. (1983). *The construction of anger in women and men* (Work in Progress No. 83-01). Stone Center Working Papers. Wellesley, MA: Stone Center for Developmental Services and Studies.

Minuchin, S. (1974). *Families and family therapy*. Cambridge, MA: Harvard University Press.

Morgan, J. P. (1991). What is codependency? *Journal of Clinical Psychology, 47*(5), 720–729.

Morgan, R. (1985). *Women who love too much: When you keep wishing and hoping he'll change*. New York: Pocket Books.

Morrow, S., & Hawxhurst, D. (1989): Lesbian partner abuse: Implications for therapists. *Journal of Counseling & Development, 68,* 58–62.

Myer, R., Peterson, S., Stoffel-Rosales, M. (1991). Co-dependency: An examination of underlying assumptions. *Journal of Mental Health Counseling, 13*(4), 449–458.

Papp, P. (1988). Couples. In M. Walters, B. Carter, P. Papp, & O. Silverstein (Eds.), *The invisible web: Gender patterns in family relationships* (pp. 200–249). New York: The Guilford Press.

Pearlman, S. (1989). Distancing and connectedness: Impact on couple formation in lesbian relationships. In E. Rothblum & E. Cole (Eds.), *Loving boldly: Issues facing lesbians* (pp. 77–88). New York: Harrington Park.

Roth, S. (1989). Psychotherapy with lesbian couples: Individual issues, female socialization, and the social context. In M. McGoldrick, C. Anderson, & F. Walsh (Eds.), *Women in families: A framework for family therapy* (pp. 286–307). New York: W.W. Norton

Schaef, A. W. (1989). *Escape from intimacy: The pseudo-relationship addictions*. San Francisco: Harper & Row.

Stiver, I. (1984). *The meanings of "dependency" in female-male relationships* (Work in Progress No. 11). Stone Center Working Papers. Wellesley, MA: Stone Center for Developmental Services and Studies.

Surrey, J. (1984). *The "self-in-relation": A theory of women's development* (Work in Progress No. 13). Stone Center Working Papers. Wellesley, MA: Stone Center for Developmental Services and Studies.

Tannen, D. (1990). *You just don't understand: Women and men in conversation*. New York: William Morrow.

Tavris, C. (1990a, March 11). One more guilt trip for women. *Star Tribune,* p. 26.

Tavris, C. (1990b). The politics of codependency. *Networker,* 43.

Vargo, S. (1987). The effects of women's socialization on lesbian couples. In The Boston Lesbian Psychologies Collective (Eds.), *Lesbian psychologies: Explorations & challenges* (pp. 161–173). Chicago: University of Illinois Press.

Walker, L. (1981). Battered women: Sex roles and clinical issues. *Professional Psychology, 12,* 81–91.

Walker, L. (1984). *The battered woman syndrome.* New York: Springer.

White, K., Houlihan, J., Costos, D., & Speisman, J. (1990). Adult development in individuals and relationships. *Journal of Research in Personality, 24,* 371–386.

Williams, D. (1985). Gender, masculinity-femininity, and emotional intimacy in same-sex friendships. *Sex Roles, 12,* 587–600.

Woititz, J. (1985). *Struggle for intimacy.* Deerfield Beach, FL: Health communications, Inc.

BALANCING RELATIONSHIPS
WITH CAREERS

Marian Stoltz-Loike

Contemporary theories of female development have postulated that women define their self-identities in relation to other people (Chodorow, 1978; Forrest & Mikolaitis, 1986; Gilligan, 1982, 1989; Miller, 1976). This theory contrasts with the masculine bias of traditional developmental theories that associate "identity" with personal independence (Lyons, 1989).

A prime focus of this chapter is the impact of women's relationships on employment issues with respect to (1) the conflict of their relational self-identity with career choices, and (2) the association of career paths and prime relationships as a member of a couple, as parents to their child(ren), or as daughters to their aging parents. Some of the following questions will be addressed: Given women's concern with relationships, what effects do marriage or childbirth have on career patterns? If women gravitate toward work that allows the expression of self in relation to others, what can be done to address issues of lack of pay equity and occupational prestige among these jobs compared with male-typed jobs? Are there differences among women who choose to work in female-typed careers compared with women who work in business, law, or medicine?

Few studies have explored the relation between career concerns and women's ethnicity (Cook, 1991; Fitzgerald & Weitzman, in press). The scant literature that does exist suggests that black women viewed high career performance as an expression of their concern for their families, rather than as a conflict with family needs (Allen & Britt, 1983), and were more likely than white women to choose traditionally male careers (Murrell, Frieze & Frost, 1991). Similarly, there is virtually no career literature on lesbian women (Fitzgerald & Weitzman, in press), although counselors have recently summarized various issues relevant to the career counseling of lesbian women (Hetherington & Orzek, 1989). Relationship issues may be different for lesbian women than for women in heterosexual relations (Eldridge & Gilbert, 1990). This chapter reflects the studies available in the literature, which typically analyze white, middle class, heterosexual women. Further studies of other groups of women would be appropriate for a truly comprehensive understanding of the association of relationship issues and women's career dimensions.

WOMEN'S CAREER DEVELOPMENT

The Nature of Women's Career Paths

Early research on the career motivation of women suggested that women worked for social reasons (considered extrinsic reasons), whereas men worked for power, money, and achievement (considered intrinsic reasons) (e.g., Ace, Graen, & Dawis, 1972; Weinberg & Tittle, 1987). Recent research, however, has shown that women expect the same rewards from work and have employment goals similar to those of men. Both men and women work to earn money and want to be productive members of society (Chester & Grossman, 1990; Grossman & Chester, 1990), value power associated with work (Grossman & Stewart, 1990), and have similar achievement goals (Chester, 1990; Travis, Phillippi, & Henley, 1991). Thus, women, like men, consider employment to be a significant part of their self-definitions (Avioli, 1985) and derive a sense of self-esteem and well-being from high-quality work (e.g., Loscocco & Spitze, 1990; Stein, Newcomb, & Bentler, 1990). Like men, women anticipate self-fulfillment from their work (Betz & Fitzgerald, 1987; Fitzgerald & Crites, 1980) and value work-related accomplishments, job security, income potential, and the respect of co-workers (Beutell & Brenner, 1986).

A generation ago, most women expected to work until they were married or had children. Today's college women plan to combine both family and career roles (Baber & Monaghan, 1988; Covin & Brush, 1991; O'Connell, Betz, & Kurth, 1989), expect their careers to be an important part of their futures (Covin & Brush, 1991; Gilbert, Dancer, Rossman, & Thorn, 1991), and anticipate that career development will be a life-span developmental process (Osipow, 1991).

Despite many similarities, men and women differ in the kinds of careers they pursue, their lifetime career achievements, and their responses to work involvement and work demands. Women's careers are more discontinuous than those of men (Voydanoff, 1987; 1988), show fewer gains from educational backgrounds (Betz & Fitzgerald, 1987), and experience a greater interaction between family and career issues (Betz & Fitzgerald, 1987; Goh, 1991; Loscocco, 1990; Loscocco & Roschelle, 1991; Nelson, Quick, Hitt, & Moesel, 1990; Williams, 1990). For example, women earned approximately 74 cents to the dollar of male wages in 1991 (U.S. Bureau of Labor Statistics, personal communication, 1992), which means that women had to work nearly seven days to gross what men earned in five days.

Education also affects women's career continuity, and more educated women are more likely to be employed (Betz & Fitzgerald, 1987). In one study, for example, 51 percent of women with BAs and 91 percent of women with PhDs in science or engineering were employed (Vetter, 1980). Nonetheless, few women were found at the levels of full professor, and university women typically earned less than their male counterparts (Ferber & Kordick, 1978). This circumstance may reflect discrimination against women or the fact that women in universities and businesses have different access to and utility of resources related to organizational success and power (Ragins & Sundstrom, 1989).

As more women enter the workplace and plan continuous lifetime employment, a more direct benefit of experience and education on lifetime earnings can be expected. Whether women will also routinely reach the prestige and income levels of their male counterparts remains debatable. To date, few women have achieved the top ranks of employment even though more than half the work force is female (U.S. Bureau of Labor Statistics, personal communication,

1989), more than half of all mothers of children under age 6 are employed (U.S. Bureau of Labor Statistics, personal communication, 1989), and approximately 70 percent of new entrants to the labor force in the next two decades will be female or members of a minority (Johnston & Packer, 1987).

A woman's motivation to achieve in her career may affect her choices about relationships. Career-committed women marry (Gilbert, Dancer, Rossman, & Thorn, 1991; Spitze, 1988) and have children (Gilbert et al., 1991; Wilk, 1986) at a later age than less career-committed women. Additionally, support for these data is evident in the finding that only 35 percent of women executives, as compared with 90 percent of male executives, have children (Schele, 1991).

Career Patterns and Women's Self-Identity

Although women work for the same reasons as men, it appears that women's career development is different and more complex than that of men (Betz & Fitzgerald, 1987; Fitzgerald & Weitzman, in press; Jenkins, 1989). This finding raises the question of whether traditional theories of career development accurately characterize women's career development (Ornstein & Isabella, 1990). Women, it is thought, may pursue a two-step career development process as compared with the one-step process of men (Betz & Fitzgerald, 1987). The first step involves establishing priorities between family and career concerns, and the second step involves career growth and development, a step similar to that taken by men.

Researchers have recently underscored the fact that although mothers perceived that parenting affects career achievement (Marshall & Jones, 1990; Olson, Frieze & Detlefson, 1990), they still experienced child raising as satisfying and rewarding (Marshall & Jones, 1990). Moreover, college women view their anticipated success at mothering as more important than success at a variety of male- and female-typed occupations (Eccles, 1986). Consequently, a life-span perspective on women's career achievement is advocated (Cotton, Antill, & Cunningham, 1990) to fully understand the relationship between self-expression and career goals for women.

112

CAREER CONCERNS

Establishing Priorities: The Importance of Gender Role Identity

Despite the assumption that women's careers are different than men's, popular magazines contain many stories of women who have made it to the top and may experience little or no conflict between family and career issues even when they do have families. While empirical data also demonstrate that many women report that they experience conflict between family and career concerns, these anecdotal stories describe women who experience little or no interrole conflict. The career histories of many of the latter group of women are continuous; some have children while others have delayed or forgone childbirth and marriage as they pursued their careers. What differentiates this latter group of women from women described by Voydanoff (1987, 1988) and other researchers who characterize women's career histories as discontinuous?

A variety of self-concept issues relate to the differences between these groups of women. Particularly important is individual gender role identity, which reflects how gender colors the way individuals perceive and interact with other people and their environments. Individual gender role identity interacts with career choices and expectations and may distinguish between career paths of different groups of women. Spence and Helmreich (1979) and Bem (1979) developed scales that are now widely used to measure gender role identity. Using self-report, Bem's Sex Role Inventory (BSRI) and Spence and Helmreich's Personality Attributes Questionnaire (PAQ) evaluate the "masculinity" (instrumental) or "femininity" (expressive) of an individual's behaviors. Since masculine and feminine scales are orthogonal, rather than opposite poles on a single scale, it is possible for a person to be high on both masculinity and femininity (androgynous), low on both (undifferentiated), or high on one and low on the other. Both men and women can be high on either scale, so the literature has adopted the nomenclature of referring to the masculine scale as the "instrumental" scale and the feminine scale as the "expressive" scale, thereby removing the stereotyped association of masculinity with male behavior and femininity with female behavior.

Among women, there is a strong association between those who are high on the instrumental scales of the PAQ or BSRI and various work-related variables (Betz & Fitzgerald, 1987; Fassinger, 1990; Mazen & Lemkau, 1990; Murrell, Frieze, & Frost, 1991). High instrumental women were less affected by negative life events (Roos & Cohen, 1987), experienced less work-related strain, and were more problem focused (Long, 1989). Career choice was also associated with gender role identity (Strange & Rea, 1983; Terborg, 1977). Furthermore, an instrumental gender role identity was associated with plans to pursue a male-typed career (Betz & Fitzgerald, 1987), so that women with high instrumental scores were more likely to pursue nontraditional majors such as math and science (Hackett, 1985) and to be involved in masculine-typed careers (Betz & Fitzgerald, 1987). In contrast, diminished career aspirations were found among women who plan to pursue family and career goals (Ragins & Sundstrom, 1989; Rix, 1987) and were characteristic of women who planned careers in female-typed jobs (Murrell, Frieze, & Frost, 1991). Even women who have pursued intellectually challenging educational curricula may choose careers that underuse their abilities (Betz, Heesacker, & Shuttleworth, 1990; Cook, 1991).

While differences between men and women may exist in various domains, studies that have held instrumentality constant have found few or no gender differences. This finding suggests that many male-female differences in career paths may actually relate to differences in the way instrumental or expressive individuals view their careers and the interrole conflict they experience between family and career roles (Betz & Fitzgerald, 1987; Murrell, Frieze, & Frost, 1991).

The interaction of gender role identity and career interest may change among women as full-time career pursuits continue to be anticipated by college-educated women. Whether gender role differences also affect male career performance is open to speculation. To date, no literature has explored the association of career interest and gender role identity among men. An interesting study might involve the comparison of gender role identities among those few men who are at home full time with an employed partner and those men who are employed outside the home.

Expression of Self via Career Choice and Performance

Many women pursue different careers than men, which may reflect women's desires to express the relational element of their self-identities within their careers (see, for example, Forrest & Mikolaitis, 1986). These female-typed jobs include teaching, nursing, social work, and office work and are characterized by lower pay and fewer opportunities for upward mobility than nonfemale-typed jobs requiring similar educational and experiential backgrounds (Murrell, Frieze, & Frost, 1991). Many women also experience a constriction of possible career opportunities because of their generally weaker math and science backgrounds (Hesse-Biber, 1985; Poole & Clooney, 1985). Consequently, some of the male-typed careers, like physician, engineer, scientist, manager, stockbroker, or architect, that pay higher incomes and have more opportunities for upward mobility may not be accessible to women (Betz & Fitzgerald, 1987; Chipman, Brush, & Wilson, 1985) even if they are interested in these careers.

Eccles (1986) proposed that understanding female career choices is related to the positive values that women place on other academic disciplines during the choice process, rather than the negative valuing they may have of math or science. Thus, Eccles views career choice as an approach-avoidance response based on valuation of different options and the anticipated compatibility of these options with other adult roles. In fact, changing the values attributed to different career pursuits would be associated with making different career choices.

In a recent review article, Cook (1991) offered three perspectives that may, in part, explain some of the different career choices of men and women and can be summarized as follows: (1) *Occupational perspectives:* Men and women may hold distinct expectations about whether a particular occupation will fulfill their work values. (2) *Perspectives on salary:* Although both sexes place similar values on salaries as a work value, women and men may use salary information differently in evaluating a job offer. (3) *Gendered context of work environment:* Women and men of the same age within the same workplace have different experiences of work environments (Fitzgerald & Weitzman, in press), of opportunities for upward mobility (Morrison & Von Glinow, 1990), and of conflicts between family and career concerns. Women may not select particular careers because they view the obstacles to achievement as overwhelming, while selecting other careers that offer greater promise of success.

Currently, many more women are pursuing careers in male-typed professions. Are these women exhibiting the independent self characteristic of their male co-workers within these jobs? Or are they changing the work force by introducing more caring, relational concerns? Magazine articles (e.g., Bernstein & Rozen, 1989) geared to businesswomen have lauded a style of management that is oriented to the worker and characterized by good listening skills, supportive behaviors, and encouragement of workers' exploring innovative performance strategies. Among physicians, as well, women who chose the specialty of surgery, which is disproportionately male dominated, reported that they hoped to change aspects of surgical practice, like improving doctor-patient relationships, rather than being attracted by the authority typically attributed to the surgeon (Grant & DuRoss, 1984).

With regard to work involvement, the different career experiences of women and men may reflect women's greater concern with relationship issues. When they worked overtime, career women experienced dissatisfaction, whereas career men felt more satisfied with their work (Sekaran, 1986). This result may relate to the greater difficulty of addressing relationship roles when fewer hours are available outside the workplace.

Role Conflict

Role conflict results when individuals must function simultaneously within multiple roles and the demands for optimal performance in each role cannot be simultaneously achieved. Role conflict can lead to stress, anxiety, or decreased levels of performance at work or at home. However, satisfaction with one's many career roles is associated with low interrole conflict (MacEwen & Barling, 1991). Role stress is related to an individual's involvement in multiple roles and may arise from external sources such as the employee's corporate culture or internal sources such as the presence of preschool children in the family. Work slowdowns or employment discontinuities are also associated with role conflicts.

Parent employees face five career dilemmas (Rapoport & Rapoport, 1976; Sekaran, 1986): (1) *Role-overload dilemmas:* Parents are responsible for housework, child care, and also planning, organizing, and coordinating family obligations. These multiple responsibilities can lead to lack of time for completion of their many tasks. (2) *Identity dilemmas:* Traditional definitions of men's and women's roles do not apply to well-functioning, equitable couples. Deriving new definitions of responsibility may lead to confusion and conflict. (3) *Role-cycling dilemmas:* Effectively identifying optimal timing for engaging in career change (e.g., relocation or promotion) or family change (e.g., childbirth or marriage) can enhance or conflict with career growth and development. (4) *Social network dilemmas:* Because couples have a limited amount of free time, they must be selective about whom to socialize with, and this can lead to conflict and guilt. (5) *Normative dilemmas:* Couples may experience negative social sanctions when they do not follow traditional gender roles.

When managing family and career becomes an essential concern of both sexes, men and women experience work and family conflicts (Bird & Ford, 1985). Nonetheless, the etiology and interpretation of this conflict appear to differ for males and females (Greenhaus, Parasuraman, Granrose, Rabinowitz, & Beutell, 1989; Loerch, Russell, & Rush, 1989).

Greenhaus & Beutell (1985) identified three antecedents of work-family conflict: (1) time-based conflict, which relates to the allocation of time to each role; (2) strain-based conflict, which involves the intrusion of strain from one role to another; and (3) behavior-based conflict, which refers to the conflict of behaviors appropriate in one role with behaviors appropriate for another role. Greenhaus and colleagues (Greenhaus, Bedeian, & Mossholder, 1987; Greenhaus et al., 1989) found that men and women experienced similar levels of stress-based and time-based conflicts from work-related sources. Individual work schedules were related to stress for men but not women. However, women, but not men, experienced increased work-family conflict when they were highly committed to their careers. In addition, men, but not women, experienced greater work-family conflict when their partners were highly committed to their careers. Loerch, Russell, and Rush (1989) found that work-family conflict was associated with total role involvement for men and with family conflict for women. Strain associated with role conflict and dual-career couple dilemmas may be reduced by prioritizing roles, reducing standards within roles, or carefully scheduling and organizing activities (Gray, 1983; Hall, 1972; Voydanoff, 1987).

Relearning gender stereotypes can be difficult for both men and women (Yogev, 1981), so that counselors can play critical roles in assisting clients to develop gender-fair ways of functioning (Stoltz-Loike, 1992a, 1992b). Moreover, counselors can underscore how the misuse of power within a relationship leads to problems for each partner and for the couple (see, for example, O'Neil and Egan's chapter on power). It is interesting to speculate that as couples rebalance the division of labor and home responsibilities, there will be a decreased effect of relationship issues on women's career continuity and an increase in the impact of this factor on men's work performance.

Counselors should also be aware that, because women have traditionally taken the role of primary caretaker, they are more likely to experience role stress or role overload between family and work roles and may leave the work force if they cannot effectively address role conflicts. Therefore, mastering effective methods for coping with role conflicts is critical to women's continued career achievements.

FACTORS INFLUENCING WOMEN'S CAREER PATHS

Three specific aspects of women's role responsibilities associated with being a wife or mother affect their career continuity: marriage, children, and housework. Attitudes of others at work regarding these factors may also play an important role in determining women's career paths.

Marriage

Evidence for the effect of relationship concerns on career achievement can be found in studies of women's career mobility and continuity. In their various studies, Philliber and Hiller (Hiller & Philliber, 1986; Philliber & Hiller, 1983; Vannoy-Hiller & Philliber, 1989) assessed how the couple's relationship affects the woman's and the couple's career paths. They found that after marriage, women either change jobs (moving from nontraditional to traditional women's employment), change from full-time to part-time employment, leave the work force, or divorce.

Both the woman's and her partner's gender role identities can affect the quality of their relationship (Vannoy-Hiller & Philliber, 1989) and the equitability of their participation in home and family roles (Nyquist, Slivken, Spence, & Helmreich, 1985). Other studies corroborated these findings, indicating that women experience significant conflicts between work and family roles (Betz & Fitzgerald, 1987; Fitzgerald & Weitzman, in press; Loscocco & Roschelle, 1991; Williams, 1990) and benefit less than men from education and job-related experiences (Barrett, 1979; Featherman & Hauser, 1976).

Men and women experience their own and spousal career commitments differently. Wives' high career commitment increases the work-family conflict for both husbands and wives (Greenhaus et al., 1989) and is negatively associated with marital success (Ladewig & McGee, 1986). Women's success at work is also associated with decreased marital adjustment (Greenhaus, Bedian, & Mossholder, 1987). In contrast, husbands' high career commitment does not have a negative impact.

These findings may be explained by exploring the different ways that career and family issues can affect partners in dual-career couples. If women define themselves in relation to others and their husbands similarly expect them to have primary responsibility for emotional support, women's high career commitment would be viewed as a salient work-family conflict for women and men. The contrasting expectations for the more "independent" man pose no conflict to his career commitment. For career-committed individuals, a range of definitions and perspectives should be explored. Learning to address the increased work-family stress both women and men experience when the woman is highly career committed and to think about the strains that may also be placed on her career and their family by the man's high career commitment can be important topics for counseling.

Just as couple relationships affect career development, work involvement may also affect the couple relationship. Studies in the late 1960s and early 1970s conscientiously tried to substantiate a direct negative impact of women's employment on marital satisfaction and child performance. Nonetheless, after two decades of studies, no such impact was found (e.g., Hoffman, 1989; Hoffman & Nye, 1974; Houseknecht & Macke, 1981; Moorehouse, 1991; Spitze, 1988; Wright, 1978). In fact, the opposite finding has often been reported (Gilbert, 1985; Voydanoff, 1987; Yogev, 1982). Career women generally spend significant time with their children at the expense of their own personal time (Spitze, 1988; Moorehouse, 1991). Those employed wives who worked out of choice, had higher educational levels, worked part-time, or received positive support for employment from their husbands were the most satisfied with their relationships (Voydanoff, 1987). Furthermore, when couples were mutually supportive of career achievement and held gender-fair attitudes, they also experienced greater marital satisfaction (Ladewig & McGee, 1986).

Specific aspects of female work may affect both partners' marital satisfaction. The wife's career attainment, the significance of her achievement, and the relationship between career achievement and household work are directly associated with the couple's marital satisfaction (Gilbert, 1985; Philliber & Hiller, 1983). Marital satisfaction generally increases with overall family income. However, when only the wife's income increases, there is a decrease in marital satisfaction (Gilbert, 1985; Hardesty & Betz, 1980). Because these results are based on self-reports of husbands and wives, various explanations can be proposed. One possibility is that women who earn higher incomes and are more involved with their careers feel more capable of expressing negative feelings about their relationships.

Children

Studies have shown that when women marry or have children they may also change their work status or leave the work force. This fact means that women may experience greater family-career conflict, work at part-time jobs with lower upward mobility but with more apparent opportunities for family time, and experience greater guilt about working when their children are young.

Although having more children at home is associated with greater career discontinuity (Fitzgerald & Weitzman, in press; Pistrang, 1984), the relationship between a woman's having a child and remaining in the work force is not clear. In fact, while children may pull at parents' heartstrings, there are no empirical data to suggest that simply becoming a parent is directly associated with change in a woman's work status. Mothers are affected by psychological as well as physical demands of parenting. Other issues, like mother's attitude toward maternal employment (DeMeis, Hock, & McBride, 1986; Hock, Gnezda, & McBride, 1984; Morgan & Hock, 1984) and the mother's work hours and level of career commitment influence the effect of children on mother's career choices (Hock, Gnezda & McBride, 1984; Morgan & Hock, 1984; Pistrang, 1984). The significance of psychological factors on work-family concerns is further reflected by the finding that even when both parents share home responsibilities, mothers typically report greater role strain than fathers (Bird & Ford, 1985).

Family demands can derail or conflict with the career of the person (typically female) responsible for these chores while giving the appearance that the relationship itself affects career development. The majority of American workers grew up during a time when it was not expected that women would work, but rather when the "motherhood mandate" was advocated and it was assumed that women's primary role involved caring for their homes and children. If women are to compete successfully in a global market, then the balance of responsibilities for home and work-related roles must be equitably negotiated (Stoltz-Loike, 1992a, 1992b). Additionally, creative solutions should be explored to address the conflict of expressing oneself in parenting and relationship roles and in career roles.

Women may benefit by self-redefinition that involves identifying a critical aspect of relationship as also being a good provider. Then career commitment does not conflict with, but rather complements, women's other relationship roles.

Housework

Factors that directly affect time available for employment may conflict with employment-related activities and career success more than simply being a partner in a relationship. Housework is a time-consuming, highly salient aspect of home life that affects career performance (Coverman & Sheley, 1986; Hardesty & Bokemeier, 1989; Nyquist, Slivken, Spence, & Helmreich, 1985). Although employed wives decrease the time that they spend in housework by about one-third, husbands of employed wives do not spend significantly more time than other husbands in housework (Berardo, Shehan, & Leslie, 1987; Loscocco & Roschelle, 1991).

At-home wives spend about 30 hours per week on housework, employed women spend about 20 hours per week, and husbands spend about 10 hours per week. Time spent on housework will directly conflict with women's ability to work longer hours or weekends or to be involved in career-related educational or professional endeavors. Most couples will primarily shoulder the burden of household responsibilities together or with children, although when couples' earnings increase they may employ household help to reduce the time spent on housework.

Equitable participation in housework may also affect relationship development and each partner's commitment to the relationship. Hochschild (1989), for example, underscores that marriages have dissolved because of conflicts over housework. However, few women would object to their husbands' assuming a greater role in home-related responsibilities. The extra housework associated with attending to couple needs or caring for children may make it appear that the relationship is affecting career performance when it is actually housework that is affecting career performance.

Interestingly, the lack of balance between the household involvement of men and women may be addressed by socialization experiences of both partners and not of either partner alone. Men and women define the equitable balance of housework differently (Gross & Arvey, 1977). For men, fair division involves performing tasks that do not take too long, whereas for women, equitability is associated with the husband's performing "traditional" women's tasks (Benin & Agostinelli, 1988; Yogev & Brett, 1985). For both men and women, sharing traditional roles may be difficult (Yogev, 1981). Furthermore, women can also derive psychological rewards from homemaking (Kibria, Barnett, Baruch, Marshall, & Pleck, 1990), and this role may enhance women's feelings of competence (Cook, 1991), contributing to their resistance to shifting role balances.

The wife's attitude toward her employment and her comfort in discussing her husband's household participation affects role balance (Barnett & Baruch, 1987; Guelzow, Bird, & Koball, 1991). When couples delayed childbirth until they reached their late 20s or early 30s, fathers were more involved in housework and child-related chores and mothers were more capable of sharing primary role responsibilities (Coltrane, 1990).

When couples engage in equitable participation in housework, they share roles and responsibilities. This means that each partner ensures that a chore is completed, even if it requires staying up late or not attending a particular evening activity (Stoltz-Loike, 1992a). In equitable relationships, it is less likely that only the female partner's career will be affected by housework. Instead, both partners' careers may be somewhat disrupted or decelerated by home and relationship demands (Stoltz-Loike, 1992b). In nonequitable couples, however, the very demanding nature of housework will selectively affect the women's career achievement.

Work Environments

Women and men receive different messages at work regarding marriage and children. Career commitment, for example, has not been found to be associated with delayed marriage or childbirth among men. Furthermore, the archetype of the corporate man is one who is dedicated to his company but is also a husband and father. In contrast, if television and movie images reflect societal values, then it may be assumed that the successful woman is one who is not married, can take care of herself, and has no children.

Identifying the relationship between work environment and career development represents highly salient counseling concerns. Types of work environment appropriate for clients will vary with their perspectives on children and children's needs for them. For example, a woman who believes that children benefit by active daily participation of parents in child care might have a very different career path and experience different levels of career satisfaction and work-family conflict in a traditional company than in one that actively advocates family-friendly policies like on-site day care, flextime, flexible work schedules, or job sharing (Stoltz-Loike, 1992b). Counselors who are attuned to these variable concerns can most directly address client counseling needs.

CONCLUSIONS

Based on the existing literature on women's career development, it can be concluded that women entering the work force today expect their careers to be a significant part of their future, anticipate that they will remain in the work force after they are married, and plan to combine family and career roles. This pattern has been documented since the early 1980s. Nonetheless, other studies have reported that family factors affect career continuity. When women expect to combine work and family roles, their choices of college majors and career expectations become more limited.

These findings underscore the effect that women's concerns with relationships may have on their career patterns. Because of these concerns, women may be seen as aberrant because men behave differently (Miller, 1976). Caution must be exercised to value women's typical behaviors of interdependence and nurturing as normative not only because these supportive behaviors characterize many women, or by definition, approximately half of the American adult population, but also because the ability to nurture and express emotions is currently viewed as healthy behavior for all adults (e.g., Silverberg, 1986). Consistent with this perspective is the association of relationship concerns with career development as a healthy and typical pattern for women and an important concern for men. For career counselors, employers, and clients, understanding this issue can be associated with increased success in the client-counselor relationship and higher performance of clients at work.

Personality factors are also strongly related to the impact of relationships on career. Women who are nontraditional and highly motivated do not show the same effect of family issues on work force continuity (see discussion above of the relationship between gender role and career paths). Instead, the career history of these women appears to parallel that of men (Fitzgerald & Weitzman, in press), while other women exhibit a more complex pattern of career development that also accommodates family roles. Consequently, different counseling strategies are appropriate for women with distinct gender role identities. Moreover, because traditional theories of career development may not address the career needs of many working women, especially those who are highly expressive, assessing gender roles should become part of the overall counseling process. Then, employment environments that differentially support either family and career roles or only career roles could more properly be considered by perspective employees.

For example, a highly expressive college woman who plans to pursue family and career goals later in life and who is highly competent in math and science may choose a career as a nurse so that she will be able to orchestrate her work schedule to combine family and career goals. A sophisticated career counselor may instead suggest that this woman consider pursuing a career as a physician or engineer, which is more commensurate with her skills, and may discuss part-time medical internships, residencies, and employment options with companies that offer flexible schedules and other family-friendly policies. Appointments with more mature physicians or engineers who have pursued family-friendly options or who themselves are expressive individuals can be advocated so that this woman can consider more diverse career opportunities. Additionally, the ways that this woman may express her concern with her patients as a physician or the importance of nurturing the talent of other engineers or technicians as a manager in an engineering concern can be discussed. Some major American corporations actively recruit female engineers and offer many female-friendly and family-friendly options, including women's support groups and part-time work at all but the highest levels of management.

Another example is a highly intelligent, capable woman who is pursuing a graduate degree and considers becoming an elementary schoolteacher rather than a university professor because she wants a career that will be easily transferable if her significant other, who is an assistant professor, does not receive tenure. This woman may benefit from discussions with female faculty members concerning how they balance dual-career roles, and from investigating career opportunities at universities that advocate the recruitment of dual-professional couples to their faculties.

In both these cases, women's options can be expanded when counselors underscore the new career sensibilities of various employers concerning couple-, parent-, and child-related family-friendly policies. Many women will choose and flourish in careers in nursing, teaching, and other traditional female pursuits. However, counselors owe their clients information on practical opportunities within diverse employment fields.

An interesting consideration also involves whether couples, like individuals, have gender role identities. For example, an expressive partner who advocates the parents' active participation in child care or the close involvement of both partners in the relationship may affect the significant other's career choices. Thus, family and career concerns may affect couples' decisions about methods of functioning. A highly instrumental couple may feel comfortable with periodic vacations together, not requiring active routine renewal of the relationship. A more expressive couple may need daily conversations to fulfil their couple needs. A more instrumental couple may feel comfortable leaving their children in the care of a trusted caretaker or day-care center while both partners pursue intense work schedules and business-related travel. A more expressive couple may instead decide to alternate travel schedules or to have one partner work at a location within minutes of the child's school or caretaking environment. Attention to couple and individual identities becomes critical to effectively address client's counseling needs. Additional studies are necessary to—

1. further enrich the understanding of the career-family interaction for parents,

2. clarify how gender differences relate and affect each individual's experiences,

3. examine how the roles assigned by society to each partner and the sociocultural expectations of each parent affect their career development, and

4. provide essential information relating to career-family and relationship issues for the father in single-parent families, father-headed families, in single-earner couples in which the father is the sole breadwinner, and in single-earner couples in which the mother is the sole breadwinner.

Since female employment has become the norm for adult women, discussion of the ways women work will revolutionize career development theories. Consideration of how women's careers represent an expression of their relational self-identities will be critical to the construction of these more complex career development theories. Moreover, understanding the effect of relationships on work-family responsibilities is associated with effectively advising both men and women about their career directions. By giving more attention to work-life issues and the ways workers select employment options to coincide with self-expression, individual gender role identities, and family and career concerns, counselors will become better equipped to assist men and women to work more capably and to derive greater satisfaction from their employment.

THE EXAMPLE OF KERI

Keri is a 27-year-old woman who recently completed a management training program at a major bank in a large northeastern city. At the time of the intake interview, she appears on time, is well-groomed, and expresses herself articulately. Keri views herself as a quick learner who understands money and people and has potential to be a high performer at the bank. Upper management at the bank corroborates this view, according to Keri, since she is routinely given challenging projects and has been recommended to pursue a part-time MBA program at the bank's expense at the well-known major university in her city.

Keri has come to see the counselor because she is thinking of leaving the bank and embarking on a major career change. At the bank she feels that she is involved primarily in projects and numbers. Keri wants to work with people. Therefore, she is considering leaving the bank and taking some education courses so that she can teach children at the local public school. In this way she feels that she can interact with and affect people more directly. Keri scored ECS (Enterprising/Conventional/Social) on the Holland code, which makes the counselor interested in further exploring Keri's motivation for and potential satisfaction with pursuing a career in education. Questions about her interest in career change, hobbies, and other interests are also explored.

Keri has been married to Jon for the last four years. They have no children and may choose to have a family in the future, although this is not a question that concerns them actively. Both Jon and Keri received their bachelor's degrees in business administration from the same college, which is where they met. Jon works as a financial analyst for a midsized company that sells stocks and bonds. His job is interesting, but his career path and future prospects within the company remain somewhat unclear. Keri has a higher income and greater growth potential at her current job than Jon does at his.

During the time that Keri was in college she did not take any courses in education because she had no interest in teaching. She explains that she has always been a good student and was interested in earning a lot of money and having a position of stature. "I love to compete," she explains to the counselor, "and the thought of being in a challenging position in a bank where I would have to perform well and work with other highly competent people was very attractive."

Keri explains that the bank has a women's group that meets once a month. She feels that her participation in the group has given her new self-perceptions. Keri views this as quite different from her experiences in college and at the bank where most of her friends were men. Now, her involvement in the women's group has exposed her to new viewpoints and allowed her to accept other ways of doing things than her hard-boiled, competitive perspectives. She values the friendships she has made with other women.

Keri has no hobbies, although she enjoys reading in her spare time. Hours at the bank are long and she has about a 1½ hour commute from work to home. Therefore, she typically leaves for work by 7:00 A.M. and rarely gets home before 8:00 P.M. After dinner with Jon at home or at a local restaurant, they both do some light housekeeping, talk to friends on the phone or watch some TV, and then go to bed by 11:00 P.M. Keri would like to be involved in a volunteer position but has not found any forum for such activities. In response to the counselor's questions she admits having had virtually nothing to do with young children for many years. She grew up as an only child and babysat briefly when she was 12 years old, but found the job boring. She agrees that it might be advisable to pursue some volunteer work with children before leaving her job to teach young children full time.

Based on the initial sessions with Keri, the counselor decides to investigate how Keri's need to express her interest in others can be utilized in work or other settings. The counselor suggests that Keri first explore whether there are management opportunities at her bank that would give her more options to interact with her co-workers and subordinates. Also, Keri might investigate whether promotional structures within the bank favor employees involved in both management and project development or promote only those employees in project development. If her bank does not promote managers, she may look to more forward-thinking banks that promote employees to upper levels from multiple tracks.

Additionally, given Keri's Holland scores, it becomes extremely important for Keri to understand the functional line of command within a school setting. She may be reluctant to deal with a school bureaucracy given her high E score on the Holland codes. The counselor would also like to explore how Keri addresses the highly structured environment of her bank.

The counselor also wishes to explore the significance of volunteer opportunities for Keri working with both children and adults.

By working with children, Keri can have an opportunity to explore whether she would find teaching children a satisfying endeavor. By working as a volunteer, Keri would have the opportunity to interact with people in a caring way, thereby expressing her relational self-identity.

Another topic of concern for counseling is the career interaction of Keri and Jon. The counselor wonders about the impact of gender stereotypes on the career choices of each spouse. For example, it would be important to analyze both Keri's and Jon's response to the fact that she earns a higher salary and has greater earning potential. Questions such as whether her decision to become a teacher is related to her career goals or instead to gender conflicts or stereotypes should be explored. By counseling Jon and Keri concurrently and exploring such dual-career couple issues as decision making as a couple or planning for success as a couple, the counselor could arrive at answers to these concerns.

REFERENCES

Ace, M. E., Graen, G. B., & Dawis, R. V. (1972). Biographic correlates of work attitudes. *Journal of Vocational Behavior, 2,* 191–199.

Allen, L., & Britt, D. W. (1983). Black women in American society: A resource developmental perspective. *Issues in Mental Health Nursing, 5,* 61–79.

Avioli, P. S. (1985). The labor-force participation of married mothers of infants. *Journal of Marriage and the Family, 47,* 739–745.

Baber, K. M., & Monaghan, P. (1988). College women's career and motherhood expectations: New options, old dilemmas. *Sex Roles, 19,* 189–203.

Barnett, R. C., & Baruch, G. K. (1987). Determinants of father's participation in family work. *Journal of Marriage and the Family, 49,* 29–40.

Barrett, N. (1979). Women in the job market: Occupations, earnings and career opportunities. In R. Smith (Ed.), *The subtle revolution: Women at work.* Washington, DC: Urban Institute.

Bem, S. L. (1979). Theory and measurement of androgyny: A reply to the Pedhazur-Tetenbaum and Locksley-Colten critiques. *Journal of Personality and Social Psychology, 88,* 354–364.

Benin, M. H., & Agostinelli, J. (1988). Husbands' and wives' satisfaction with the division of labor. *Journal of Marriage and the Family, 50,* 349–361.

Berardo, D. H., Shehan, C. L., & Leslie, G. R. (1987). A residue of tradition: Jobs, careers, and spouses' time in housework. *Journal of Marriage and the Family, 49,* 381–390.

Bernstein, A. J., & Rozen, S. C. (1989). Thirteen ways to re-energize your staff. *Working Woman,* 1989, 45–46.

Betz, N. E., & Fitzgerald, L. F. (1987). *The career psychology of women.* Boston, MA: Academic Press.

Betz, N. E., Heesacker, R. S., & Shuttleworth, C. (1990). Moderators of the congruence and realism of major and occupational plans in college students: A replication and extension. *Journal of Counseling Psychology, 37,* 269–276.

Beutell, N. J., & Brenner, O. C. (1986). Sex differences in work values. *Journal of Vocational Behavior, 28,* 29–41.

Bird, G. W., & Ford, R. (1985). A source of role strain among dual-career couples. *Home Economics Research Journal, 14,* 187–194.

Chester, N. L. (1990). Achievement motivation and employment decisions: Portraits of women with young children. In H. Y. Grossman and N. L. Chester (Eds.), *The experience and meaning of work in women's lives.* Hillsdale, NJ: Lawrence Erlbaum Associates.

Chester, N. L., & Grossman, H. Y. (1990). Introduction: Learning about women and their work through their own accounts. In H. Y. Grossman and N. L. Chester (Eds.), *The experience and meaning of work in women's lives.* Hillsdale, NJ: Lawrence Erlbaum Associates.

Chipman, S. F., Brush, L., & Wilson, D. (Eds.) (1985). *Women and mathematics: Balancing the equation.* Hillsdale, NJ: Lawrence Erlbaum Associates.

Chodorow, N. (1978). *The reproduction of mothering: Psychoanalysis and the sociology of mothering.* Berkeley, CA: University of California Press.

Coltrane, S. (1990). Birth timing and the division of labor in dual-earner families. *Journal of Family Issues, 11,* 157–181.

Cook, E. P. (1991). Annual Review: Practice and research in career counseling and development, 1990. *The Career Development Quarterly, 40,* 99–131.

Cotton, S., Antill, J. H., & Cunningham, J. D. (1990). The work attachment of mothers with preschool children. *Psychology of Women Quarterly, 14,* 255–270.

Coverman, S., & Sheley, J. F. (1986). Changes in men's housework and child-care time, 1965-1975. *Journal of Marriage and the Family, 48,* 413-422.

Covin, T. J., & Brush, C. C. (1991). An examination of male and female attitudes toward career and family issues. *Sex Roles, 25,* 393-415.

DeMeis, D. K., Hock, E. E., & McBride, S. L. (1986). The balance of employment and motherhood: Longitudinal study of mothers' feelings about separation from their first-born infants. *Developmental Psychology, 22,* 627-632.

Eccles, J. (1986). *Gender roles and women's achievement.* Paper presented at annual meeting of the American Educational Research Association, San Francisco.

Eldridge, L. S., & Gilbert, L. (1990). Correlates of relationship satisfaction in lesbian couples. *Psychology of Women Quarterly, 24,* 43-62.

Fassinger, R. (1990). Causal models of career choice in two samples of college women. *Journal of Vocational Behaviors, 36,* 225-248.

Featherman, D. L., & Hauser, R. M. (1976). Sexual inequalities and socioeconomic achievement in the US, 1962-1973. *American Sociological Review, 41,* 462-483.

Ferber, M., & Kordick, B. (1978). Sex differentials in the earnings of PhD's. *Industrial and Labor Relations Review, 31,* 227-238.

Fitzgerald, L. S., & Crites, J. O. (1980). Toward a career psychology of women: What do we know? What do we need to know? *Journal of Counseling Psychology, 27,* 44-62.

Fitzgerald, L., & Weitzman, L. (in press). Women's career development: Theory and practice from a feminist perspective. In Z. Leibowitz & D. Lea (Eds.), *Adult career development: Concepts, issues, and practices* (2nd ed.). Arlington, VA: American Association for Counseling and Development.

Forrest, L., & Mikolaitis, N. (1986). The relational component of identity: An expansion of career development theory. *The Career Development Quarterly, 35,* 76-88.

Gilbert, L. (1985). *Men in dual-career families: Current realities and future prospects.* Hillsdale, NJ: Lawrence Erlbaum Associates.

Gilbert, L., Dancer, L. S., Rossman, K. M., & Thorn, B. L. (1991). Assessing perceptions of occupational-family integration. *Sex Roles, 24,* 107-119.

Gilligan, C. (1982). *In a different voice.* Cambridge, MA: Harvard University Press.

Gilligan, C. (1989). Teaching Shakespeare's sister: Notes from the underground of female adolescents. In C. Gilligan, N. P. Lyons, & T. Hanmer (Eds.), *Making Connections: The relational worlds of adolescent girls at Emma Willard School.* Cambridge, MA: Harvard University Press.

Goh, S. C. (1991). Sex differences in perceptions of interpersonal work style, career emphasis, supervisory mentoring behavior, and job satisfaction. *Sex Roles, 24,* 701–710.

Grant, L., & DuRoss, D. J. (1984). Expected rewards of practice and personal life priorities of men and women medical students. *Sociological Focus, 17,* 87–104.

Gray, J. D. (1983). The married professional woman: An examination of her role conflicts and coping strategies. *Psychology of Women Quarterly, 7,* 235–243.

Greenhaus, J. H., & Beutell, N. J. (1985). Sources of conflict between work and family roles. *Academy of Management Review, 10,* 76–88.

Greenhaus, J. H., Bedeian, A. G., & Mossholder, K. W. (1987). Work experiences, job performance, and feelings of personal and family well-being. *Journal of Vocational Behavior, 31,* 200–215.

Greenhaus, J. H., Parasuraman, S., Granrose, C. S., Rabinowitz, S., & Beutell, N. J. (1989). Sources of work-family conflict among two-career couples. *Journal of Vocational Behavior, 34,* 133–153.

Gross, R. H., & Arvey, R. D. (1977). Marital satisfaction, job satisfaction, and task distribution in the homemaker job. *Journal of Vocational Behavior, 11,* 1–13.

Grossman, H. Y., & Chester, N. L. (1990). *The experience and meaning of work in women's lives.* Hillsdale, NJ: Lawrence Erlbaum Associates.

Grossman, H. Y., & Stewart, A. J. (1990). Women's experience of power over others: Case studies of psychotherapists and professors. In H. Y. Grossman, and N. L. Chester (Eds.), *The experience and meaning of work in women's lives.* Hillsdale, NJ: Lawrence Erlbaum Associates.

Guelzow, M. G., Bird, G. W., & Koball, E. H. (1991). An exploratory path analysis of the stress process for dual-career men and women. *Journal of Marriage and the Family, 53,* 151–164.

Hackett, G. (1985). Role of mathematics self-efficacy in the choice of math-related majors of college women and men: A path analysis. *Journal of Counseling Psychology, 32,* 47–56.

Hall, D. T. (1972). A model of coping with role conflict. *Administrative Science Quarterly, 4,* 471–486.

Hardesty, C., & Betz, N. (1980). The relationships of career salience, attitudes toward women, and demographic and family characteristics to marital adjustment in dual-career couples. *Journal of Vocational Behavior, 17,* 242–250.

Hardesty, C., & Bokemeier, J. (1989). Finding time and making do: Distribution of household labor in nonmetropolitan marriages. *Journal of Marriage and the Family, 51,* 253–267.

Hesse-Biber, S. (1985). Male and female students' perceptions of their academic environment and future career plans. *Human Relations, 38,* 91–105.

Hetherington, C., & Orzek, A. (1989). Career counseling and life planning with lesbian women. *Journal of Counseling and Development, 68,* 52–55.

Hiller, D. V., & Philliber, W. W. (1986). Determinants of social class identification for dual-earner couples. *Journal of Marriage and the Family, 48,* 583–587.

Hochschild, A., with Machung, A. (1989). *The second shift: Working parents and the revolution at home.* New York: Viking.

Hock, E., Gnezda, M. T., & McBride, S. L. (1984). Mothers of infants: Attitudes toward employment and motherhood following birth of the first child. *Journal of Marriage and the Family, 46,* 425–431.

Hoffman, L. W. (1989). Effects of maternal employment in the two-parent family. *American Psychologist, 44,* 283–292.

Hoffman, L. W., & Nye, F. I. (1974). *Working mothers.* San Francisco: Jossey-Bass.

Houseknecht, S. K., & Macke, A. S. (1981). Combining marriage and career: The martial adjustment of professional women. *Journal of Marriage and the Family, 43,* 651–661.

Jenkins, S. R. (1989). Longitudinal prediction of women's careers: Psychological, behavioral, and socio-structural influences. *Journal of Vocational Behavior, 34,* 204–235.

Johnston, W. B., & Packer, A. H. (1987). *Workforce 2000: Work and workers for the 21st century.* Indianapolis, IN: Hudson Institute.

Kibria, N., Barnett, R. C., Baruch, G. K., Marshall, N. L., & Pleck, J. H. (1990). Homemaking role quality and the psychological well-being and distress of employed women. *Sex Roles, 22,* 327–347.

Ladewig, B. H., & McGee, G. W. (1986). Occupational commitment, a supportive family environment, and marital adjustment: Development and estimation of a model. *Journal of Marriage and the Family, 48,* 821–829.

Loerch, K. J., Russell, J. E., & Rush, M. C. (1989). The relationship among family domain variables and work-family conflict for men and women. *Journal of Vocational Behavior, 35,* 288–308.

Long, B. C. (1989). Sex-role orientation, coping strategies, and self-efficacy of women in traditional and nontraditional occupations. *Psychology of Women Quarterly, 13,* 307–324.

Loscocco, K. A. (1990). Career structures and employee commitment. *Social Science Quarterly, 71,* 53–68.

Loscocco, K. A., & Roschelle, A. R. (1991). Invited contribution: Influences on the quality of work and nonwork life: Two decades in review. *Journal of Vocational Behavior, 39,* 185–225.

Loscocco, K. A., & Spitze, G. (1990). Working conditions, social support and the well-being of female and male factory workers. *Journal of Health and Social Behavior, 31,* 313–327.

Lyons, N. P. (1989). Listening to voices we have not heard: Emma Willard girls' ideas about self, relationships, and morality. In C. Gilligan, N. P. Lyons, & T. Hanmer (Eds.), *Making connections: The relational worlds of adolescent girls at Emma Willard School.* Cambridge, MA: Harvard University Press.

MacEwen, K. E., & Barling, J. (1991). Effects of maternal employment experiences on children's behavior via mood, cognitive difficulties, and parenting behavior. *Journal of Marriage and the Family, 53,* 635–644.

Marshall, M. R., & Jones, C. H. (1990). Childbearing sequence and the career development of women administrators in higher education. *Journal of College Student Development, 31,* 531–537.

Mazen, A. M., & Lemkau, J. P. (1990). Personality profiles of women in traditional and nontraditional occupations. *Journal of Vocational Behavior, 37,* 46–59.

Miller, J. B. (1976). *Toward a new psychology of women.* Boston, MA: Beacon Press.

Moorehouse, M. J. (1991). Linking maternal employment patterns to mother-child activities and children's school competence. *Developmental Psychology, 27,* 295–303.

Morgan, K. C., & Hock, E. (1984). A longitudinal study of psychosocial variables affecting the career patterns of women with young children. *Journal of Marriage and the Family, 46*, 383–390.

Morrison, A. M., & Von Glinow, M. A. (1990). Women and minorities in management. *American Psychologist, 45*, 200–208.

Murrell, A. J., Frieze, I. H., & Frost, J. L. (1991). Aspiring to careers in male- and female-dominated professions: A study of black and white college women. *Psychology of Women Quarterly, 15*, 103–126.

Nelson, D. L., Quick, J. C., Hitt, M. A., & Moesel, D. (1990). Politics, lack of career progress, and work/home conflict: Stress and strain for working women. *Sex Roles, 23*, 169–185.

Nyquist, L., Slivken, K., Spence, J. T., & Helmreich, R. L. (1985). Household responsibilities in middle-class couples: The contribution of demographic and personality variables. *Sex Roles, 12*, 15–34.

O'Connell, L., Betz, M., & Kurth, S. (1989). Plans for balancing work and family life: Do women pursuing nontraditional and traditional occupations differ? *Sex Roles, 20*, 35–45.

Olson, J. E., Frieze, I. H., & Detlefson, E. G. (1990). Having it all? Combining work and family in a male and a female profession. *Sex Roles, 23*, 515–533.

Ornstein, S., & Isabella, L. (1990). Age vs stage models of career attitudes of women: A partial replication and extension. *Journal of Vocational Behavior, 36*, 1–19.

Osipow, S. (1991). Invited contribution: Observations about career psychology. *Journal of Vocational Behavior, 39*, 291–296.

Philliber, W. W., & Hiller, D. V. (1983). Relative occupational attainments of spouses and later changes in marriage and wife's work experience. *Journal of Marriage and the Family, 45*, 161–170.

Pistrang, N. (1984). Women's work involvement and experience of new motherhood. *Journal of Marriage and the Family, 46*, 433–448.

Poole, M. E., & Clooney, G. H. (1985). The relationship between interest-occupation congruence and job satisfaction. *Journal of Vocational Behavior, 26*, 251–263.

Ragins, B. R., & Sundstrom, E. (1989). Gender and power in organizations: A longitudinal perspective. *Psychological Bulletin, 105*, 51–88.

Rapoport, R., & Rapoport, R. N. (1976). *Dual-career families re-examined: New integrations of work and family.* London: Martin.

Rix, S. E. (Ed.) (1987). *The American Woman: 1987–88: A report in depth.* New York: Norton.

Roos, P. E., & Cohen, L. H. (1987). Sex roles and social support as moderators of life stress adjustment. *Journal of Personality and Social Psychology, 52,* 576–585.

Schele, A. (1991, December). Career Strategies: The mommy-track trap. *Working Woman,* pp. 28–31.

Sekaran, U. (1986). *Dual-career families.* San Francisco: Jossey-Bass.

Silverberg, R. A. (1986). *Psychotherapy for men: Transcending the masculine mystique.* Springfield, IL: Charles Thomas.

Spence, J. T., & Helmreich, R. (1979). The many faces of androgyny: A reply to Locksley and Colten. *Journal of Personality and Social Psychology, 37,* 1032–1046.

Spitze, G. (1988). Women's employment and family relations: A review. *Journal of Marriage and the Family, 50,* 595–618.

Stein, J. A., Newcomb, M. D., & Bentler, P. M. (1990). The relative influence of vocational behavior and family involvement on self-esteem: Longitudinal analyses of young adult women and men. *Journal of Vocational Behavior, 36,* 320–338.

Stoltz-Loike, M. (1992a). *Dual career couples: New perspectives in counseling.* Alexandria, VA: American Association for Counseling and Development.

Stoltz-Loike, M. (1992b). The working family: Helping women balance the roles of wife-mother and career woman. *The Career Development Quarterly,* in press.

Strange, C. C., & Rea, J. S. (1983). Career choice considerations and sex role self-concept of male and female undergraduates in nontraditional majors. *Journal of Vocational Behavior, 23,* 219–226.

Terborg, J. R. (1977). Women in Management: A research review. *Journal of Applied Psychology, 6,* 647–664.

Travis, C. B., Phillippi, R. H., & Henley, T. B. (1991). Gender and causal attributions for mastery, personal, and interpersonal events. *Psychology of Women Quarterly, 15,* 233–249.

Vannoy-Hiller, D., & Philliber, W. W. (1989). *Equal partners: Successful women in marriage.* Newbury Park, CA: Sage Publications.

Vetter, B. M. (1980). Working women scientists and engineers. *Science, 207,* 28–34.

Voydanoff, P. (1987). *Work and family life.* Beverly Hills, CA: Sage Publications.

Voydanoff, P. (1988). Work role characteristics, family structure demands and work/family conflict. *Journal of Marriage and the Family, 50,* 749–761.

Weinberg, S. L., & Tittle, C. K. (1987). Congruence of real and ideal job characteristics: A focus on sex, parenthood status, and extrinsic characteristics. *Journal of Vocational Behavior, 30,* 227–239.

Wilk, C. A. (1986). *Career women and childbearing: A psychological analysis of the decision process.* New York: Van Nostrand Reinhold.

Williams, J. C. (1990). Sameness feminism and the work/family conflict. *New York Law School Law Review, 35,* 347–360.

Wright, J. D. (1978). Are working women really more satisfied? Evidence from several national surveys. *Journal of Marriage and the Family, 40,* 301–313.

Yogev, S. (1981). Do professional women have egalitarian marital relationships? *Journal of Marriage and the Family, 43,* 865–871.

Yogev, S. (1982). Happiness in dual-career couples: Changing research, changing values. *Sex Roles, 8,* 593–605.

Yogev, S., & Brett, J. (1985). Perceptions of the division of housework and child care and marital satisfaction. *Journal of Marriage and the Family, 47,* 609–618.

DEPRESSION IN WOMEN

Kathleen Y. Ritter

Everyone knows what it is like to feel "blue" or sad from time to time. But at what point do these low times in life become labeled *depression?* Nolen-Hoeksema's (1990) comprehensive literature review on depression indicates that "there is no definitive answer to this question," but that "even moderate levels of depression appear to significantly impair functioning in work and school settings and in social situations" (p. 5).

The Diagnostic and Statistical Manual of Mental Disorders (DSM-III-R) (American Psychiatric Association, 1987) lists nine symptoms of a major depressive syndrome, five of which must be present for two or more weeks for a diagnosis. One of these five must be a depressed mood or a diminished loss of interest or pleasure (p. 222).

Many people who exhibit symptoms of depression (1) meet fewer than five of the DSM-III-R criteria for a major depressive syndrome, and/or (2) do not seek help from a mental health professional and receive a psychiatric diagnosis. For the purposes of this chapter, the term *depression* will encompass "the many varieties of mood on a continuum from feeling blue at one extreme, to being overwhelmed and suffering from hopelessness, helplessness, feelings of guilt, self-recrimination, and low self-esteem, at the other" (Formanek and Gurian, 1987, p. xiii). The intent of the chapter is to focus on the relationship between gender and depression, since "after puberty, women show more depression than men" (Nolen-Hoeksema, 1990, p. 6). Interestingly, the largest gender differences are found for the less severe symptoms (McGrath, Keita, Strickland, & Russo, 1990).

Depression "is overwhelmingly a women's disorder" (Kaplan, 1991, p. 206). There are currently at least 7 million women in the United States with a diagnosable depression (McGrath et al., 1990), and the number of depressed women exceeds that of men by an average of 2:1 in over 30 countries and in all Western cultures (Abramson & Andrews, 1982; Bernard, 1982; Nolen-Hoeksema, 1990; Weissman, 1980; Weissman & Klerman, 1987). The sex ratios for bipolar disorders are about equal, but for all other categories of depression, the rate for women is double that of men (Nolen-Hoeksema, 1990; Weissman & Klerman, 1987). This sex difference in depression "is one of the most consistent findings in the literature" and "holds for White, Black, and Hispanic women and persists when income level, education, and occupation are controlled" (McGrath et al., 1990, p. 1). Further, there is little evidence that this difference is attributable to the fact that men are less likely to discuss feelings or admit to depression than women or that they become alcoholic rather than depressed (Nolen-Hoeksema, 1990).

FACTORS CONTRIBUTING TO DEPRESSION IN WOMEN

Kaplan (1991) believes that there is a "fundamental overlap between the central dynamics of depression and key dimensions in the nature of women's psychological development" and that "the frequency of depression in women suggests that depression may not be an 'illness' superimposed on an alien or indifferent personality structure, but rather may be...an exaggeration of the normative state of being female in Western society" (p. 207). The evidence for biological factors in women's depressions is weak and not well supported. Further, "there does not seem to be as great an increase in risk for depression during periods of hormonal change as is commonly believed" (Nolen-Hoeksema, 1990, pp. 75–76). There is little evidence to relate altered endocrine balance or specific hormones to mood changes (Weissman, 1980; Weissman & Klerman, 1987).

There is considerable research showing a relationship between hormonal abnormalities and *some* depressions during the premenstrual phase, but very few women who are depressed at this time show symptoms *only* at this phase in their cycles. They also have symptoms at other stages, and many who have severe premenstrual depression have a personal or family history of depressions unrelated to the menstrual cycle. Further, they are often women who expect that unpleasant moods will accompany monthly phases (Nolen-Hoeksema, 1990). Similarly, most mood changes in pregnancy or the lack of a pregnancy occur in women who are predisposed to affective disorders. Pregnancy and infertility both occur in a social context, and when women are depressed at these times, it is important to examine their prior mental health history as well as their attitudes and feelings about their situation (McGrath et al., 1990).

Low moods or "blues" after childbirth are self-limiting for the majority of women, and it seems likely "that most studies of postpartum blues have overestimated the incidence of this problem" (Nolen-Hoeksema, 1990, p. 64). Given that there is no evidence that serious depressions are hormonally based, women who experience stressful events in addition to childbirth are at high risk for depression. For women vulnerable to emotional disorders, childbirth seems to overload the circuits, with hormonal fluctuations interacting with life stresses to result in extended or serious depression (McGrath et al., 1990; Nemtzow, 1987; Nolen-Hoeksema, 1990). In the same vein, "depression may be a precursor rather than a consequence of menopausal difficulties" (McGrath et al., 1990, p. 13). In fact, depressed women are apt to have negative impressions of menopause (Avis cited in Adler, 1991; Formanek, 1987a) and are twice as likely as nondepressed women to report menopausal symptoms. As in pregnancy, infertility, or childbirth, women prone to depression frequently experience recurrences of the disorder at these times (Nolen-Hoeksema, 1990).

Thus, reproductive events are not key factors in the higher rate of female depression. Rather, the developmental, psychological, and sociocultural conditions of women's lives have a greater impact than biology on their emotional states. Four factors contributing to depression in women will be discussed in the following sections: (1) the importance of relationships in women's lives; (2) their cognitive and behavioral styles; (3) their unique social and socioeconomic life stressors; and (4) the oppressive conditions under which many women live. After a summary of the literature pertaining to these four factors and before a section addressing issues related to counseling with depressed women, a discussion dealing with young people at risk for depression will be provided. Two of these populations will be given special treatment: adolescent girls and children of depressed mothers.

Relationships in Women's Lives

Girls whose primary caretaker is generally female experience themselves as less differentiated and more relationally connected than boys, who tend to be pushed toward early separation (Chodorow, 1978, 1989; Fischer, 1986). "Male gender identity is threatened by intimacy while female gender identity is threatened by separation" (Gilligan, 1982, p. 8). Because females have a prolonged attachment to mother (Chodorow, 1978; Fischer, 1986), this early relationship becomes a prototype for later relationships, and internalization of the caretaker's empathetic attitude (or the lack of it) and the quality of their mutuality contribute to the capacity for later mutuality (Jordan, 1991). In the reproduction of this "mothering" in later life, if a woman's need for mutuality is not met or if her relational capacity is impaired, she becomes depressed.

Relationship Orientation

Women become depressed when their lives do not have an adequate relational context or they are unable to combine self-development with intimacy (Jack, 1991; Stiver, 1991a, 1991b). "...when women are severely constricted in the full development of their relational capacities, and when women are strongly discouraged or punished for self-expression, the conditions are established that can lead to depression" (Kaplan, 1991, p. 209). According to Lerner (1987, 1988), it is not women's relationship orientation that predisposes them to depression, but what happens to them in relationships. Stiver (1991a) believes that women experience a continuous sense of loss when opportunities for mutual empathy and mutual empowerment are limited. The culture of inequity makes it difficult for women to maintain a positive sense of self (i.e., to keep her "self" in relation [Jack, 1987a]). Further, the feminine assets of empathy and flexible ego boundaries, as well as concern for others, are strengths valued by relational feminists, but they carry with them a vulnerability to depression (Jack, 1991; Miller, 1976).

Caring function. Women provide nurturance and support to others more frequently than men and are named disproportionately as confidantes and companions by both men and women (Rubin, 1985). Women's "range of caring" exposes them to a greater risk of depression than men. As mentioned previously, "women are expected to respond to the pain and needs of others, whether or not their own needs for support and validation are met" (McGrath et al., 1990, p. 22). They suffer from a "contagion of stress" when people they care about are distressed (McGrath et al., 1990) and bear the heavy weight of the social system, which can "literally grind down the spirit" (Bernard, 1982, p. 8).

Marriage. Marriage seems to "protect" men more than women, with husbands more often than wives reporting being affirmed and understood by their partners. Unhappily married women experience more depressive symptoms than either happily married or unmarried women (McGrath et al., 1990). A feeling of powerlessness or inequality in a marriage (relative to decision making on household chores), as well as feeling frustrated, isolated, and lonely within their relationships, seems to increase women's propensity to depression (McGrath et al., 1990; Nolen-Hoeksema, 1990). Being unable to communicate with a spouse and have their relational needs met by that person can be depressing for most women (Klerman & Weissman, 1985), but especially for those who have endowed their marital partners with some magical ability or strength to protect and take care of them (Caplan, 1985).

An unhappy marriage is "a grave risk to a woman's mental health" (McGrath et al., 1990, p. 23). Men become more depressed when single, widowed, or separated; women become more depressed when married, especially if they are unable to make "the kinds of connection they want and often cannot get" (Stiver, 1991a, p. 264). A woman's vulnerability to depression is compounded when she is the mother of young children, increases with the number of children living at home, and is greatly affected when she is the caretaker for aging parents or in-laws, whether or not she is still caring for her own children at the time. This "role overload" can often be offset by a low level of marital strain, an affirming job, or both (McGrath et al., 1990; Nolen-Hoeksema, 1990). The quality of a woman's relationship with her partner appears to mediate her experience of painful events or chronic conditions (Jack, 1987b).

Satisfying employment can help women deal with marital stress, and women with marital problems who work outside the home are less depressed than those who do not (Nolen-Hoeksema, 1990). Multiple roles can compensate for one another in times of difficulty, and full-time homemakers often rely on their spouses and children as their primary sources of gratification. If the marital relationship is poor or unsupportive, depression is often a result (Klerman & Weissman, 1985).

Aneshensel (1986) found that the most depressed group among nine categories of women was nonemployed wives with high marital strain. These women were five times more depressed than the least depressed group, employed wives with a combination of low marital strain and low employment strain. Several other studies have found that "housewives" are the most depressed group of women (Young-Eisendrath & Wiedemann, 1987) and are more depressed than their employed husbands, particularly if they do not feel affirmed in their marriages or if they lack a certain level of intimacy in their primary relationship. Higher income housewives can afford to hire others to perform some of the noxious tasks of homemaking, and therefore have more outlets for alternative sources of affirmation than low-income housewives. Thus, they are less prone to experience depression (Nolen-Hoeksema, 1990).

Older widows generally have an easier time adjusting to their role loss than widowers, probably because of the ongoing nature of their support systems. Additionally, discontinuity affects women throughout the life span, but these constantly changing circumstances serve to protect women from depression in old age (Tallmer, 1983). There are some true stresses in later life (such as poverty, poor health, and the losses of a partner, friends, and home), but first-onset depression is rare after age 65, and it is speculated that most long-term depressed older women were also depressed as young women. In other words, some women carry into their later years a vulnerability that, when combined with stressors in the social environment, can lead to depression (Formanek, 1987b; McGrath et al., 1990).

De-selfing

Mothers (and other early caretakers) often collude with the culture and teach their daughters to silence or diminish themselves in order to stay in relationship with the caretaker or others. Self-alienation with a cutting off of emotions leads to presentation of a false self (Jack, 1987b). This "loss of self" (Jack, 1991) or loss of "voice" (Gilligan, 1982) and the self-censoring and self-denying process that accompanies it leads to what Jack (1991) calls "compliant relatedness." This loss of self in unsatisfactory relationships is like a self-betrayal of which a woman is deeply ashamed. This loss of relationship with the self is often more painful and more depressing than loss of any illusion, hope, or external other. Yet women often make the choice to muffle their voices and stifle the self in order to stay in relationships (Gilligan, 1991; Lerner, 1985).

When too much of the self becomes negotiable under relationship pressures, a "de-selfing" occurs. The "we" overtakes the "I," and this loss is accompanied by depression and often anger in "nice ladies" (Lerner, 1985, 1987, 1991). A woman's denial of whole parts of herself often includes a "model of goodness" (Jack, 1987b), in which goodness is equated with self-sacrifice. In order to be kept safe from anxiety about abandonment, women adopt the rigid cultural stereotypes of "ought," "should," "good," and "bad" that define a good woman (Gilligan, 1982; Jack, 1987b). If a woman acts according to masculine or societal definitions of "goodness" and becomes independent, assertive, and competent, she often does so at the cost of her "womanhood." Being a good woman (i.e., submissive, passive, and dependent) places her in a double bind because "to be a healthy woman by society's standards is to be a sick adult" (Heriot, 1985, p. 12).

Preservation of the relational self becomes all-important, and for that, women often inhibit the expression of anger (Kaplan, Brooks, McComb, Shapiro & Sodano, 1985). According to Jack (1991), "there is a basis to women's fears of negative consequences to the relationship if they express either anger and dissatisfaction or fear to their partners" (p. 43). Thus, they attempt to build up the other at the expense of self. "This leads eventually to lowered self-esteem, to feelings of self-betrayal, and to deep anger" (Jack, 1991, p. 139). To keep from expressing this anger, they carefully monitor and judge their thoughts and silence their voices. If they do express the anger, they are sometimes labeled immature or neurotic. Sometimes this inner rage and growing resentment explodes at partners or children. Feeling guilty or fearful at the potential loss of the relationship, they often alternate between being overly nice and "good" or angry and withholding, but depressed in either case (Jack, 1991).

Cognitive and Behavioral Styles

Not only do relationships serve different functions for women than for men, but the genders also are socialized to different styles of thinking and behaving. The curbing of ambition and resulting competence loss, the lack of instrumentality in their lives and concomitant helplessness, and a self-blaming attributional style predispose many women to depression and even suicide.

Restriction of Action

In addition to curbing anger, women are also socialized to curtail their action and assertion. "This pattern of women severely inhibiting their own strivings and actions so as to preserve relational ties emerges over and over again in clinical work with depressed women" (Kaplan, 1991, p. 213). Fear of loss of love or attachments keeps women fearing the success that may bring about differentness or separation from loved ones (Lebe, 1983). This potential for loss of relational ties affects women from childhood on, and female aspirations often strain the maternal bond (Bernay, 1983; Marcus, 1987). Mothers encourage differentiation in a boy but push for sameness in a girl. Likeness is frequently equated with closeness, and this situation, for many a woman, sets up a lifelong pattern in which she "hovers close and tries to please" (Jack, 1991, p. 40). The fact that women's strivings for achievement often *do* threaten their relationships (Miller, 1976) only reinforces their fears.

In many ways, women learn that their self-enhancement, ambition, or achievement will harm their relationships with others (Lerner, 1987) and, hence, learn to inhibit actions that will further their own goals (Kaplan, 1991). Being viewed by self or others as selfish or being threatened with loss of love or abandonment keeps women's goals and hopes for themselves contained. This loss of a "life dream," something they especially wanted to do in life, causes deep regret and often mourning (Weenolsen, 1988). The loss of the competent self they could have become and the accompanying loss of positive feedback for their achievements leads to a hopelessness and helplessness that is depressing for many women (Bernay, 1983).

Learned Helplessness

Helplessness is a characteristic of depression, and when women adopt stereotyped images of femininity in addition to an accompanying cognitive set against assertion, they are especially predisposed to depression (Weissman, 1980; Weissman & Klerman, 1987). The concept of learned helplessness, taken from the work of Seligman (1975), describes the conditioning of women to passivity and waiting to be fulfilled rather than to the traditionally masculine attitudes of independence and action. This lack of instrumentality or mastery is considered an indicator of reduced mental health (McGrath et al., 1990). Without a sense of efficacy in their lives, women frequently feel at the mercy of others and the situations that befall them. More so than men, women's locus of control is external, and they believe that forces "out there" have more determining effects on their lives than do their own efforts (Young-Eisendrath & Wiedemann, 1987). They expect to be taken care of and are dependent upon the feedback of others when judging themselves or their abilities (Gurian, 1987).

Depression, then, becomes "an almost unavoidable response to an environment that allows women little control over most of the important things in life and little hope that life will improve" (Belle, 1982, p. 241). This learned helplessness leaves women with a limited response or problem-solving repertoire when under stress and, hence, extremely vulnerable to depression (Weissman, 1980). The sadness is often associated with heavy drinking. Depression is the most common diagnosis of alcoholic women, and the chemically dependent "can present as depressed because of the mood-altering affects of alcohol and other drugs" (McGrath et al., 1990, p. 93). Only after months or even years of sobriety can an underlying diagnosis of depression be made. Additionally, more women than men become alcoholics during or following a bout of depression.

Attributional Style

"Women and girls exhibit attributional styles commonly observed in depressed and/or helpless people, whereas men and boys exhibit attributional styles commonly observed in nondepressed and/or mastery-oriented people" (Abramson & Andrews, 1982, p. 90). Because of their conditioning to passivity and helplessness, women often develop pessimistic explanatory styles in which they come to expect that they cannot control outcomes. From their perspectives, they do not have the ability or it is not within their power to attain highly valued outcomes or to avoid adverse ones. Further, they engage in a ruminative response set when depressed that serves to amplify symptoms and extend depressive episodes. Men, on the other hand, are socialized to distract themselves from depression by engaging in physical activity. The tendency of males toward distraction when distressed may lead some to maladaptive extremes such as excessive consumption of alcohol, aggressive behavior, or a dampening of emotions altogether. On the other hand, women's tendency to ruminate and "hold on" to depression interferes with instrumental behavior and may only increase feelings of helplessness and increase depressive explanations for their behavior (McGrath et al., 1990; Nolen-Hoeksema, 1990).

Negative cognitions. There appear to be gender-related differences in cognitive processing, and even mild depression in women can induce the production of further negative cognitions. A vicious cycle is then created in which women move from a mild depression to a severe one through a process of rumination of unpleasant thoughts (Joseph, 1987). Girls and women blame themselves for bad events (internal), believe that whatever characteristics they possess that caused the negative happenings must be permanent aspects of their characters (stable), and think that these faults pervade all of their beings (global) (Abramson & Andrews, 1982; Gurian, 1987). Self-directed hostility and shame result from this internal, global, and stable attributional set (Gurian, 1987). Dichotomous thinking also characterizes the cognitive patterns of "good" women (e.g., either stay in relationship or act on my own needs; either care for others or care for myself; either be selfless [and good] or selfish [and bad] [Jack, 1987b]). This good/bad girl split interacts with women's reduced instrumentality, helplessness, attributional style, and self-directed blame/shame and leads to what feels like a permanent condition of depression (Jack, 1991).

Eating disorders. Depression is related to several eating disorders in women, specifically anorexia nervosa, bulimia, and "bulimarexia," but whether depression is a correlate, cause, or consequence of an eating problem is unclear (McGrath et al., 1990). Regardless, the premorbid personalities of eating-disordered women tend to be like those of the depressed (i.e., "rigid, perfectionistic, overachieving, compliant, 'good' girls" [Finkelstein, 1987, p. 105]). Also, like depressed women, they think dichotomously and are helpless, dependent, and conforming to the wishes of others and to the culturally stereotyped definition of femininity.

Intrusive and unempathic parental overinvolvement is almost universal in women with eating disorders. Under these conditions, women have difficulty achieving independent self-regulation and a necessary sense of omnipotence or power. This lack leaves them with a pervasive sense of ineffectuality and inner hunger, which manifests itself in an eating disorder. Surrey (1991) believes that the internalized mother-daughter relationship is disrupted and eating is an attempt to reinstate the sense of connection. "Because they arise from similar developmental deficits that result in object loss, eating disorders and...depression can be thought of as two faces of the same intrapsychic...dilemma" (Finkelstein, 1987, p. 110).

Suicide. For far too many women, depression leads to attempts to take their lives. Although more males commit suicide than females

(2:1 at 21 years rising to 10:1 at 60 years), the gender differential is reversed for suicide attempts. Three times as many adult women attempt suicide than men, and ten times as many adolescent girls as boys. Female suicide deaths, however, are increasing at a faster rate than male suicide deaths (Neuringer, 1987).

Compared with other groups, professional women are a relatively advantaged group. They nonetheless commit suicide at rates that are either comparable to or higher than their male peers. In spite of their freedom, options, education, resources, and educational level, they struggle with a variety of conflicts and stressors that increase their risk for depression. Many professional women have difficulty reconciling their achievement and affiliation needs and fear that their career will threaten male self-esteem or jeopardize marital prospects. Further, single self-reliant women are often lonely and isolated as they struggle with unmet relational and emotional needs. Suicide is often the result (McGrath et al., 1990).

Like depressed women, suicidal women think dichotomously, but even more so. They tend to view everything in terms of bipolar opposites. If they are disappointed, they respond as if they had failed completely or been utterly rejected. This dichotomous thinking is impervious to change and sustains negative affect. They feel helpless to change their depressed emotions and hopeless about any future improvement. Being totally weary and completely depressed, the women see suicide as the only way to end the pain (Neuringer, 1987).

Social and Socioeconomic Status

The life situations of many women are depressing because "real social discriminations make it difficult for them to achieve mastery by direct action and self-assertion, which only further contributes to their psychological distress. . . .these inequities lead to legal and economic helplessness, dependency on others, chronically low self-esteem, low aspirations, and ultimately, clinical depression" (Klerman & Weissman, 1985, pp. 502–503; Weissman, 1980; Weissman & Klerman, 1987). Compared with men, they lack the power necessary to attain goals they might set for themselves, and the kind of work they do is evaluated more negatively and taken far less seriously. As a group, they are segregated into low-paying jobs where subtle discrimination and sexual harassment are prevalent. Yet, they often learn to ignore or accept injustices as a way of surviving because they often cannot afford to quit their jobs or leave relationships (Nolen-Hoeksema, 1990).

According to the U.S. Department of Labor (1992), women earn 74 cents for every dollar a man earns, and inequalities as broad as this have persisted for more than 30 years. Far more women than men are the single parents of minor children, and fewer than half of the 60 percent of fathers who are required by divorce decrees to pay child support payments do so on a regular basis. Further, the standard of living of divorced women and their children drops about 70 percent in the first year after a divorce (it rises 42 percent for men) (Nolen-Hoeksema, 1990). Poverty is a "pathway to depression," and 75 percent of the U.S. poverty population is women and children (McGrath et al., 1990, p. xii). Poverty is a high correlate of psychological distress (Golding, 1988; McGrath et al., 1990), and high levels of depression are common "among women without confidants, child-rearing assistance or employment and among women experiencing chronic stressful conditions, particularly those reflecting economic problems" (Belle, 1990, p. 385). Belle (1990) further notes that income level is predictive of depression because it predicts financial, parenting, and child care problems. After studying several hundred low-income mothers, Belle concluded that unaltered stressful life conditions often take a toll not only in the form of depression, but also as attempted suicides, mental breakdowns, health problems, and children's adjustment problems (1982). "The long-term problems of poverty, burdensome responsibilities, and foreclosed opportunity contribute more heavily to the depression of low-income mothers than a single crisis or tragic event" (Belle, 1982, p. 241).

Oppression and Depression

Oppression exists in a variety of forms. Just as poverty and its accompanying life stressors oppress many women and predispose them to depression, so do three other sets of conditions, discussed below. They include the presence of violence and physical violation in the lives of many women, as well as being members of a stigmatized group in society. In this regard, the oppressive life conditions of lesbian and ethnic minority women will be discussed.

Victimization by Violence

The overall presence of victimization is significantly higher for women than for men and is likely to be understated. Estimates of childhood sexual assault range from 21.7 to 37 percent of women, partner battering from 25 to 50 percent, and rape between 12 and 46 percent (Nolen-Hoeksema,1990). As many as 71 percent of working women may experience sexual harassment. "Victimization in interpersonal relationships is a significant risk factor in the development of depressive symptomatology in women" (McGrath et al., 1990, p. 28).

Some depressions may result from battering-related head injuries, but being physically violated in a personal relationship, in and of itself, sets up a vulnerability for depression. Estimates of the rate of suicide attempts in battered women range from 25 to 42 percent (Nolen-Hoeksema,1990). Additionally, from 30 to 75 percent of women who abuse alcohol and drugs do so to repress traumatic experiences of sexual and physical abuse and incest. After the first year of sobriety, memories of these events can begin to emerge, and 18 months after sobriety is often a crisis point for recall (McGrath et al., 1990).

Careful diagnosis is crucial in identifying and treating depression, and an assessment must take into consideration a concurrent personality disorder (which may occur in 40 percent of depressed individuals). Childhood physical or sexual abuse in women is associated with a high proportion of borderline personality disorders, along with depression and suicidal symptoms. In any case, a history of assault and violence must be considered when working with depressed, suicidal, or bulimic women (McGrath et al., 1990).

Lesbian Women

Depression is the most common reason that lesbians seek counseling (McGrath et al., 1990; Rothblum, 1990). The high rate of suicide attempts among Caucasian lesbians (41 percent) is 2½ times that of the 26 percent of white heterosexual women who have either seriously considered or attempted suicide. Latina and black lesbians commit suicide at rates of 28 and 27 percent higher than do white lesbians. Stigmatization and shame contribute to the 25 percent of black lesbians who consider or attempt suicide. These rates are higher than for black heterosexual women (19 percent) or black heterosexual men (2 percent). The 24 percent of black gay men and 37 percent of white gay men (compared with 13 percent of nongay white men) are also very high rates, but the rates of attempted or completed suicides for comparable populations of women are even higher. Adolescent lesbians attempt suicide at about three times the rate of adult lesbians because of social isolation, rejection by family or peers, self-hatred, and depression (McGrath et al., 1990; Rofes, 1983; Rothblum, 1990). Lesbian women also may use chemicals to escape stigma, lack of social supports, and internalized shame, with rates of substance abuse reported to be approximately 30 percent in lesbian and gay populations (McGrath et al., 1990).

Clearly, being of lesbian orientation places a woman at high risk not only for depression, but for suicide and chemical abuse as well. Even though lesbian women carry with them the same reduced societal and socioeconomic status as their heterosexual sisters, their life experiences differ in some significant ways from those of nonlesbian women. "The double burden of being a lesbian in this society and [for women of color] differing demographically from the lesbian community may increase rates of depression" (McGrath et al., 1990, p. 88).

As has been discussed previously, lack of social support and depression are related. For fear of rejection and misunderstanding, only 28.4 percent of lesbians come out to their mothers and 19.3 percent to their fathers. Thus, for a majority of lesbians, parents are not included among their support network, while the reverse is true for most heterosexual women (McGrath et al., 1990; Rothblum, 1990). Further, fear of stigmatization and job loss keeps many lesbian women and their partners closeted or isolated, and for women not affiliated with a lesbian network, their lover may be their only confidante. "Thus, depression may be a greater risk factor for rural lesbians or lesbians who are not out to many people outside of their partner" (Rothblum, 1990, p. 71).

The coming-out process is stressful for many lesbians, but once women are out, there is a protective advantage both psychologically and socially. As is true for nonlesbian women, being in a supportive relationship is related to positive mental health for lesbians, but disruption in a primary relationship is a risk factor for depression. Being mothers of young children may be somewhat protective, but societally homophobic treatment of their offspring, coming out to children and fear of their rejection, and ongoing custody battles (which 80 percent of lesbians lose in lower courts) are precursors of depression (Rothblum, 1990).

Satisfying work serves to mitigate against depression in heterosexual women, but discrimination and job insecurity are common in lesbians. Most occupations are closed to people who are openly lesbian or gay, and leading a double life at work, in the family, and in society often takes its toll on mental health. Traditional religion has judged lesbians and gay men as sinners and labeled them as "objectively disordered" or perverted. About 80 percent of all lesbians consult a mental health professional at some point in their lives, and they often receive inadequate treatment, with the goals of counseling frequently being to cure them of their "affliction" or to convert or reorient them to heterosexuality. A woman may find a lesbian-affirming counselor or at least one who sees her orientation as somewhat normative, but many women leave counseling more hopeless and depressed than before (Ritter & O'Neill, 1989). Given all the oppressive conditions under which lesbian women live, it is amazing that they have coped as well as they have (Rothblum, 1990).

As mentioned previously, alcoholism and other chemical abuse is related to depression in lesbians, with 30 to 35 percent, compared with 5 percent of nonlesbian women, reporting drinking alcohol excessively (Glaus, 1989; Nicoloff & Stiglitz, 1987; Rothblum, 1990). When lesbians first come out, bars may be the only place they know to meet other women like themselves. They may also see chemicals as helping to anesthetize the sometimes chronic anxiety resulting from isolation; fear of disclosure; constant monitoring of behavior, thoughts or conversation; and low self-esteem or shame resulting from societal, religious, or self-condemnation (Nicoloff & Stiglitz, 1987; Ritter & O'Neill, 1989).

Lesbians who are nonwhite, older, adolescent, or working-class may feel particularly isolated. Their sisters who are more educated, white, urban, and have some job security or self-employment often have access to lesbian-affirming information and positive role models within the lesbian community. Members of ethnic minority groups may not be aware of lesbianism within the history of their own culture or may not see lesbian women of color to emulate. As if being a stigmatized subgroup within an already oppressed population were not sufficient to render them vulnerable to depression, it is estimated that half of all black and Latina lesbians have been physically abused (Rothblum, 1990).

Ethnic Minority Women

Just as any form of oppression is associated with depression in women, so is race or ethnicity. Before beginning this discussion, it is important to keep in mind that data reporting correlations between ethnic subpopulations and depression reflect many factors, cultural/racial background being only one. "Ethnic minority women are more likely than Anglo women to share a number of socioeconomic risk factors for depression, including racial/ethnic discrimination, lower educational and income levels, segregation into low-status and high-stress jobs, unemployment, poor health, larger family sizes, marital dissolution, and single parenthood" (McGrath et al., 1990, p. 76). Thus, in the absence of clear cultural differences in rates of depression in men and women, the discussion below could be more reflective of any of the above-mentioned variables than of ethnicity per se.

Discrimination-provoked violence is a risk factor for depression in any low-status or stigmatized group of women, lesbian and ethnic minority women being the most common examples. Additionally, black and Hispanic women are particularly likely to be poor. Women of color, particularly black and native American women, frequently have serious health problems resulting from alcoholism, but they may also drink heavily to escape depressing socioeconomic conditions and conflicts (McGrath et al., 1990). The suicide rate for adolescent women of color is higher than for white women of the same age (which is already 10 times higher than for boys) (Rofes, 1983).

Black women. Discrimination has severe emotional consequences, with the long-lasting pain affecting children and childrearing strategies (Belle, 1982). Black women face a number of mental health problems as a result of a more than 300-year history of racism in American society. Possible misdiagnosis is a concern among ethnic minority groups in general, and in one study (cited in McGrath et al., 1990), the rate of a depression diagnosis was 42 percent higher for black than for white women. Whether sociocultural variables and/or discrimination affect the rates of depression in black women to this extent or whether many of the subjects were inappropriately diagnosed is unclear (McGrath et al., 1990).

Hispanic women. Hispanic women are overrepresented among lower socioeconomic classes and younger ages, and many have living arrangements incongruent with gender stereotypes in their culture. More than one out of two has no husband present, and a large number are separated or divorced. These circumstances carry with them gender role conflicts (McGrath et al., 1990).

Traditional cultural expectations of passivity and obligation predispose Latinas to depression, since they are expected to be simultaneously responsible for the outcome of their marriages and unassertive toward father, husband, and other authority figures. Confusion about sexuality affects women's intimate relationships, and traditional cultural expectations frequently do not allow cooperative and supportive heterosexual relations to develop. As a result, Hispanic women often become "overly involved" with their children and transmit their own "psychocultural vulnerability to depression to their daughters" (McGrath et al., 1990, p. 77).

Migration, culture shock, and adjustment to a foreign civilization are often depressing for Latinas. Given the value that Hispanic cultures place on family and extended community networks, immigration and social alienation are often predictive of depression in women from these groups. Before interpreting the Hispanic/white differences in depression as reflecting differences in cultural values, however, it is important first to control for economic, social class, and age differences (McGrath et al., 1990).

Asian and Pacific Islander women. Asian American women are a diverse group, ranging from those whose educational and economic profile compares favorably with American women in general to those first-generation immigrant women with eight or fewer years of education. Nonetheless, because of perceived similar characteristics of all women of Asian origin, they are often subject to the same gender stereotyping of docility and subservience and suffer similar ethnic and racial discrimination.

Asian women are inclined to handle difficult situations by being accommodating rather than assertive and have a greater predisposition to depression than their male counterparts. In other words, the higher female to male ratios of depression found virtually worldwide hold for Asian and Pacific Islander women. Many Southeast Asian refugee women suffer from another risk factor as well. Many have been sexually abused, and for them, "rape is a secret issue surrounded by an extreme reticence to reveal details during evaluation and treatment" (McGrath et al., 1990, p. 79). Extreme trauma, not only from abuse but also from extensive cruel and dehumanizing treatment to which they were subjected before and during immigration, has left many depressed and suffering from posttraumatic stress disorder (McGrath et al., 1990).

Native American women. These women are among the least visible and researched group in American society. Much information from government-based agencies is not necessarily sensitive to the native American experience of being driven off their lands and placed on reservations. Nor is there much empirical research on native American women, but without a doubt, their health and mental health status is "bleak" (McGrath et al., 1990, p. 79). Their death rate from alcoholism, cirrhosis/liver disease, homicide, suicide, accidental death, and motor vehicle accidents is from 2 to 10 percent higher than for other American women.

As with all other ethnic minority women, culturally sanctioned gender roles predispose native American women to depression, as do poverty, lack of education, and large numbers of children. Further, many have experienced incest, rape, and sexual assault. In response to the numerous stressors affecting native American women, a large number self-medicate with alcohol and drugs (McGrath et al., 1990).

YOUTH AT RISK FOR DEPRESSION

Adolescent Girls

"Adolescence has traditionally been considered a period in which most young people go through distressing self-analysis and experience frequent periods of anxiety and depression" (Nolen-Hoeksema, 1990, p. 24). Before adolescence, however, the depression rates of boys and girls are essentially similar, with boys slightly more likely to report depression than girls. Although the female and male rates of depressive symptoms rise substantially from childhood to adolescence, gender differences begin to emerge in early adolescence. There is a rapid rise in the rate of depression in girls during the high school years, and by age 14 or 15, girls are much more likely to be depressed than boys. At the end of adolescence, the adult female to male depression ratio of 2:1 is established (Kurash & Schaul, 1987; McGrath et al., 1990; Nolen-Hoeksema, 1990).

Women who were depressed as girls are significantly more likely to be depressed as adults than those who were not depressed at younger ages. Girls are at increased risk for depression in early puberty, but as hormonal production becomes stabilized after age 12, depression levels decline, and the higher rates of depression in girls compared with boys do not emerge until age 14 or 15 (Nolen-Hoeksema, 1990). A number of negative influences, such as low parental support, authoritarian and unstable families, depressed parents, physical or sexual abuse, dissatisfaction with their maturing bodies, and competence loss, are better predictors of adolescent female depression than hormonal levels. If negative life events occur simultaneously with the physical changes of puberty, the risk for depression is increased, however (Kurash & Schaul, 1987; McGrath et al., 1990; Nolen-Hoeksema, 1990).

Gender intensification occurs during adolescence, when girls feel pressure to assume feminine sex role characteristics. According to Kurash and Schaul (1987), a mother's own degree of psychological individuation is a crucial variable in handling her daughter's adolescence. She must be able to separate her own needs from those of the young girl, respect the differences between them, allow for the adolescent's repudiation of the mother's projections, and still remain affectively connected. Adolescent girls often feel the influence from parents, especially fathers, who expect them to conform to sex role stereotyping in careers and who also restrict their range of independence compared with boys their age (Marcus, 1987).

Peer pressure to conform to culturally prescribed norms of femininity also operates. Girls are commonly expected to devalue their own abilities and accomplishments and rely on others for their self-esteem. They are not to appear competent or assertive and often go to great lengths not to violate their sex roles. Thus, female de-selfing begins at adolescence, when the most intelligent girls are often more depressed than other girls their age (Nolen-Hoeksema, 1990). "Thus, it appears as though female adolescents are in double jeopardy. Instrumentality and competence lower the risk for depression over the life cycle. However, if female adolescents are instrumental and competent in their activities and interactions, they are at increased risk for rejection by their peers, which may increase risk for depression" (McGrath et al., 1990, p. 83).

Gilligan (Gilligan, Lyons, & Hanmer, 1990) believes that adolescence poses a crisis of connection for girls and is "a watershed in female development, a time when girls are in danger of drowning or disappearing" (p. 10). "At the edge of adolescence, eleven- and twelve-year-old girls observe where and when women speak and when they are silent" (p. 25). Girls are not only in danger of losing connection with others, but also of losing their voices. Thus, they often end up losing authentic connection both with others and with self (Gilligan, 1991).

Children of Depressed Mothers

Depressed children are likely to have depressed mothers, and the younger and more dependent the children, the more influence their mothers have on them. Because mothers and daughters are of the same gender, mothers tend not to experience female children as separate from themselves. Traditionally, mothers are more intensely involved with young daughters than young sons, and two- and three-year-old girls spend more time close to mothers than do their brothers. Girls' attachments to their mothers last longer than do those of boys, their relationships are more interdependent, and their process of separation more complex (Fischer, 1986). Hence, young girls are often more vulnerable than boys to the effects of maternal depression and attributional style, although children of both genders are at high risk for future depressions (Gurian, 1987).

"Mothers of young children are highly vulnerable to depression; the more children in the house, the more depression is reported" (McGrath et al., 1990, p. xii). Likewise, the children of highly stressed mothers are at an increased risk for depression (Formanek, 1983). Parenting is a difficult task for depressed women. They are more demanding of their children, less tolerant of disobedience, and use more shouting and physical punishment than nondepressed mothers. They are also less responsive and nurturant and more hostile (Belle, 1982). The result is that their children are predisposed to depression and all its possible manifestations, including learning problems, antisocial conduct, attention-deficit disorders, aggressive behaviors, withdrawal, hyperactivity, somatic complaints, hopelessness, low self-esteem, chemical abuse, and suicide.

IMPLICATIONS FOR COUNSELING

Perspective and Assessment

Before discussing approaches and strategies for counseling depressed women, other considerations must be addressed. The first is one of a framework for counselors working with this population. Second, from this feminist perspective, a careful socioculturally relevant assessment is mandatory before beginning the counseling process.

Feminist Perspective

When counseling depressed women, it is important to work within a sociocultural framework, or from what has been referred to as a feminist perspective (McGrath et al., 1990). Whether or not clients or counselors identify with the term *feminist*, the concept implies that therapists must take the sociocultural matrix into account when working with depressed women. A feminist philosophy of counseling is not a treatment approach per se, but rather serves as a framework to guide therapists through the helping process.

A counselor is a companion through this journey, a member of a "politically radical conspiracy" in which the "ear of the therapist becomes connected to the client's voice" that long ago was driven "underground" (Gilligan, 1991). Gilligan (1991) contends that women listen to themselves through others and that counseling involves joining with their lost voices. This view implies that the relationship between a woman and her counselor is egalitarian (McGrath et al., 1990) and thus unlike most of the other relationships in the client's life, in which she is in a position of lesser status. The therapist may be an expert on counseling theory and practice, but the client is the most knowledgeable about herself and her own problems and solutions. Thus, not only does the therapeutic relationship itself empower, but so do the interventions of the therapist, "which enhance clients' self-confidence, self-direction, autonomy, and sense of personal power" (Gilbert, 1980, p. 256).

Assessment and Consultation

A comprehensive history, including a careful and thorough assessment, is the starting point in counseling a depressed woman. The context-relevant assessment should include patterns of alcohol and drug use; history of abuse, violence, or victimization; current or past suicidal ideation or behaviors; sexual orientation status and degree of identity development in this regard; employment patterns; reproductive history and associated depressions; socioeconomic level or condition; racial/ethnic discrimination, childbearing and child-rearing patterns; relationship status and its nature; family history of depression; course of the depression; and social support network. In addition, any psychopathology must be diagnosed and the client's attributional style, coping skills, instrumentality, strengths, and resources assessed (McGrath et al., 1990).

Women have higher rates than men of certain medical illnesses associated with depression. Therefore, a recent physical examination and consultation with a physician is important if there are concurrent medical issues. Special attention should be paid to medication usage, especially that of psychotropic drugs, since "approximately 70 percent of the prescriptions for antidepressants are given to women, often with improper diagnosis and monitoring" (McGrath et al., 1990, p. xiii). Nonetheless, medication can help some women use counseling more effectively by relieving disabling anxiety or depression, thus allowing them to concentrate on using available energy for understanding or solving problems (McGrath et al., 1990). Misdiagnosis and improper dosages of antidepressants are real dangers for depressed women, and it is crucial to work closely with a physician if a client is taking medication for her depression or any associated conditions.

After a working alliance is formed with a depressed woman, counseling should begin with the most life-threatening or critical issues highlighted on the assessment inventory (e.g., an underlying or concurrent medical condition; alcohol, drug, or medication misuse/abuse; suicidal thoughts or behaviors; child abuse; serious financial difficulties; unemployment; or currently being in a violent or battering relationship). Once appropriate referrals have been made and the immediate situation is stabilized, counseling can address some of the issues contributing to the manifestations of depression.

Counseling Approaches and Strategies

The discussion of counseling approaches and strategies is organized around two of the four factors contributing to depression in women, the centrality of relationships in their lives and the nature of their cognitive and behavioral styles. Interpersonal (or relationally related) approaches are discussed first, with accompanying strategies for helping women move beyond depression. Behavioral and cognitive perspectives follow. A brief rationale for the choices of techniques is included.

Interpersonal Approaches

Given women's development and embeddedness in relationships, the counseling process itself not only takes place in that context, but also deals with the interpersonal aspects of clients' lives.

Relational issues such as disconnecting or reconnecting with significant others as the client progresses through the counseling process must be addressed and assistance provided for the grieving and healing involved. Counselors may need to help women join or form new support communities or to deal with unresolved family of origin issues. This section will discuss these interpersonally related approaches to counseling with depressed women.

Disconnecting and reconnecting. Assisting women in the counseling relationship to reconnect their lost voices with feelings often creates (or increases) disruptions in their interpersonal connections. As they begin to find their "I" and to express opinions or buried anger, they or significant others may fear that counseling is making them worse instead of better. Family, friends, and even co-workers may need to be invited to sessions in order to recalibrate relationships and find new or different balances. The pressures upon a woman to return to her "old (self-less) self" may be intense, and she may need help in establishing new self-definitions and ego boundaries while still keeping her self-in-relation. Some abusive, devaluing, or non-growth-enhancing relationships may end when women gain a renewed sense of self, and clients may need special help with the loss and mourning issues involved.

Supported grieving. In this regard, women can be helped to see that "all our relationships are part of who we are" (Weenolsen, 1988, p. 499), and even if a connection involved a great deal of negative emotion, the part of self that was lost must be grieved and a new one reborn. The transition from powerless giving to empowered relating is a difficult one and involves "a loss of old ways of seeing and interacting and, for many women, includes the mourning of a self and of relationships that have been lost...." (Jack, 1991, p. 195).

Counselors can help to attribute a different meaning to this grieving than was given to the original depression. The first depression undoubtedly felt purposeless and hopeless, but transition-related mourning can be purposeful and hopeful if counselors can provide an appropriate framework for the process. This one is "a passage through the pain of loss and uncertainty to a healing transformation that holds new possibilities of relatedness" (Jack, 1991, p. 205).

Especially painful is the coming out process for lesbian women, in which an old self must be grieved before a new and stronger one can emerge (O'Neill & Ritter, 1992; Ritter & O'Neill, 1989). Depression is common as women move from denial or confusion about their sexual orientation through stages leading to the establishment of a positive lesbian identity (Cass, 1979; Coleman, 1982). Counselors and support groups can assist in this painful journey by reframing it as a process that reverses de-selfing and leads to a stronger and more authentic self.

Transition journeys for all women need to be supported by a community composed not only of counselors, but also of friends and even support or therapy groups. Since women are relational by nature, some experts see group counseling or self-help groups as crucial to healing in depressed women (McGrath, 1991; McGrath et al., 1990). Groups of all kinds for women, both therapy and support, are conducted in communities across the country. Counselors should recommend these groups as adjuncts to therapy for women who are recovering from abuse, battering, incest, divorce, or loss of any kind, or who might need extra support for a variety of concerns.

Family of origin. Lerner (1987, 1988) believes that the de-selfing process of women begins in their first family and continues into later relationships. By understanding the legacies of previous generations they bring into adulthood, women can be helped to consolidate a clearer and more separate sense of self. Through the process of gathering family facts and understanding multigenerational patterns and triangles, women can gain a more objective perspective on their own lives. If counselors help women to be more mindful and conscious about relationship choices, rather than being passively conditioned or led into them, many depressions can be alleviated.

Behavioral and Cognitive Approaches

A growing amount of data show that behavioral/cognitive behavioral approaches either independently or combined with interpersonal/self-in-relation perspectives (both of which are conducted from a feminist framework) can help women alter the negative cognitions and low sense of personal efficacy underpinning their depression. Distraction, mastery, and action strategies can also help alleviate depressive symptoms and empower women (McGrath et al., 1990). The following section will deal first with behavioral approaches, namely action strategies and skills training, and conclude with a discussion of using cognitive therapy with depressed women.

Action strategies. Counseling can help provide alternatives to feeling hopeless, overwhelmed, and inadequate, and this counseling often includes action approaches to therapy. McGrath (1991) believes that if counselors are simply talking with depressed women, they are not doing enough, and she suggests that counselors move clients into action initially and help them reconnect with feelings later. As mentioned earlier in this chapter, women ruminate and tend toward inactivity when depressed, whereas men distract themselves with activity. Counselors can ask women to deal with their depression much as a man would. The activity could be in the form of walking, exercise, swimming, or anything that stimulates the body physiologically and increases energy flow. Depressed clients often resist suggestions for activity, and therapists may need to be fairly insistent.

Lowen (1976; Lowen, Meichenbaum, Watzlawick, & Wolpe, 1990) believes that depressed people exhibit one third as much body movement as nondepressed people and, thus, have little energy available to respond to life. He contends that there is a loss of love in early life behind every depression. Women, especially, compensate for this by being "good," thinking that by pleasing others they can get the love they want. This constricting process eventually leads to depression, which Lowen tries to open up with breathing exercises in order to move energy and emotion. Even if counselors are not trained in bioenergetics per se, they can still help depressed clients learn to breathe deeply and slowly. This breathing process can be turned into practice exercises, or even into relaxation training, especially with clients who have debilitating anxiety accompanying their depression.

Action strategies can also include empowerment activities. Women often need assistance seeking and securing a job (Josefowitz,

1980), increasing their own sense of authority (Young-Eisendrath & Wiedemann, 1987), and learning to be "real" rather than "good." In this regard they could undoubtedly benefit from understanding the personal change process and learning how to trust themselves enough to take responsibility for their lives (Bepko & Krestan, 1990; Dowling, 1988; Heriot,1985).

Skills training. Depressed women frequently need an enhanced set of relationship skills before they can initiate new or different kinds of actions and activities. They often may need help in broadening their range of problem-solving and coping skills and may need special assistance with vocational training and job-seeking skills (Josefowitz, 1980), specific communication skills, or assertiveness training (Alberti & Emmons, 1990).

By using step-by-step procedures, detailed examples, and practice exercises, counselors can often help women feel safe in learning new skills and behaviors. Years of passivity and fear have usually preceded the depression and helplessness. By moving too rapidly, counselors can inadvertently compound a woman's fear or increase her self-blame if the client believes she has failed either the task or the counselor. In order to counteract a lack of instrumentality and self-efficacy, therapists need to graduate the tasks so clients feel challenged by goals and yet can still control the outcomes (Kobasa, 1985). In other words, the practice needs to be structured so women can succeed and experience a sense of mastery (Blechman, 1980). A listing of specific materials is beyond the scope of this chapter, but many books and skills-training guides are available (Alberti & Emmons, 1990; Cudney & Hardy, 1991; Phelps & Austin, 1987; Preston, 1989).

Cognitions. Cognitive therapy is recommended when working with depressed women in order to alter their negative attributional style. These clients tend to have a depressing cognitive schema or way of viewing the world, which, combined with a scarcity of vocational, assertive, or efficacy skills, often results in their getting little positive feedback for their accomplishments. This low level of desired feedback often feeds a negative schema, which depresses them further and has them emitting fewer behaviors that can be positively reinforced by others. Thus, a downward cycle is set up in which their depressed perception of reality actually gets increasing reinforcement (Krantz, 1983; Hollon, 1983).

Cognitive therapies can reverse this downward spiral and alter the internal dialogue that feeds it (McGrath et al., 1990). These strategies can help a woman gain a sense of power and mastery over her own life by learning to control her cognitions. Simply presenting depression as a problem of faulty thinking is empowering to many women and allows them to focus on changing their thought processes rather than involuntarily being ruled by their emotions. There are many cognitive behavioral books available for both counselors and clients (Beck, 1976; Burns, 1981, 1990; Emery, 1982, 1988; Meichenbaum & Cameron, 1982).

Combined with other activities carefully designed to increase women's sense of instrumentality, cognitive therapy can be of great benefit to depressed women. By learning to target the specific thoughts that are associated with negative emotions and replacing them with affirming or coping statements, women find that they are able to be more instrumental in their lives than they had previously believed. This increased competency, combined with action or skills training or both, gives clients more control over what happens to them. Thus, they are less depressed and have the self-esteem and resources necessary to confront the sometimes extremely difficult circumstances of their lives.

CONCLUSION

Girls and women have a tendency to blame themselves for negative events and attribute the results to some defect of theirs (Abramson & Andrews, 1982; Gurian, 1987). For many, it is a great relief to learn that the depression is not their fault, but rather a natural response to gender role conditioning, devaluing or violent relationships, abuse, poverty, a stigmatized sexual orientation, racism, discrimination, role strain, or oppression. Stressed clients often come to therapy wondering if their depression indicates they are losing their minds or going crazy. Women, especially those with an external locus of control, will ask, "Am I right to feel this way?" They frequently feel empowered in learning that millions of women are depressed for exactly the same reasons as they and that others think and feel the same as they do.

With knowledge of the sociocultural influences on all women's depressions, a woman can come to feel less ashamed and blaming of herself for her own depression, less personally inadequate, less guilty for her "weakness," less pathological, and more normal. This increased objectivity can allow her to see her life and that of other women through a new set of eyes and "evaluate herself by different standards" (Jack, 1991, p. 196). A shift of perspective away from *self* and self-condemnation to the *situation* can free energy for the actual work of moving through and out of depression.

THE EXAMPLE OF VIVIAN

Vivian is a 30-year-old divorced African-American woman. She has four children (ages 5, 7, 9, and 11) and is the oldest child and only daughter of a widowed mother. Her father was killed in a factory accident when she was 6. Vivian assisted her mother in raising her two brothers, one of whom (Sam) is developmentally disabled and lives in the family home. The whereabouts of the younger brother, Leroy, are unknown. Vivian's Aunt Lottie lives in town, but the rest of the extended family remained in the South when the two sisters came north some years back to find work in the factories.

Vivian's mother worked in the factory until she was widowed. By that time, the demands of a full-time job and caring for three small children, one of whom required constant assistance, left her exhausted. Her husband's and children's Social Security benefits and extra income from child care supported her and the family. Vivian was a "good girl" and was never the burden that Sam was or a troublemaker like Leroy. Even after she married Henry at 18, Vivian continued to serve as her mother's helper. Sam could never be left alone, so Vivian ran Mom's errands for her and watched Sam while Mom went to church. Aunt Lottie and the churchwomen helped from time to time, but they had families and troubles of their own; thus, Mom depended on Vivian for most of her physical and emotional support.

Henry left Vivian for another woman shortly after their fourth child was born. Even though the other children were 2, 4, and 6 years old, finances necessitated that Vivian continue in her job at the convalescent center where she had worked her way up to shift supervisor. The kids stayed at Mom's house, often overnight, since Vivian took advantage of every possible opportunity to work double shifts and receive the extra pay. She and Henry had never gotten along well, and Henry's employment was sporadic. When he was unemployed, he would frequently get drunk and become verbally or physically abusive to Vivian. She has neither heard from him since he left nor received any financial support for the children.

When Vivian first presented for counseling, she reported that she had felt depressed most of her life, but that the emotions had become more intense in recent months. Some days, she could barely climb out of bed, get the children dressed, fed, and over to Mom's house, and drive herself to work. Vivian described few friendships ("no time for them and besides, they just end up hurting you anyway"), much loneliness and sadness, and a life that seemed to hold few pleasures except for eating. She told of feeling responsible for so many others—Mom, her children, Aunt Lottie, and the patients at work—and of having no time for herself. She said she sometimes had an impulse to take an overdose of the medicine in the supply closet at the convalescent center, but that the thought of the others trying to survive without her kept her from killing herself.

Vivian worried continually about money, her son who was having trouble paying attention in school, her daughter who cried every time she left, and her own future, which seemed bleak and burdensome. These thoughts continued day and night, and she had not been able to stop them. When asked to describe her life in one word, she said she felt "trapped" with no way out. To her, the situation seemed hopeless as she felt powerless to change the course of events.

Vivian blamed herself for falling for Henry and getting herself in the mess she was in. She was also mad at herself for her saying "yes" to everyone's requests for fear of their not liking her and for her inability to "make waves" or stand up for herself. Additionally, she was angry at Henry for leaving after she tried so hard to make the marriage work and at Mom and the children for needing her so much. It seemed that she had given so much to these relationships and got so little back. She found herself snapping at her kids, and on a "couple" of occasions, she reported feeling out of control and spanking them "a bit too hard." She then felt guilty and scared. It terrified her to think of being alone for the rest of her life, and she would do anything to avoid that possibility.

The work with Vivian was preceded by a careful assessment of factors that might present obstacles to the counseling process. Her history reflected a family pattern of depression but no alcohol, drug, or medication abuse on her part. Food appeared to be her drug of choice. Medical records indicated a moderately high blood pressure for which she was currently taking medication. Suicide and Axis II disorders were ruled out, and the possibility of reportable abuse of her children would be monitored weekly. Vivian's strengths included abilities to remain financially solvent despite a limited income, to parent four young children as a single mother, to acquire a credible employment history including a recent promotion, and to handle multiple responsibilities adequately. She was referred to a psychiatrist who prescribed an anti-depressant medication that has been shown to counteract obsessive thinking.

The counseling process began with the counselor describing to Vivian the nature of women's depression and its frequency in single, financially stressed mothers like herself. As the two of them discussed her many responsibilities and her conditioning as an African-American woman to try her best to meet the expectations of both herself and others, Vivian was able to be somewhat more objective about her situation and to blame herself less. In other words, she had been doing what she was expected to do, and depression was a natural result.

The counselor explained to Vivian that she would be a companion on her journey and not an authority with additional expectations for her, as so many in her life had been. Her role during counseling would be to assist Vivian in connecting with a "voice" she had lost long ago and to help her remain in relationships with her family and colleagues at work without feeling that she was continually compromising her integrity. At one point during the six-month process, Mom and Aunt Lottie joined a session, and the counselor assisted Vivian in negotiating some boundaries for her caretaking of them. After Vivian explained to them her stressful situation, they agreed to rely more on each other and their church friends for assistance rather than calling on Vivian for help. Vivian promised to limit the amount of time she expected Mom to babysit to work hours and two evenings a week. During these nights, she was to be with friends from the single mothers' support group at a local community center that primarily served the African-American population. Her additional child care would come from trade-offs she would negotiate with other women from the group. Before any of these discussions took place, Vivian and the counselor would often practice the encounter so she would have the skills she needed once she was in the actual situation. Rehearsals with colleagues were also conducted so that Vivian was more able to set limits when others would ask for assistance or coverage when they wanted extra days off. These exercises were carefully designed with graduated tasks so that Vivian experienced a sense of mastery rather than additional failure.

It was determined that both Vivian and her children carried much unresolved grief from their past. Vivian was helped to write a letter to Henry inviting him to a session, but her limited efforts to locate him proved futile. Instead, his sister came and told Vivian about the pain of their childhoods; after this, she came to see herself as less victimized and Henry as also a victim. She was able to mourn her "sweetheart" and her lost childhood. The children came to one session, and the five of them grieved their lost family and renewed hope in their present one. With this transition-related mourning, Vivian was able to begin appreciating the birth of a new self.

Vivian and the counselor worked in a systematic manner with her cognitive style. Each distortion or thought that led to or reinforced depressing thinking was carefully identified. She was taught thought-stopping techniques and methods for substituting precise and affirming coping statements for those that had previously led to anger or guilt. Homework charts that she could use to record and substitute thoughts were constructed.

Vivian was encouraged to use the exercise room at work three lunch hours a week, and she also began taking walks on weekends. A woman at work agreed to give Vivian a massage on Saturdays in return for an afternoon of child care. Additionally for tension reduction, Vivian was taught deep-breathing exercises and relaxation in which she was to engage when she felt stressed. Vivian had always wanted to be a registered nurse, and a long-term plan to help her reach this goal was developed. She contacted a legal aid society that located Henry and forced him to help with child support. A counselor at the community college was willing to work with her over the next several years in securing loans, work-study positions, and reservations in the campus child care cooperative. She took a class in assertiveness training and developed the ability to read many of the self-help books related to depression, assertiveness, parenting, and self-esteem. At the end of counseling, the case was turned over to the college counselor, who assured Vivian that she was in good hands and well on her way to overcoming depression.

REFERENCES

Abramson, L. Y., & Andrews, D. E. (1982). Cognitive models of depression: Implications for sex differences in vulnerability to depression. *International Journal of Mental Health, 11,* 77–94.

Adler, T. (1991, July). Women's expectations are menopause villains. *APA Monitor,* p. 14.

Alberti, R. E., & Emmons, M. L. (1990). *Your perfect right: A guide to assertive living* (6th ed.). San Luis Obispo, CA: Impact.

American Psychiatric Association. (1987). *Diagnostic and statistical manual of mental disorders* (3rd ed., rev.). Washington, DC: Author.

Aneshensel, C. (1986). Marital and employment role-strain, social support, and depression among adult women. In S. Hobfoll (Ed.), *Stress, social support, and women* (pp. 99–114). Washington, DC: Hemisphere.

Beck, A. T. (1976). *Cognitive therapy and the emotional disorders.* New York: International Universities Press.

Belle, D. (Ed.). (1982). *Lives in stress: Women and depression.* Beverly Hills, CA: Sage.

Belle, D. (1990). Poverty and women's mental health. *American Psychologist, 45,* 385–389.

Bepko, C., & Krestan, J. (1990). *Too good for her own good: Searching for self and intimacy in important relationships.* New York: Harper and Row.

Bernard, J. (1982). Foreword. In D. Belle (Ed.), *Lives in stress: Women and depression* (pp. 7-8). Beverly Hills, CA: Sage.

Bernay, T. (1983, August). *Separation and the sense of competence-loss in women.* Paper presented at the ninety-first annual convention of the American Psychological Association, Anaheim, CA.

Blechman, E. A. (1980). Behavior therapies. In A. M. Brodsky, & R. T. Hare-Mustin (Eds.), *Women and psychotherapy* (pp. 217-244). New York: Guilford Press.

Burns, D. (1981). *Feeling good: The new mood therapy.* New York: Signet.

Burns, D. (1990). *The feeling good handbook.* New York: Plume.

Caplan, P. J. (1985). Between women: Lowering the barriers. In J. H. Robbins & R. J. Siegel (Eds.), *Women changing therapy: New assessments, values, and strategies in feminist therapy* (pp. 51-79). New York: Harrington Park Press.

Cass, V. C. (1979). Homosexual identity formation: A theoretical model. *Journal of Homosexuality, 4,* 219-235.

Chodorow, N. J. (1978). *The reproduction of mothering: Psychoanalysis and the sociology of gender.* Berkeley, CA: University of California Press.

Chodorow, N. J. (1989). *Feminism and psychoanalytic theory.* New Haven, CT: Yale University Press.

Coleman, E. (1982). Developmental stages of the coming out process. In J. C. Gonsiorek (Ed.), *Homosexuality and psychotherapy* (pp. 31-43). New York: The Haworth Press.

Cudney, M. R., & Hardy, R. (1991). *Self-defeating behaviors.* San Francisco: Harper.

Dowling, C. (1988). *Perfect woman: Hidden fears of inadequacy and the drive to perform.* New York: Summit Books.

Emery, G. (1982). *Own your own life.* New York: New American Library.

Emery, G. (1988). *Getting undepressed.* New York: Touchstone.

Finkelstein, S. (1987). Eating disorders: Why women and why now? In R. Formanek & A. Gurian (Eds.), *Women and depression: A lifespan perspective* (pp. 101-116). New York: Springer.

Fischer, L. R. (1986). *Linked lives: Adult daughters and their mothers.* New York: Harper and Row.

Formanek, R. (1983, August). *Children and depression.* Paper presented at the ninety-first annual convention of the American Psychological Association, Anaheim, CA.

Formanek, R. (1987a). Depression and menopause: A socially constructed link. In R. Formanek & A. Gurian (Eds.), *Women and depression: A lifespan perspective* (pp. 255–271). New York: Springer.

Formanek, R. (1987b). Depression and the older woman. In R. Formanek & A. Gurian (Eds.), *Women and depression: A lifespan perspective* (pp. 272–281). New York: Springer.

Formanek, R., & Gurian, A. (Eds.). (1987). *Women and depression: A lifespan perspective.* New York: Springer.

Gilbert, L. A. (1980). Feminist therapy. In A. M. Brodsky & R. T. Hare-Mustin (Eds.), *Women and pyschotherapy: An assessment of research and practice* (pp. 245–265). New York: The Guilford Press.

Gilligan, C. (1982). *In a different voice: Psychological theory and women's development.* Cambridge, MA: Harvard University Press.

Gilligan, C. (1991, August). *The psyche lives in a medium of culture: How shall we talk of love?* Paper presented at the ninety-ninth annual convention of the American Psychological Association, San Francisco, CA.

Gilligan, C., Lyons, N. P., & Hanmer, T. J. (Eds.). (1990). *Making connections: The relational worlds of adolescent girls at Emma Willard School.* Cambridge, MA: Harvard University Press.

Glaus, K. O. (1989). Alcoholism, chemical dependency and the lesbian client. In E. D. Rothblum & E. Cole (Eds.), *Lesbianism: Affirming nontraditional roles* (pp. 131–144). New York: The Haworth Press.

Golding, J. M. (1988). Gender differences in depressive symptoms: Statistical considerations. *Psychology of Women Quarterly, 12,* 61–74.

Gurian, A. (1987). Depression and young girls: Early sorrows and depressive disorders. In R. Formanek & A. Gurian (Eds.), *Women and depression: A lifespan perspective* (pp. 57–83). New York: Springer.

Heriot, J. (1985). The double bind: Healing the split. In J. H. Robbins & R. J. Siegel (Eds.), *Women changing therapy: New assessments, values, and strategies in feminist therapy* (pp. 11–28). New York: Harrington Park Press.

Hollon, S. (1983, August). *New perspectives on the cognitive model of depression: Research/practice.* Symposium discussant at the ninety-first annual convention of the American Psychological Association, Anaheim, CA.

Jack, D. (1987a). Self-in-relation theory. In R. Formanek & A. Gurian (Eds.), *Women and depression: A lifespan perspective* (pp. 41–45). New York: Springer.

Jack, D. (1987b). Silencing the self: The power of social imperatives in female depression. In R. Formanek & A. Gurian (Eds.), *Women and depression: A lifespan perspective* (pp. 161–181). New York: Springer.

Jack, D. C. (1991). *Silencing the self.* Cambridge, MA: Harvard University Press.

Jordan, J. V. (1991). The meaning of mutuality. In J. V. Jordan, A. G. Kaplan, J. B. Miller, I. P. Stiver, & J. L. Surrey (Eds.), *Women's growth in connection: Writings from the Stone Center* (pp. 81–96). New York: Guilford Press.

Josefowitz, N. (1980). *Paths to power: A woman's guide from first job to top executive.* Reading, MA: Addison-Wesley.

Joseph, S. (1987). Cognitive theory. In R. Formanek & A. Gurian (Eds.), *Women and depression: A lifespan perspective* (pp. 46–53). New York: Springer.

Kaplan, A. G. (1991). The "self-in-relation": Implications for depression in women. In J. V. Jordan, A. G. Kaplan, J. B. Miller, I. P. Stiver, & J. L. Surrey (Eds.), *Women's growth in connection: Writings from the Stone Center* (pp. 206–222). New York: Guilford Press.

Kaplan, A. G., Brooks, B., McComb, A. L., Shapiro, E. R., & Sodano, A. (1985). Women and anger in psychotherapy. In J. H. Robbins & R. J. Siegel (Eds.), *Women changing therapy: New assessments, values, and strategies in feminist therapy* (pp. 29–40). New York: Harrington Park Press.

Klerman, G. L., & Weissman, M. M. (1985). Depressions among women: Their nature and causes. In J. H. Williams (Ed.), *Psychology of women: Selected readings* (2nd ed.) (pp. 484–513). New York: W. W. Norton.

Kobasa, S. C. (1985). Stressful life events, personality and health: An inquiry into hardiness. In A. Monet & R. S. Lazarus, (Eds.), *Stress and coping: An anthology* (2nd ed.) (pp. 174–188). New York: Columbia University Press.

Krantz, S. E. (1983, August). *When negative thoughts reflect negative realities.* Paper presented at the ninety-first annual convention of the American Psychological Association, Anaheim, CA.

Kurash, C. L., & Schaul, J. F. (1987). Depression and adolescent girls. In R. Formanek & A. Gurian (Eds.), *Women and depression: A lifespan perspective* (pp. 84–100). New York: Springer.

Lebe, D. (1983, August). *Women's depressions across the lifespan.* Symposium discussant at the ninety-first annual convention of the American Psychological Association, Anaheim, CA.

Lerner, H. G. (1985). *The dance of anger.* New York: Harper and Row.

Lerner, H. G. (1987). Female depression: Self-sacrifice and self-betrayal in relationships. In R. Formanek & A. Gurian (Eds.), *Women and depression: A lifespan perspective* (pp. 200–221). New York: Springer.

Lerner, H. G. (1988). *Women in therapy.* New York: Jason Aronson.

Lerner, H. G. (1991, August). *The dances of anger and intimacy: Reflections on change.* Paper presented at the ninety-ninth annual convention of the American Psychological Association, San Francisco, CA.

Lowen, A. (1976). Bioenergetics. London: Penguin Books.

Lowen, A., Meichenbaum, D., Watzlawick, P., & Wolpe, J. (1990, December). *Treatment of depression and anxiety.* Panel discussion at the second Evolution of Psychotherapy Conference, Anaheim, CA.

Marcus, B. F. (1987). Object relations theory. In R. Formanek & A. Gurian (Eds.), *Women and depression: A lifespan perspective* (pp. 27–40). New York: Springer.

McGrath, E. (1991, August). *Women, men, and the depressions—What you need to know.* Paper presented at the ninety-ninth annual convention of the American Psychological Association, San Francisco, CA.

McGrath, E., Keita, G. P., Strickland, B. R., & Russo, N. F. (Eds.). (1990). *Women and depression: Risk factors and treatment issues.* Washington, DC: American Psychological Association.

Meichenbaum, D., & Cameron, R. (1982). Cognitive-behavior therapy. In G. Wilson & C. Franks (Eds.), *Contemporary behavior therapy* (pp. 310–338). New York: The Guilford Press.

Miller, J. B. (1976). *Toward a new psychology of women.* Boston: Beacon Press.

Nemtzow, R. (1987). Childbirth: Happiness, blues, or depression? In R. Formanek & A. Gurian (Eds.), *Women and depression: A lifespan perspective* (pp. 132–146). New York: Springer.

Neuringer, C. (1987). Suicidal self-destruction in women. In R. Formanek & A. Gurian (Eds.), *Women and depression: A lifespan perspective* (pp. 239–252). New York: Springer.

Nicoloff, L. K., & Stiglitz, E. A. (1987). Lesbian alcoholism: Etiology, treatment, and recovery. In Boston Lesbian Psychologies Collective (Eds.), *Lesbian psychologies: Explorations and challenges* (pp. 283–293). Urbana, IL: University of Illinois Press.

Nolen-Hoeksema, S. (1990). *Sex differences in depression.* Stanford, CA: Stanford University Press.

O'Neill, C., & Ritter, K. (1992). *Coming out within: Stages of spiritual awakening for lesbians and gay men.* San Francisco: Harper.

Phelps, S., & Austin, N. (1987). *The assertive woman: A new look* (2nd ed.). San Luis Obispo, CA: Impact.

Preston, J. (1989). *You can beat depression.* San Luis Obispo, CA: Impact.

Ritter, K. Y., & O'Neill, C. W. (1989). Moving through loss: The spiritual journey of gay men and lesbian women. *Journal for Counseling and Development, 68,* 9–15.

Rofes, E. E. (1983). *"I thought people like that killed themselves": Lesbians, gay men and suicide.* San Francisco: Grey Fox Press.

Rothblum, E. D. (1990). Depression among lesbians: An invisible and unresearched phenomenon. *Journal of Gay and Lesbian Psychotherapy, 1,* 67–87.

Rubin, L. B. (1985). *Just friends: The role of friendship in our lives.* New York: Harper and Row.

Seligman, M. E. P. (1975). *Helplessness: On depression, development and death.* San Francisco: W. H. Freeman.

Stiver, I. P. (1991a). The meaning of care: Reframing treatment models. In J. V. Jordan, A. G. Kaplan, J. B. Miller, I. P. Stiver, & J. L. Surrey (Eds.), *Women's growth in connection: Writings from the Stone Center* (pp. 250–267). New York: Guilford Press.

Stiver, I. P. (1991b). The meanings of dependency in female-male relationships. In J. V. Jordan, A. G. Kaplan, J. B. Miller, I. P. Stiver, & J. L. Surrey (Eds.), *Women's growth in connection: Writings from the Stone Center* (pp. 143–161). New York: Guilford Press.

Surrey, J. L. (1991). Eating patterns as a reflection of women's development. In J. V. Jordan, A. G. Kaplan, J. B. Miller, I. P. Stiver, & J. L. Surrey (Eds.), *Women's growth in connection: Writings from the Stone Center* (pp. 237–249). New York: Guilford Press.

Tallmer, M. (1983, August). *Depression in older women.* Paper presented at the ninety-first annual convention of the American Psychological Association, Anaheim, CA.

U.S. Department of Labor. (1992). *Employment and earnings* (p. 221). (Vol. 39). Washington, DC: U.S. Government Printing Office.

Weenolsen, P. (1988). *Transcendence of loss over the life span.* New York: Hemisphere.

Weissman, M. M. (1980). Depression. In A. M. Brodsky & R. T. Hare-Mustin (Eds.), *Women and psychotherapy* (pp. 97–112). New York: Guilford Press.

Weissman, M. M., & Klerman, G. L. (1987). Gender and depression. In R. Formanek & A. Gurian (Eds.), *Women and depression: A lifespan perspective* (pp. 3–15). New York: Springer.

Young-Eisendrath, P., & Wiedemann, F. L. (1987). *Female authority: Empowering women through psychotherapy.* New York: Guilford Press.

WOMEN'S REPRODUCTIVE LIFE CYCLE ISSUES

Melanie A. Warnke and Contributors

INTRODUCTION

Women's reproductive life cycle issues are those reproductive-related concerns, processes, and the associated choices women face that are the result of physical, psychological, and social development. These issues are not simply individual considerations, but are imbedded in the context of women's experiences as a group. This chapter describes how the "common themes" of individual physical and psychological development, interpersonal relationships, sociocultural climate, and the interactions among these various factors relate to women's reproductive life cycle issues.

Issues discussed in this chapter are by definition related to individuals' bodies: therefore, women's physical development, health and medical implications, and choices about their bodies are important aspects to understand. Women's psychological development and characteristics also influence their considerations of reproductive issues. Because they have an impact upon women's daily lives and long-term life plans, such choices can be stressful. To understand the meaningfulness of these issues for a woman, counselors need to place her choices in the context of her life as a whole, including her relationships with others and sociocultural attitudes concerning reproductive life cycle issues. Many of the issues discussed here are by their very nature relationship oriented: for example, birth control.

Throughout her life, a woman must also contend with the expectations and reactions of others to her reproductive decisions. Such communications from others can certainly complicate her personal decision making.

On a broader level, societal attitudes, norms, and institutions (e.g., legal, medical, and political systems) prescribe gender role standards influencing women's perceptions of their life roles, bodies, sexual attitudes and behaviors, and identities. Traditional gender role attitudes maintain that motherhood is central to female identity. While men's gender identity can be established in a variety of ways, women's identity is established primarily through childbearing and child rearing. Alternative perceptions of gender roles are today being developed, but are not yet clearly defined. Both traditional and nontraditional gender role conceptualizations can influence women's decisions about reproductive issues throughout their lives.

The purpose of this chapter is to present some of the reproductive life cycle issues that women experience in the 1990s and to provide a framework of common themes for understanding these issues. Each of the issues presented involves choices many women make as a result of their physical, psychological, and social development.

First, as women become sexually active, they must address a variety of issues. Dr. Suzanne Hedstrom explains how the HIV/AIDS (human immunodeficiency virus/acquired immunodeficiency syndrome) epidemic has dramatically changed the potential health risks to all sexually active women and has promoted the use of condoms for safer sex. Dr. Melanie Warnke indicates how a variety of factors affect women's preferences to have or not have children. However, difficulties may occur in fulfilling women's childbearing preferences. Dr. Ellen Cook describes the experiences of women who cope with infertility. Dr. Mary Armsworth presents issues related to women's choices to have or not have abortions. To avoid the possibility of unplanned pregnancies, women may choose to prevent unplanned pregnancies permanently. Dr. Pamela Smith describes factors associated with women's considerations of voluntary sterilization procedures. Finally, reproductive life cycle issues do not occur exclusively during traditional childbearing years. Dr. Diane Prosser presents menopause as a developmental reproductive life cycle issue that women experience at mid-life. All of the authors contributed counseling suggestions for working with women who are addressing reproductive life cycle issues. These counseling implications will be discussed at the end of the chapter.

HIV/AIDS AND SAFER SEX

Gender role prescriptions are imbedded in women's sexual activity and use of contraceptives. Croteau, Nero, and Prosser (1991) suggest that sexist gender role socialization lead to some women's limited willingness and ability to assert their contraceptive options. These issues are especially salient for women who rely on men's cooperation to reduce the risks of contracting HIV and AIDS. Some women who insist upon using certain types of contraceptives have experienced negative sanctions, hostility, and violence. At the same time, however, society holds women responsible for preventing reproduction and sexually transmitted diseases. Choice related to contraceptive usage are serious decisions for sexually active women. A woman's awareness of contraceptive devices, health risks, attitudes toward sexual behaviors and sexual partners, and gender role standards is crucial to making informed decisions about sexual behaviors.

Beginning in the 1960s, a number of contraceptive technologies were mass-produced for women to prevent unplanned pregnancies. Female and male sterilization and oral contraceptives are the most commonly used methods of contraception; condoms have become the third leading method of contraception among sexually active women (Forrest & Fordyce, 1988). The increase of condom usage is the result of a growing interest in preventing the life-threatening epidemic of HIV/AIDS. American women purchased approximately 40 percent of the condoms sold in 1987 (Mays & Cochran, 1988); however, only one in six sexually active women used condoms at all during that year (Forrest & Fordyce, 1988). These statistics are especially important since one study examining heterosexual transmission among partners of HIV-positive individuals found that use of condoms decreased the rate of seroconversion among spouses of persons with AIDS from 82 percent for couples not using condoms consistently to 14 percent among couples using condoms consistently (Fischl, Dickenson, Segal, Flannagan, & Rodriguez, 1987). Consistent condom usage is presently the safest method of preventing HIV infection among heterosexual sexually active women, but condoms do not eliminate risk.

Many people believe that HIV/AIDS is a "gay disease" that does not afflict women (Bell, 1989); however, women have been diagnosed since the beginning of the epidemic. Of the nearly 180,000 diagnosed cases of AIDS in the United States through June 1990, 11 percent occurred in women (HIV/AIDS Surveillance Report, 1991). In 1988, HIV/AIDS was the eighth leading cause of death among all American women aged 25 to 40 (Centers for Disease Control, 1991). Ybarra (1991) estimates that more than 130,000 women are HIV-positive and currently asymptomatic. Despite these data, there has been a lack of attention to the threat of HIV/AIDS to women. The women most likely to be at risk for acquiring an HIV infection are among the least advantaged groups in American society: poor, urban, and ethnic minorities (Mays & Cochran, 1988). More than half of the women with AIDS are African American, and another 21 percent are Hispanic/Latino (HIV/AIDS Surveillance Report, 1991). Mays and Cochran (1988) underscore the importance of ethnic, racial, cultural, and religious factors that influence sexual behavior patterns.

Intercourse with infected male intravenous (IV) drug users is the second leading source of HIV infection among American women: women's own IV drug usage is the primary cause of transmission (HIV/AIDS Surveillance Report, 1991). In the past 10 years, women's risk for contracting the virus solely through sexual contact with males who engage in high-risk behaviors has increased (HIV/AIDS Surveillance Report, 1991). In addition, there is an increasing potential risk of contracting the virus indirectly through sexual activities with individuals who were previously sexually involved with partners who engaged in high-risk behaviors. During heterosexual contact, women are 17.5 times more likely to contract the HIV virus from infected men than vice versa, even when the number of sexual contacts is controlled (Padian, Shiboski, & Jewell, 1991). The data point to the urgent need for women to change their patterns of sexual behavior to promote health and defend against acquiring HIV.

Studies have suggested that while knowledge of information about HIV/AIDS is important to the control of this epidemic, information alone has not led to a change in sexual practices (Baldwin & Baldwin, 1988; Gray & Saracino, 1989). The researchers have found that individuals do not believe that the threat of the virus applies to them. There are a number of other reasons why women may not change their sexual behaviors. Dominant social norms socialize women to devalue their bodies and to behave passively in sexual activities. Women who insist on sexual practices that meet their standards of safety go against traditional gender role expectations. Standards for condom usage overtly address these gender role expectations because they require coordination with male partners. To increase safer sex practices, women need to analyze cultural messages and evaluate their personal attitudes concerning their role in sexual activities. In addition, it is necessary for women to behave assertively with partners.

Women may need assistance in developing assertion, communication, and problem-solving skills to help them raise the issues of using condoms or pursuing alternatives to intercourse, to rebut partners' refusal to cooperate, and to learn to choose partners wisely (Cochran & Mays, 1989). With health-promoting attitudes and necessary interpersonal skills in place, a woman is more likely to enact the behavioral changes that reduce the likelihood of HIV infection. Every sexual encounter entails possible risk factors that women must acknowledge to protect themselves and their sexual partners.

CHILDBEARING PREFERENCES

Childbearing status has a dramatic and long-term effect on women's life-styles and life plans. A decision to have or not have a child is a complex, and frequently difficult, process connected to a variety of interrelated individual, interpersonal, and sociocultural factors. McKaughan (1987) contends that women's concerns related to childbearing are universal and based on their unique daily lives, backgrounds, and personalities. An understanding of universal concerns and the unique influences these issues have upon individual women helps counselors provide assistance and support to those who are developing childbearing plans. Given that women's thinking about the costs and benefits of having children is more complex than the thinking of men (Baber, 1983), it is especially important to address the many factors women consider in their childbearing plans.

A woman's childbearing preference is influenced by her understanding of her own personal characteristics. Women who prefer having children tend to express more traditional gender role values (Scott & Morgan, 1983). Callan (1986) found that women who want to become mothers are more likely to identify values in the role of mother and perceive fewer benefits of a childfree life-style; the reverse is true of women who prefer to remain childfree. Some women consider their physical health or the physical experience of pregnancy and childbirth as salient issues in their plans; other women do not.

Women usually consider their financial status, employment situations, and ages when developing childbearing preferences. However, the impact of these factors on women's preferences seems to vary considerably. For example, Warnke's (1991) study has suggested that child-anticipated, childfree-anticipated, and undecided women of a similar age range describe the importance of age in different ways. Age affected how long child-anticipated participants perceived they could attempt to have a child and how long undecided participants perceived they could wait to decide about childbearing. In contrast, childfree-anticipated women could not imagine having children at their ages. Women employed outside the home are more likely to be childfree than women who are not paid employees (Ramu & Tavuchis, 1986). In addition, childfree-committed women are more likely than child-anticipated women to believe they must choose between having a child and pursuing a career (Holahan, 1983; Warnke, 1991).

Other demographic variables seem to influence women's childbearing preferences. A woman's race (Beckman, 1979), level of education (Ramu & Tavuchis, 1986), number of siblings (Holm, 1984), and religious affiliation (Ramu & Tavuchis, 1986) have been found to affect childbearing considerations. The few studies that have examined race as a variable suggest that women of various races differ in their perceptions of reasons for having children (Beckman, 1979). Women with no religious affiliation prefer fewer children (Ramu & Tavuchis, 1986), and although fertility preference differences among women from Catholic, Protestant, and Jewish faiths have decreased, Catholic women prefer to have more children (Weller & Bouvier, 1981). Scott and Morgan (1983) have found that educational attainment is negatively related to perceived ideal family size.

Relationships with and opinions of partners and secondarily those of parents appear to influence women's considerations strongly (Warnke, 1991). Women frequently indicate that their partner's willingness to share household responsibilities and perceived willingness to share parenting responsibilities play an important part in their considerations. Some women indicate that the presence or absence of a grandchild in the family affects their attitudes toward childbearing. Women often discuss their mothers' attitudes toward and experiences of parenting as influential in their considerations. Other women's experiences as mothers or childfree individuals also affect a woman's own decision about having or not having children. Female family members', friends', and acquaintances' personal experiences and life-styles provide models for a woman who is developing childbearing plans.

Women's childbearing intentions are also affected by sociocultural attitudes and norms. The role of parent is more closely linked to social identity for women than for men. Investment in the parental role is more likely to limit other roles for women than for men in our culture. Dominant societal attitudes and norms affect childbearing preferences by subtly creating barriers to certain options for women. Women are aware of expectations for them to become mothers, and they often discuss whether or not their plans fit with these societal standards. According to Warnke's (1991) study, however, women typically do not indicate that these societal attitudes have a significant impact on their childbearing preferences. It seems that sociocultural assumptions about women and motherhood are subtle "givens" to which women adjust or internalize, thereby making the assumptions seem less influential.

Women's childbearing considerations appear to be based on individual, interpersonal, and sociocultural factors. Personal characteristics, values of having or not having children, financial status, employment circumstances, age, and relationships with significant others are common issues that women identify as salient to their plans. For some women, health issues related to childbearing and child rearing are important concerns. In addition, sociocultural standards associated with women and their social roles create expectations that affect women as a group. A woman's unique life experiences, personal characteristics, and childbearing preferences determine how these universal factors affect her and which factors she perceives as most salient to her decision. A counselor can help women sort out the influences of these universal factors in their unique process of developing childbearing preferences.

Infertility

Becoming a mother is an unquestioned part of many women's life plans, yet 15 percent of the childbearing-aged population may wish to conceive but cannot do so (Bellina & Wilson, 1985). The discovery of infertility can provoke a biopsychosocial crisis that is difficult to resolve. The term *biopsychosocial* indicates that the crisis involves an interaction among physical conditions predisposing difficulties in conception and childbearing, medical interventions intended to correct the infertility, social assumptions about parenthood, reactions of others, and the individual's psychological characteristics (Cook, 1987).

Infertility is generally defined as the inability to conceive and carry to term a pregnancy after at least one year of unprotected, regular sexual intercourse. Physical causes can be identified in all but 10 percent of couples, with men and women equally likely to have problems with infertility (Bellina & Wilson, 1985). Contrary to popular belief, there is no firm evidence that infertility is generally caused by emotional problems, stress, or the need to relax (see reviews in Cook, 1987). The typical infertile couple is one in which the spouses are physically healthy, have made a decision to start a family, assumed they would conceive easily, and have been trying to conceive without medical assistance for some time. Couples pursuing medical interventions usually find no easy solutions to their difficulties; a protracted period of testing and interventions for months or years is more typical.

Cook (1987) described common psychological reactions among individuals coping with infertility: (1) denial that infertility may actually be happening to them (especially when others seem to conceive readily); (2) anxiety, renewed with each menstrual cycle; (3) anger due to loss of control over a life option; (4) isolation and alienation from others, especially partners and fertile friends and family, as the stress intensifies; (5) feelings of guilt, inadequacy, and low self-esteem because of their childless status; and (6) depression and grief, often suffered in private and over long periods of time. Individuals wishing to become parents can experience infertility as a bereavement: of a child who may never be and of their life dream of bearing and rearing their own children. The stress that infertile lesbian women face is compounded by difficulties in conceiving and mothering children within a system that does not recognize their needs and relational commitments as valid (Brown, 1991).

Women appear to experience the crisis of infertility as being more profound than do men. A number of studies have documented that women in infertile couples report more negative effects than their husbands (see review in Abbey, Andrews, & Halman, 1991). In two recent interview studies, wives saw infertility as more stressful and devastating to their lives than did their husbands. Wives were more likely to take the lead role in pursuing information, support, and medical intervention for the infertility, and to see themselves as responsible for the infertility (Abbey et al., 1991; Greil, Leitko, & Porter, 1988; Shapiro, 1988).

Women's daily lives are usually more disrupted by infertility; medical interventions require women to monitor their menstrual cycle daily. More extensive interventions may require frequent physician visits, pills, injections, x-rays, and so on. Women commonly have to go through such demanding procedures even if it is the man's physical condition that causes the infertility. Women may feel angry and ambivalent about the inconvenience to them (Sparks & Hamilton, 1991).

Women may experience a greater crisis than men because of the broader social norms concerning reproduction. Miall (1985) notes that "in a society that values fertility, childlessness becomes an attribute of the individual which can be discrediting or stigmatizing. ...Involuntary childlessness is regarded as a deficient or abnormal condition" (p. 384). Women are especially likely to experience this stigmatization because they are expected to embrace childbearing and rearing as central life tasks. A couple's difficulties in bearing children have often been seen as a woman's problem: her curse and her fault. Infertility continues to be attributed to women's choices or psychological problems (Sandelowski, 1990). Such a view today takes a more sophisticated form in blaming women for actions predisposing them to infertility (e.g., waiting to start a family until their thirties; engaging in sexual activity; increasing the chances of complications from birth control or diseases) (Sandelowski, 1990). The implication is the same: Women can be blamed for their infertility. Unfortunately, women may feel responsible despite medical evidence that clearly establishes the physical causes as being outside of their control.

The nature of the reactions and support of others are crucial to a woman's experiences of infertility. Congruence between the social support that an infertile woman needs and actually receives may be important in influencing the amount of depression she experiences (Fouad & Fahje, 1989). Yet, because of the social stigma still attached to infertility, infertile women frequently report being misunderstood, excluded, devalued, and/or rejected by others (Abbey et al., 1991). Apart from overt stigmatization, others may simply not be aware of the personal struggles that a woman is experiencing. Infertility involves the most private aspects of a woman's physiology and relationship with her partner. Infertile individuals may not feel comfortable sharing such information with others, especially if they feel guilty or inadequate because of infertility. They may prefer to avoid everyday social conversations, holidays, and baby showers, which painfully remind them of life possibilities that may never be open to them. Thus, infertile women may be isolated from essential interpersonal support, both by others' attitudes and behaviors and by their own efforts to cope with infertility.

Counselors should not underestimate the magnitude of the infertility crisis on every aspect of a woman's life. Her relationships with others may be vitally enhanced or disrupted by the crisis; how she defines herself as a woman in today's society may be affirmed or disconfirmed. Sensitivity to gender issues can help women to emerge from the crisis with a renewed sense of purpose and self-image, whatever its outcome.

Abortion

Decisions related to a woman's choice to terminate an unwanted pregnancy bring home the power and complexity of societal, cultural, political, and personal variables involved in the choice. David (1988) has underscored this complexity, stating, "No other elective surgical procedure has evoked as much world-wide debate, generated such emotional and moral controversy, or received greater sustained attention from the public and the media" (p. 9) as this form of fertility regulation. Issues regarding abortion are intertwined in multiple levels of influence affecting not only the choice of the individual, but her responses and the responses of others toward her.

Since the U.S. Supreme Court's landmark decision in *Roe v. Wade* (1973), abortion has been a legal surgical procedure in all states. A first-trimester abortion, which is medically safer than normal childbirth, is protected by the right of privacy and is determined by the woman and her physician. Beyond the first trimester, the state "may regulate the abortion procedure in ways that are reasonably related to the preservation and protection of maternal health:" (*Roe v. Wade,* 1973, p. 732). In the third trimester, the state may regulate or prohibit an abortion because of the viability of the fetus, with abortion permitted only to preserve the life or health of the mother.

The *Roe v. Wade* (1973) decision has been under attack by legislative and judicial branches of government since its existence (Faludi, 1991). More than 50 bills were proposed to enact restrictions to abortions during the first year following the decision; in 1974, there was an effort to pass a constitutional amendment banning the rights provided in the *Roe v. Wade* decision. In 1976, the Hyde Amendment blocked federal funding for abortions; a majority of states have enacted legislation to block use of state funding for abortions. Legislation in more than 30 states has led to prohibitive rules, including consent and notification regulations. There have been countless legal challenges to the *Roe v. Wade* (1973) decision which culminated at the U.S. Supreme Court's 1989 *Webster v. Reproductive Health Services* decision upholding state restrictions on abortions and the 1991 *Rust v. Sullivan* ruling allowing government to prohibit employees of federally funded clinics from speaking about abortion. A recent (July 1992) U.S. Supreme Court decision has supported state restrictions on abortion while narrowly upholding *Roe v. Wade*. The debate concerning women's abortion rights is likely to continue in the arenas of public opinion, legislation, and the judiciary.

The nature of women's responses to abortion has been the topic of legal and medical policy decisions throughout history. Prior to the 1973 legalization of abortion, researchers' conclusions were frequently influenced by Freudian theory that viewed the denial of pregnancy as unnatural for women, therefore resulting in severe trauma (Simon & Senturia, 1966). Research hypotheses were developed from Freudian views of the role of motherhood for women and exclusively examined unpleasant emotions such as depression, anxiety, guilt, shame, and regret. The majority of studies conducted during this time focused on the possible psychopathology of the woman who sought an abortion or the possible pathology that resulted from an abortion (Turell, Armsworth, & Gaa, 1990).

This view has underscored a long-running debate related to whether or not women suffer from severe traumatic responses to abortion, which would be detrimental to society. Arguments that abortions threaten mental health have been used to support restrictive legislation or counsel women against abortion (Public Interest Directorate, American Psychological Association, 1991). Recent reviews of the empirical literature (Adler, David, Major, Roth, Russo,

& Wyatt, 1990; Turell et al., 1990) find no evidence to support traumatic response to abortion for the majority of women. In fact, most women experience the abortion as a relief, and their responses are best understood in the context of coping with stressful life events (Adler et al., 1990).

Reviews indicate that for women who have difficulty adjusting adjusting to abortion, personal and social factors appear to be most influential (Turell et al., 1990). Younger and unmarried childfree women are more likely to experience negative responses to abortion than those who are older or have already had children. Women who have negative responses may have a history of psychological disturbance prior to the abortion; may have had a second-trimester abortion, which is a more difficult procedure; or may blame themselves for the pregnancy (Public Interest Directorate, American Psychological Association, 1990). In addition, women whose religion or culture prohibits abortion and those who attend church frequently are more likely to experience difficulty with post-abortion adjustment (Adler, 1975).

Numerous authors stress the importance of the decision-making process at the time the woman is attempting to choose an outcome for an unwanted pregnancy (Adler et al., 1990; Turell et al., 1990). Studies consistently find that women who are satisfied with their choice or who report little difficulty in making the decision to abort show more positive post-abortion responses. More negative post-abortion reactions are associated with greater reported difficulty in decision making and include feelings of guilt (Osofsky & Osofsky, 1972) and anxiety (Bracken, 1978). Major, Mueller, and Hildebrandt (1985) also found that women who were satisfied with their decisions to abort had not intended to become pregnant and did not place deep meaning on the pregnancy.

Social support from significant others is the predominant social variable related to abortion responses (Turell et al., 1990). Both perceived and actual social support have been associated with more favorable adjustments to abortion (Bracken, Hachamovitch, & Grossman, 1974). This study found that for older women, partner support was more important; for younger women, parental support was more important. The complexity of social support is evidenced in a study by Major et al. (1985). Their study found that women who were accompanied to the clinic on the day of abortion were significantly more depressed and reported more physical complaints after the abortion than were women who were not accompanied. Women who were accompanied tended to be younger and expected to cope less well than those who were not accompanied. It appears that perceived support is more critical than actual presence of individuals.

Armsworth (1991) and Marecek (1987), however, have indicated that pervading social pressures and interpersonal fears may prohibit a woman from seeking professional help at this critical time. She may fear judgment from others, fear revealing the pregnancy, and attempt to deny the pregnancy altogether. Continued efforts at open, objective discussion of this topic are needed to remove barriers to seeking help.

Voluntary Sterilization

A woman's decision to undergo a surgical sterilization procedure, or tubal ligation, as a permanent means of birth control seems to be straightforward. However, this decision is met with much controversy and presents many issues that relate to a woman's personal experiences, interpersonal relationships, and societal acceptance. These issues are complex and reflect the changing roles of women and conflict in society's recognition and acceptance of these changing roles. With the advent of laser surgery technology, the risk of complications from sterilization procedures has been reduced. Women's sterilization increased through the 1980s (Groat, Neal, & Wicks, 1990) and was the leading method of birth control among women in the late 1980s (Forrest & Fordyce, 1988). Male sterilization is a less intrusive and safer procedure than female sterilization; however, the number of male sterilizations has decreased (Kneen, 1988).

Women frequently request an end to their childbearing functioning because they wish to reduce the stress and anxiety associated with the responsibility for and health risks of other birth control techniques. Once the burden of an unplanned pregnancy is lifted, many women feel free to pursue other areas of their lives that were previously more difficult to plan and accomplish. Women who undergo sterilization are typically over 30 years of age, married, have at least one child, and perceive that their childbearing years are coming to an end (Groat et al., 1990). Satisfaction with the current family structure and desire to begin or maintain other life roles affect these women's decisions. Other women request tubal ligations because they do not wish to have any children. They have considered their life plans and are comfortable in settling into childfree life-styles without the risk of pregnancy. Each woman's life-style preferences and personal goals are affected by her gender role orientation and cultural gender role standards.

Life events influence women's views about themselves and sterilization. It is not uncommon for women to opt for sterilization when they are experiencing significant life stresses, particularly those associated with loss and grief (Kohn, 1986). Sterilization may be a way to cope following the death or serious illness of a child or the birth of a disabled child. Women frequently request tubal ligations following abortions, miscarriages, and stillbirths (Rank, 1985). Sterilization may be a method of self-protection from similar traumas (Kohn, 1986). Because society holds women responsible for birth control and for the physical health of children, women often experience events such as abortions, miscarriages, or illnesses of children as evidence of their failures. Under such circumstances, the choice of sterilization may be a form of self-punishment.

Although voluntary sterilization decisions are personal ones, they are affected by other individuals. The individuals who appear to have the greatest influence on women's voluntary sterilization considerations are partners, children, and parents. Significant relationship conflict with partners may relate to women's decision-making processes, particularly if women take responsibility for the tensions. Women may be concerned that pregnancy could make them more dependent on their partners or that it could be used by partners to control them. Women may believe that they would be more desirable to partners if there were no risk of pregnancy (Bean, Clark,

Swicegood, & Williams, 1983). The number of children a woman's partner desires may also affect her sterilization plans.

Relationship issues with children may surface when voluntary sterilization is considered. Women who are satisfied with and enjoy the role of mother have more difficulty deciding about sterilization (Groat et al., 1990). A number of women desiring sterilization express general dissatisfaction with parenting; the procedure frees them from the risk of parenting additional children (Kohn, 1986). Some women believe that they would be dissatisfied or unsuccessful mothers and therefore should not have children. The association between women's desires to have children and relationships with parents has been contradictory (Haskell, 1985; Reading & Amatea, 1986). Dissatisfaction with one's parents may enter into the decision to select sterilization, particularly for those women who fear that they would pass on inadequate parenting to the next generation.

Contradictory societal attitudes and norms simultaneously expect women to bear children and discriminate against them for doing so. Segments of society express negative attitudes toward sterilization procedures and individuals who request these procedures. Yet many women believe that it is necessary to choose between parenting and career goals (Bean et al., 1983). Some women believe that workplaces provide them greater career advancement opportunities if pregnancy is not possible.

Medical professionals and government policies affect the process of women's elective sterilization. In order to receive federal financial assistance for sterilization surgery, women must receive counseling and wait 30 days after signing a consent (Federal Register, cited in Kohn, 1986). The U.S. Department of Health and Human Services does not require such stringent eligibility criteria for any other surgical procedure. Most private physicians may also require counseling prior to the procedure to protect themselves from future litigation. Counselors need to assess whether a woman is electing to seek counseling concerning her decision-making process or is required to attend counseling before a sterilization procedure will be scheduled. If a woman is seeking assistance during the decision-making process, counselors can examine her views on self and sterilization, life experiences, relationships, and social attitudes that are influential in her decision.

MENOPAUSE

The chance that women will seek counseling concerning issues arising at mid-life is likely to rise dramatically in the next decade, especially since there are more middle-aged women than ever living in the United States. Women may seek assistance in adjusting to the physiological, psychological, and interpersonal changes they ex-perience and support in dealing with negative sociocultural percep-tions of women and aging.

Women at mid-life face negative societal attitudes toward aging women. Fertility has been so closely connected to femininity that menopausal women may be perceived as individuals without value as their "biological purpose" comes to an end. Social norms for judging the worth of women that emphasize attractive physical appearance and youth as the standard for beauty result in perceptions of mid-life women as less valuable. Sexist and ageist messages contribute to a sense that menopause is something to hide (Dickson, 1990). While it is understandable that women feel reluctant to discuss their menopause, silence serves to perpetuate the biased views. Unless these negative societal attitudes are examined and discarded, they may be internalized by many women.

Menopause is often viewed as a single point in time, marked by the end of menstrual periods. Actually, menopause occurs over several years, with fluctuations in body chemistry, emotions, and sense of self. A number of health issues have been associated with the endocrine changes during menopause: (1) osteoporosis, a degenerative bone disease; (2) hot flashes and night sweats; (3) sleep disturbances as a result of night sweats and cerebral responses to changing hormone levels; (4) changes in skin, vaginal tissues, and weight distribution; and (5) transitory mood changes. While some research suggests that 80 to 90 percent of women experience at least some of the stressful signs of menopause (Sheehy, 1991), others (McKinlay, McKinlay, & Brambilla, 1987) have suggested that menopause has little effect on women's physical or mental health.

Previous assumptions that menopausal women experience extreme psychological and physiological dysfunction have not been supported (Matthews et al., 1990). Periodic mood fluctuation is transitional, and menopause has not been associated with depression (Hunter, 1990; Jackson, Taylor, & Pyngolil, 1991). While most women do not experience menopause as highly stressful, many consider medical treatment to reduce some of the complications associated with the transition.

Consideration of estrogen replacement therapy (ERT) is one of the most personal decisions facing perimenopausal women. Unfortunately, current medical evidence on the effects of ERT is limited, complex, and contradictory (Sheehy, 1991). ERT has been associated with reductions in cardiovascular disease (Stampfer et al., 1991) and prevention of osteoporosis (Goldman & Tosteson, 1991), but it may increase the risk of breast (Kelsey & Gammon, 1990) and endometrial (Goldman & Tosteson, 1991) cancers. While cyclical administration of progesterin with estrogen has been found to decrease rates of breast cancer, it also blocks some of the favorable effects of estrogen on the cardiovascular system and increases the risk of endometrial cancer (Goldman & Tosteson, 1991). This cyclical approach also artificially induces menstrual periods, which some women wish to avoid. Women may seek counseling as they interpret medical information, weigh risks, and make choices about ERT. Exploring personal values as women make judgments about critical health issues may be an important focus of counseling.

Physical changes during menopause may lead a woman to reconsider aspects of her personal identity. Women may experience a sense of loss as their childbearing opportunities end and as they move beyond the years associated with youth. Yet mid-life can also be viewed as an opportunity for developing new perceptions of self and new life roles. The average woman lives for 30 years after menopause, a time span approximately equal to the years during which she experiences a menstrual cycle. Women at mid-life have an opportunity to adapt and flourish as they deal with physiological changes, societal views of these changes, and the ways these issues influence their identities.

The developmental changes caused by menopause and the resulting redefinition of self also affects women's relationships with others. Relationships are affected by changes in the personal meanings each person attaches to the relationship and by the way that each of them is affected by societal meanings assigned to women over 50. Menopausal mothers may be faced with challenges in developing mutually satisfying adult relationships with their children. The recognition that the woman is aging may cause both mother and adult child to confront mortality issues.

Long-term partnerships may also be strained at mid-life as each partner evaluates past choices and considers new opportunities. If a relationship has become unsatisfactory, partners may choose to revitalize the relationship, seek new relationships, or focus more energy on other aspects of their lives. Sexual relationships may be another area of concern for some menopausal women. Partners' support related to sexuality can be very important during this transition. Diminished sexual desire, reduced comfort during intercourse resulting from biological changes in vaginal tissues and secretions, and negative perceptions of a woman's body by one or both partners have been reported by women as difficulties during menopause. All contribute to changes in a woman's sexual identity and her approach to sexual expression. Perceptions of female sexuality at mid-life and beyond may affect a woman's relationship with her sexual partner or her motivation to seek an intimate partner, should that be a goal. Counselors' knowledge and support of these issues may assist clients in discussing sexual concerns they might experience during menopause.

COUNSELING IMPLICATIONS

Social scientists and counselors have given little attention to women's reproductive life cycle issues, and historically the literature has presented them as crises rather than developmental concerns. A majority of the literature has assumed that a woman who does not want or is not able to have a child must be disturbed in some way. However, more recent literature suggests that while some women's psychological responses to reproductive life cycle issues are disruptive to their lives, a majority of women do not respond in a way that is dysfunctional or pathological. Unless there is clear evidence to the contrary, counselors should assume that difficulties women experience are due to adjustment to developmental and/or situational circumstances rather than individual deficits.

Counselors must continuously examine their own biases, values, and expectations toward women and reproductive issues. It may be helpful, and sometimes necessary, for counselors to state their views so a woman can decide whether a particular counselor will be helpful to her. Counselors should be aware of community resources and referrals who provide supplemental or alternative services. In addition, counselors need to have a solid knowledge base for understanding these issues. They should access accurate information about the related health concerns, medical technologies, and physical risks.

Counselors also need to assess the effects of gender on an individual woman's experiences. Gender role analysis of reproductive life cycle issues provides a framework for addressing individual, interpersonal, and societal factors by examining sociocultural messages; a woman's own beliefs; and her interpersonal relationships associated with gender roles, her body, and reproductive life cycle issues. Such an analysis allows for exploration of normative life events associated with gender-related issues without blaming individuals for their participation in the socialization process (Brown, 1986). Implementing a gender role analysis allows women to examine and understand their feelings and thoughts about the complex factors that influence their reproductive life cycle issues. In addition, women have an opportunity to discuss a full range of options available to them so they can feel increased control in their lives and maintain positive attitudes toward themselves and their reproductive life cycle concerns. Finally, this process may give women a sense of empowerment because it allows them to make more informed choices based on an understanding of a variety of factors and because it reduces the likelihood that they will blame themselves for the difficulties they experience in making choices.

The first component of gender role analysis focuses on sociocultural messages. Analyses of social attitudes toward women and toward their control of their own sexual or reproductive behaviors are critical in understanding how the sociocultural environment creates a context for women's reproductive life cycle issues. The dominant culture's messages about women's roles, their bodies, their rights to make decisions related to sexuality and reproduction, and their responsibility for reproduction reduce women's sense of control over their decisions and their sense of themselves. A woman's examination of relevant legal, legislative, and medical policies and practices is also important in her understanding of how society weighs upon her considerations. Counselors need to have current information concerning policies and practices associated with women's reproductive issues. Women's awareness of societal barriers may reduce some of the influence of these barriers, thus increasing women's sense of personal power over their life choices. Counselors can assist a woman by examining how the sociocultural environment simultaneously creates reinforcers and barriers to any fertility choice she makes and how these issues affect her.

Second, in the gender role analysis, a woman needs to discuss her feelings, thoughts, and experiences related to reproductive life cycle concerns, her sense of self, gender role attitudes, and gender role behaviors to enhance her sense of empowerment. Sensitivity to women's diverse racial, ethnic, and socioeconomic backgrounds is important in examining these topics. Counselors can support, legitimize, and validate women's thoughts and women's rights to make decisions concerning these issues. Clients frequently need to explore their beliefs about the value of having and not having children, their gender role attitudes, their personal characteristic related to childbearing considerations, and their rights to make their own fertility choices. Examination of internalized cultural messages is likely to increase women's sense of self-empowerment and decision-making abilities. When women have an opportunity to discuss these topics in the context of their broader life plans, they are better able to make decisions. Counselors may assist in the development of decision-making skills for some women who find it especially difficult to choose among options available to them. After decisions are made, some women may need assistance in implementing decisions they make.

Finally, gender role analysis looks at women's interpersonal relationships. Implementation of reproductive life cycle decisions often relates directly to partners. For example, women use interpersonal skills in discussing sexual behaviors or infertility with partners. Some women may need help in developing communication skills, assertiveness skills, problem-solving strategies, and mutual goal setting in order to feel empowered to implement their plans.

Women need support from other significant individuals in their lives. Learning how to enhance support from family members, friends, and members of organizations developed for individuals experiencing specific reproductive issues increases a woman's sense of personal power in addressing these issues. Women may need assistance in understanding how others' behaviors can support or disrupt their sense of control over these issues and how to increase their chances of receiving support from significant others. Counselors need to assist a woman in exploring how relationships with partners, family members, friends, and acquaintances affect her childbearing considerations while validating her own fertility choices.

Women as a group are influenced by common factors in addressing reproductive life cycle issues. However, the meanings each woman places on specific issues and the salience attributed to the various factors depend on her unique experiences, background, and personal characteristics. A counselor needs to be responsive to the common sociocultural, individual, and interpersonal influences as well as to the unique meanings of these factors for each woman. Sensitivity to a woman's special set of considerations or needs resulting from her individual racial, cultural, socioeconomic, marital, and sexual/affectional orientation background is very important.

Counselors also need to become involved in the process of identifying and changing sociocultural structures that limit women's sense of empowerment related to reproductive life cycle issues. Counselors can advocate for relevant legislation, or they can report on the negative influence of institutional gender role standards on women's options to women's groups or government, legal, and organizational policymakers. Counselors may support educational and primary prevention programs that (1) provide accurate information about sexually and reproductive-related issues for women and men; (2) encourage broader gender role attitudes; and (3) teach everyone care, choices, rights, and responsibilities related to sexual behavior and reproductive life cycle issues. Counselors can advocate for development of medical treatments and contraceptive devices that provide healthier alternatives for women than those that currently exist. Counselors can also conduct and support related research applying a variety of methodologies.

CONCLUSIONS

A majority of the research and intervention strategies described in the literature on reproductive life cycle issues is based on women who are white, middle or upper class, heterosexual, and married. In most cases, the literature typically reflects a dominant cultural attitude concerning which women have children and whose issues are of value.

We have very little information about how ethnic/racial differences are associated with reproductive life cycle issues. Minority women are either excluded from or "lumped in" with the responses of all participants in most research studies. Ethnic/racial differences may not be significant in themselves, but these differences may connote certain sociocultural norms (e.g., family size) or may be confounded with socioeconomic differences. However, race/ethnicity may shape the context of women's reproductive life cycle issues.

Most of the literature does not address the effects of marital status or sexual/affectional orientation on women's choices. The way infertility is defined implies that infertility is an issue for heterosexual women in monogamous relationships. Little information concerning childbearing preferences and use of reproductive technologies among single women and lesbians is available. Nor has there been much discussion of the sexual transmission of the HIV virus among lesbians.

A number of the issues presented in this chapter are strongly affected by women's socioeconomic status. Treatment of infertility complications is financially prohibitive for many women, especially since federal government agencies categorize most treatments as experimental, and insurance companies typically do not reimburse for experimental medical interventions. We do not have information about how women experience infertility when they do not financially have the treatment choices available to those who can afford expensive medical interventions. Women who are economically disadvantaged are likely to have more difficulty in paying for an abortion, and government assistance for the procedure is virtually unavailable (Faludi, 1991). This constraint may increase the likelihood of poor women undergoing tubal ligations. However, sterilization procedures may be an economic hardship among women who cannot receive federal assistance for the procedure. Ethnic/racial minority and economically disadvantaged women may receive greater support from social institutions for undergoing sterilization procedures, especially with the HIV/AIDS epidemic, since these women have higher rates of contracting the virus than other groups of women.

Government policy associated with funding for reproductive issues has a greater impact on economically disadvantaged women. New Jersey has recently implemented a policy that denies increased state financial general assistance when a child is born in the family. At the same time, the federal government has restricted the use of tax dollars for abortions, and women must receive counseling and wait 30 days before federal monies can be used to pay for their sterilization procedure. Women who have the money to pay for medical treatment related to reproductive issues clearly have more options. The impact of women's economic status on their preferences and decisions clearly deserves more attention.

Women's reproductive life cycle issues are directly related to their physical, psychological, and social development. As developmental specialists, counselors can assist women in understanding life stages and the options available to them at these stages. Counselors play an important role in helping women explore the personal, interpersonal, and sociocultural context of their reproductive issues and the salience of these issues in their choices. In addition, counselors have a significant role in advocating relevant structural change to meet the reproductive life cycle needs of women.

THE EXAMPLE OF KATE

Kate was a 34-year-old white, married, upper middle class woman who was seeking counseling to discuss her decision to have a child or remain childfree. She had recently been diagnosed with noncancerous fibroid uterine tumors. Her physician had told her that she could have surgery to remove the tumors, but they would likely return in the future; or she could have a hysterectomy. Her physician indicated that if she wanted to bear a child, she should have the tumors removed and attempt to conceive as soon as possible. Kate had earlier thought that she would prefer to maintain her childfree life-style, but she had not made a definite commitment. She was feeling a time constraint in making a decision, and she came to counseling requesting assistance in making a definite decision. Kate had been married for 7 years and employed full-time as a biologist for 10 years. She was one of two female biologists in her workplace. Her husband had also remained uncommitted about childbearing and had recently stated that his concerns were related more to Kate's physical well-being than to their childbearing status. Kate had moved to the community two years earlier, and she and her husband had established a few close friendships and numerous acquaintances. She described herself as a private person who did not discuss childbearing or physical illness with many people.

The counselor believed that it was important to structure a gender role analysis in the counseling sessions by examining Kate's own beliefs, the sociocultural messages, and her interpersonal relationships associated with gender roles, her body, and the reproductive decisions she was attempting to make. The gender role analysis began by examining Kate's beliefs about her body, her gender role orientation, and her choices associated with reproduction. One of the first issues in counseling was the need for accurate information concerning the physical illness and health risks to Kate and to a possible fetus. Kate also needed to discuss her fears and concerns related to the physical problems and her beliefs that her earlier behaviors (i.e., use of birth control) had caused these physical difficulties.

Kate described her values regarding having a child or remaining childfree and how her gender role attitudes/behaviors and personal characteristics affected her childbearing considerations. She perceived herself as holding nontraditional gender attitudes in many aspects of her life; however, she believed that a woman should be in the home full time with a child for the child's first five years of life. If she were to decide to have a child, she thought that she or a full-time nanny should be with the child through the preschool years. These beliefs had direct implications for her employment and financial concerns. While her place of employment had a good maternity leave policy and part-time employment opportunities, she believed that her position was such that any time away from the job would put her behind others in the workplace. She did not believe that she could leave the workplace for five years and keep up with the field of biology, and she did not know whether she could afford to have a full-time nanny on her present salary. She took great pride in her career role and was not sure that she wanted to make changes in that role to accommodate being a mother. Kate believed that she had a right to make her own decisions concerning reproduction, yet she acknowledged that others' attitudes influenced her more than she would like.

A second component of a gender role analysis in the counseling sessions focused on how relationships with and observations of a variety of people in Kate's life influenced her childbearing considerations. She indicated that her relationship with her husband was important to her considerations and that although they maintained relatively egalitarian responsibilities, she would likely have greater child-rearing responsibilities. Her perceptions of her parents' and sisters' experiences and degrees of satisfaction with parenting also influenced her fertility plans. She indicated that her two sisters' having children took the pressure off of her to have a grandchild for her parents. Kate's younger sister was one of the few people with whom Kate had discussed her medical difficulties and childbearing considerations; Kate perceived her sister as supportive of whatever decisions Kate made.

Kate's friends' and acquaintances' life-styles as related to their child-rearing status also influenced Kate's considerations. Kate had talked to two friends about her circumstances, and they had both expressed support of her regardless of her choice. She indicated that approximately half of the individuals she spent time with had no children or had grown children. She indicated that the activities with individuals who were parents were likely to include the children, and she frequently felt out of place when she and her husband were one of the few couples who did not have children. Although most friends and acquaintances did not make direct comments concerning Kate's childbearing status, Kate believed that her fertility plans were in question among her social contacts. She indicated that her co-workers did not have much influence on her considerations, in part because she was not close to them and in part because most of them were men.

In addition to individual and interpersonal components of a gender role analysis, the impact of sociocultural messages related to women and reproduction were important to discuss in counseling. Kate discussed how her daily life experiences were affected by the societal norm to bear children. She was very cognizant of the ambiguous societal attitudes toward mothers, infertile women, and voluntarily childfree women during her decision-making process. Her sensitivity was heightened by the fact that if she did not have a child, she was not sure whether she would consider herself infertile or voluntarily childfree, nor was she sure how others would perceive her. She described her dilemma in making her medical situation and consequent decisions known to others. She expressed concerns that if she was perceived as experiencing fertility difficulties because of her health situation, she would be treated with pity about her "deficit"; and if she was perceived as choosing to remain childfree, she would experience negative sentiment toward her. Given the ambiguity of her physical condition, she was aware of the negative societal attitudes toward women without children regardless of the reasons. She described social pressure to have a child, even with the increased medical risks she would experience.

Through a structural analysis of gender roles, the counseling sessions addressed how a wide variety of medical, personal, interpersonal, and sociocultural influences affected Kate's childbearing considerations. After Kate understood the broad gender role context of her decision, the most salient factors to Kate were identified. In the process of discussing the relationship between the context of childbearing considerations and her life goals, Kate decided that she wanted to maintain her childfree life-style and schedule a hysterectomy. After these decisions were made, Kate continued counseling to discuss how a hysterectomy would change her perceptions of herself, how her plans would be seen by others, and how and with whom she was going to discuss her medical problems and surgery.

REFERENCES

Abbey, A., Andrews, F. M., & Halman, L. J. (1991). Gender's role in response to infertility. *Psychology of Women Quarterly, 15,* 295-316.

Adler, N. E. (1975). Emotional responses of women following therapeutic abortion. *American Journal of Orthopsychiatry, 45,* 446-454.

Adler, N. E., David, H. P., Major, B. N., Roth, S. H., Russo, N. F., & Wyatt, G. E. (1990). Psychological responses after abortion. *Science, 248,* 41-44.

Armsworth, M. W. (1991). Psychological response to abortion. *Journal of Counseling and Development, 69,* 377-379.

Baber, K. M. (1983). Delayed childbearing: The psychosocial aspects of the decision-making process. *Dissertation Abstracts International, 44,* 3174A.

Baldwin, J. D., & Baldwin, J. I. (1988). Factors affecting AIDS-related sexual risk-taking behavior among college students. *Journal of Sex Research, 25,* 181-196.

Bean, F. D., Clark, M. P., Swicegood, G., & Williams, D. (1983). Husband-wife communication, wife's employment, and the decision for male or female sterilization. *Journal of Marriage and the Family, 45,* 395-403.

Beckman, L. J. (1979). The relationship between sex roles, fertility, and family size. *Psychology of Women Quarterly, 4,* 43-60.

Bell, N. K. (1989). AIDS and women: Remaining ethical issues. *AIDS Education and Prevention, 1,* 22-30.

Bellina, J. H., & Wilson, J. (1985). *You can have a baby: Everything you need to know about fertility.* New York: Crown.

Bracken, M. B. (1978). A causal model of psychosomatic reactions to vacuum aspiration abortion. *Social Psychiatry, 13,* 135-145.

Bracken, M. B., Hachamovitch, M., & Grossman, G. (1974). The decision to abort and psychological sequelae. *Nervous and Mental Disease, 158,* 154-162.

Brown, L. S. (1986). Gender-role analysis: A neglected component of psychological assessment. *Psychotherapy, 23,* 243-248.

Brown, L. S. (1991). Therapy with an infertile lesbian client. In C. Silverstein (Ed.) *Gays, lesbians, and their therapists: Studies in psychotherapy* (pp. 15-30). New York: Norton.

Callan, V. J. (1986). The impact of the first birth: Married and single women preferring childlessness, one child, and two children. *Journal of Marriage and the Family, 48,* 261-269.

Centers for Disease Control. (1991, February). The HIV challenge continues. *CDC: HIV/AIDS Prevention Newsletter,* pp. 1-3, 5.

Cochran, S. D., & Mays, V. M. (1989). Women and AIDS-related concerns: Roles for psychologists in helping the worried well. *American Psychologist, 44,* 529-535.

Cook, E. P. (1987). Characteristics of the biopsychosocial crisis of infertility. *Journal of Counseling and Development, 65,* 465-470.

Croteau, J. M., Nero, C. I., & Prosser, D. J. (1991). Social and cultural sensitivity in group specific HIV/AIDS programming. Manuscript submitted for publication.

David, H. P. (1988). Overview: A brief history of abortion and studies of denied abortion. In H. P. David, Z. Dytrych, Z. Matejcek, & V. Schuller (Eds.) *Born unwanted: Developmental effects of denied abortion* (pp. 9-22). New York: Springer.

Dickson, G. L. (1990). A feminist poststructuralist analysis of the knowledge of menopause. *Advances in Nursing Science, 12,* 15-21.

Faludi, S. (1991). *Backlash: The undeclared war against American women.* New York: Crown.

Fischl, M. A., Dickenson, G. M., Segal, A., Flannagan, S., & Rodriguez, M. (1987, June). Heterosexual transmission of Human Immunodeficiency Virus (HIV), relationship of sexual practices to seroconversion. Paper presented at the Third International Conference on AIDS, Washington, DC.

Forrest, J. D., & Fordyce, R. R. (1988). U.S. women's contraceptive attitudes and practice: How have they changed in the 1980s? *Family Planning Perspectives, 20,* 112-118.

Fouad, N. A., & Fahje, K. K. (1989). An exploratory study of the psychological correlates of infertility on women. *Journal of Counseling and Development, 68,* 97-101.

Goldman, L., & Tosteson, A.N.A. (1991). Uncertainty about post menopausal estrogen: Time for action, not debate. *New England Journal of Medicine, 325,* 800-802.

Gray, L. A., & Saracino, M. (1989). AIDS on campus: A preliminary study of college students' knowledge and behaviors. *Journal of Counseling and Development, 68,* 199-201.

Greil, A. L., Leitko, T. A., & Porter, K. L. (1988). Infertility: His and hers. *Gender & Society, 2,* 172-199.

Groat, H. T., Neal, A. G., & Wicks, J. W. (1990). Sterilization anxiety and fertility control in the later years of childbearing. *Journal of Marriage and the Family, 52,* 249-258.

Haskell, W. A. (1985). The role of the mother-daughter relationship in the choice regarding motherhood. *Dissertation Abstracts International, 46,* 1561A.

HIV/AIDS Surveillance Report. (1991, July 10). *United States AIDS activity.* Atlanta, GA: Centers for Disease Control, Center for Infectious Disease.

Holahan, C. K. (1983). The relationship between information search in the childbearing decision and life satisfaction for parents and nonparents. *Family Relations, 32,* 527-535.

Holm, C. F. (1984). Housing aspirations and fertility. *Sociology & Social Research, 68,* 350-363.

√ Hunter, S. (1990). Psychological and somatic experience of the menopause: A prospective study. *Psychosomatic Medicine, 52,* 357-367.

Jackson, B. B., Taylor, J., & Pyngolil, M. (1991). How age conditions the relationship between climacteric status and health symptoms in African American women. *Research in Nursing & Health, 14,* 1-9.

Kelsey, J. L., & Gammon, M. D. (1990). Epidemiology of breast cancer. *Epidemiological Reviews, 12,* 228-240.

Kneen, H. (1988). A decline in vasectomies. *Maclean's, 10.*

Kohn, I. (1986). Counseling women who request sterilization: Psychodynamic issues and interventions. *Social Work in Health Care, 11,* 35-57.

Major, B., Mueller, P., & Hildebrandt, K. (1985). Attributions, expectations, and coping with abortion. *Journal of Personality and Social Psychology, 48,* 585-599.

Marecek, J. (1987). Counseling adolescents with problem pregnancies. *American Psychologist, 42,* 89-93.

Matthews, K. A., Wing, R. A., Kuller, L. H., Meilahn, E. N., Kelsey, S. F., Costello, E. J., & Caggiula, A. W. (1990). Influences of natural menopause on psychological characteristics and symptoms of middle-aged healthy women. *Journal of Consulting and Clinical Psychology, 58,* 345-351.

Mays, V. M., & Cochran, S. D. (1988). Issues in the perception of AIDS risk and risk reeducation activities by Black and Hispanic/Latina women. *American Psychologist, 43,* 949-957.

McKaughan, M. (1987). *The biological clock: Balancing marriage, motherhood, and career.* New York: Penguin.

McKinlay, J. B., McKinlay, S. M., & Brambilla, D. (1987). The relative contributions of endocrine changes and social circumstances to depression in middle-aged women. *Journal of Health and Social Behavior, 28,* 345-363.

Miall, C. E. (1985). Perceptions of informal sanctioning and social stigma of involuntary childlessness. *Deviant Behavior, 6,* 383-403.

Osofsky, J., & Osofsky, H. (1972). The psychological reaction of patients to legalized abortion. *American Journal of Orthopsychiatry, 42,* 48-60.

Padian, N. S., Shiboski, S. C., & Jewell, N. P. (1991). Female-to-male transmission of Human Immunodeficiency Virus. *Journal of the American Medical Association, 266,* 1664-1667.

Public Interest Directorate, American Psychological Association. (1990). *Psychological issues in the abortion debate.* Legislative briefing sheet. Washington, DC: American Psychological Association.

Public Interest Directorate, American Psychological Association. (1991). *Psychological responses following abortion.* Washington, DC: American Psychological Association.

Ramu, G. N., & Tavuchis, N. (1986). The valuation of children and parenthood among the voluntarily childless and parental couples in Canada. *Journal of Comparative Family Studies, 17,* 99-116.

Rank, M. (1985). *Free to grieve.* Minneapolis, MN: Bethany House.

Reading, J., & Amatea, E. S. (1986). Role deviance or role diversification: Reassessing the psychosocial factors affecting the parenthood choice of career-oriented women. *Journal of Marriage and the Family, 48,* 255-260.

Roe v. Wade, 410 U.S. 705 (1973).

Rust v. Sullivan, 222 S.Ct. 1759 (1991).

Sandelowski, M. J. (1990). Failures of volition: Female agency and infertility in historical perspective. *Signs: Journal of Women in Culture and Society, 15,* 475-499.

Scott, W. J., & Morgan, C. S. (1983). An analysis of factors affecting traditional family expectations and perceptions of ideal fertility. *Sex Roles, 9,* 901-914.

Shapiro, S. A. (1988). Psychological consequences of infertility. In J. Offerman-Zuckerberg (Eds.), *Critical psychophysical passages in the life of a woman: A psychodynamic perspective* (pp. 269-289). New York: Plenum.

Sheehy, G. (1991, October). The silent passage: Menopause. *Vanity Fair,* pp. 222-227, 252-254, 256, 258, 260-263.

Simon, N., & Senturia, A. (1966). Psychological sequelae of abortion. *Archives of General Psychiatry, 15,* 378-389.

Sparks, C. H., & Hamilton, J. A. (1991). Psychological issues related to the alternative insemination. *Professional Psychology, 22,* 308-314.

Stampfer, M. J., Colditz, G. A., Willet, W. C., Manson, J. E., Rosner, B., Speitzer, F. E., & Hennekens, C. H. (1991). Postmenopausal estrogen therapy and cardiovascular disease: A ten-year follow-up from the nurses' health study. *New England Journal of Medicine, 325,* 756-762.

Turell, S. C., Armsworth, M. W., & Gaa, J. P. (1990). Emotional response to abortion: A critical view of the literature. *Women & Therapy, 9,* 49-68.

Warnke, M. A. (1991). A psychosocial investigation of factors women consider in their childbearing preferences. *Dissertations Abstracts International, 51,* 5644B.

Webster v. Reproductive Health Services, 492 U.S. 490 (1989).

Weller, R. H., & Bouvier, L. F. (1981). *Population: Demography and policy.* New York: St. Martin's.

Ybarra, S. (1991). Women and AIDS: Implications for counseling. *Journal of Counseling and Development, 69,* 285-287.

WOMEN AND THEIR BODIES: EATING DISORDERS AND ADDICTIONS

Laurie B. Mintz and Deborah M. Wright

Many women in our culture struggle with eating disorders and addictions to alcohol and drugs. Much has been written about the etiology and treatment of these concerns. Unfortunately, however, much of this writing adopts a unidimensional perspective, focusing solely on either sociocultural, personality, or family factors contributing to these issues. This chapter is among the first attempts to explore the contribution of each of these three factors to the development and maintenance of eating disorders and addictions in women and to suggest treatment strategies and goals based on the consideration of these factors.

It must first be noted, however, that these categories are broad and overlapping. By *sociocultural factors,* we are referring to features of the broader social environment, such as societal expectations regarding the roles of women. *Relational factors* include salient features of women's relationships with others, such as family and peers. *Personal factors* include biological factors, psychodynamic factors, personality features, and life history events unique to an individual woman. There is much overlap among these factors. For example, incest could be classified as a personal history factor, a family relations factor, or a societal factor related to the devaluation of women in our culture. Hence, in discussing sociocultural, personal, and relational factors related to eating disorders and addictions among women, it is important to keep in mind that the placement of issues in one or another category was not always a clear-cut decision.

The grouping together of eating disorders and addictions also requires explanation. There is much overlap between the two disorders in terms of etiology, associated personality characteristics, life history events, and treatment needs. For example, both addictions and eating disorders can be considered ways of coping with societal, relational, and personal factors in women's lives. In this view, the function that the substance serves is more important than the choice of the substance itself, and alcohol, food, and drugs are all thought to serve the same function for the individual (Brisman & Siegel, 1984). Furthermore, many women simultaneously or sequentially suffer from issues with both food and substances (Katz, 1990). For example, one-quarter to one-third of patients with eating disorders have a prior or current addiction to alcohol (Mitchell, Hatsukami, Eckert, & Pyle, 1985). Counselors are therefore wise to be aware of counseling issues and strategies for working with both women with eating disorders and women with substance abuse issues.

EATING DISORDERS

Many scholarly and popular press articles have concluded that eating disorders have reached epidemic proportions (Mintz & Betz, 1988). Unfortunately, however, just what comprises an eating disorder is a question fraught with confusion. This confusion is due to several factors, including a lack of consistent operational definitions used in eating disorder research, the change in eating disorder criteria between the *Diagnostic and Statistical Manual of Mental Disorders* (DSM-III) and the *Diagnostic and Statistical Manual of Mental Disorders, Third Edition Revised* (DSM-III-R), and the fact that eating and weight concerns have become normative among women (Mintz & Betz, 1988). Due to the lack of clarity and confusion in previous writings and research, brief definitions of several eating disorders will be presented. For more precise criteria and definitions, refer to the DSM-III-R (American Psychiatric Association, 1987).

The DSM-III-R includes Anorexia Nervosa, Bulimia Nervosa, and Eating Disorders not Otherwise Specified. Anorexia Nervosa is an eating disorder characterized by an extreme preoccupation with thinness and a loss of at least 25 percent of one's body weight. Since anorexia nervosa is mainly a disorder of adolescence, it will not be discussed in this chapter. For information, see classic works by Bruch (1973; 1978), Garfinkel and Garner (1982, 1985), and Minuchin and colleagues (1978).

Bulimia is an eating disorder characterized by recurrent episodes of binge eating over which there is a feeling of loss of control, followed by self-induced vomiting, laxative use, rigorous dieting, fasting, or excessive exercise to counteract the effects of binge eating. The DSM-III-R also includes a category of Eating Disorders not Otherwise Specified, which includes non-anorexic individuals who purge but do not binge and individuals who binge but do not purge. The latter group is often referred to as compulsive overeaters or binge eaters. It is important to note that compulsive overeating is not synonymous with obesity (Brown, 1985). Most compulsive overeaters are not obese, but are 10 to 20 pounds overweight and preoccupied with food and eating (Black, 1990). While compulsive overeating can lead to obesity, so can physiological factors. Thus, it is erroneous to assume that obese women have eating disorders or that normal-weight women do not have such disorders. Rather than being related to weight per se, bulimia and compulsive overeating are characterized by a woman's relationship to food and her body.

To help clarify the difference between an eating disorder and the concern shared by most women in our culture about eating and their bodies, the notion of an eating disorder continuum has been proposed (Striegel-Moore, Silberstein, & Rodin, 1986; Squire, 1983). This continuum ranges from "no concern with weight and normal eating, to normative discontent with weight and moderately disregulated eating, to bulimia" (Striegel-Moore et al., 1986, p. 246). Other points on the continuum include chronic dieting, binge or compulsive overeating, and occasional dieting.

Research has sought to differentiate between women at different points along the eating disorder continuum, and clear evidence has emerged that women at different points on the continuum differ in terms of their psychological makeup and treatment needs (e.g., Katzman & Wolchik, 1984; Mintz & Betz, 1988). More specifically, as eating behavior becomes more severe (i.e., bulimia or anorexia), so do associated problems (e.g., personality issues, suicidal ideation). Nevertheless, even within a specific eating disorder category, there may be a great degree of heterogeneity in terms of etiology and treatment needs (Rybicki, Lepkowsky, & Arndt, 1989). For example, for one woman, bulimia may be related mainly to endorsement of sociocultural pressures toward thinness, whereas for another it may be related to a history of sexual victimization. In working with eating-disordered women in counseling, then, it is important to thoroughly assess the range of underlying factors and to treat accordingly.

The following sections focus on sociocultural, personal, and relational factors associated with the development and maintenance of both bulimia and compulsive overeating. Much of what is presented also applies to other groups along the eating disorder continuum, such as chronic dieters. Nevertheless, it is important to keep in mind the heterogeneity of women with eating disorders and the need to see each client as an individual with her own unique history and treatment needs.

Sociocultural Context and Factors

Bulimia and compulsive overeating are overwhelmingly issues that affect women, and hence it is critical to examine the cultural and societal forces that contribute to these disorders. An examination of these forces reveals that there is a clear relationship between women's oppression in general and any specific woman's relationship to food and her body (Laidlaw, 1990). Two related aspects of women's oppression associated with the development and maintenance of eating disorders are the societal pressure to attain an ideal body shape and the more global socialization of women in our culture.

There is much pressure on women in our culture to attain a culturally defined ideal body shape encompassing both thinness, and more recently, fitness. Furthermore, "current sociocultural influences teach women not only what the ideal body looks like, but also how to attain it, including how to diet, purge, and engage in other disregulating behaviors" (Striegel-Moore et al., 1986, p. 256). Our cultural belief system purveys the message that anyone who diets hard enough and works out long enough can attain the ideal look. Such a view not only ignores biological realities, but sets women up to feel ashamed and defeated, since it implies that not achieving this ideal is a woman's fault and that weight control is equal to self-control (Katzman, Weiss, & Wolchik, 1986; Striegel-Moore et al., 1986).

Given these sociocultural pressures toward thinness and fitness, most women in our culture diet, and dieting is often the entry point for bulimia and other eating disorders (Smead, 1984). Restrictive dieting often precedes and leads to binge eating, which itself is often followed by increased attempts to lose weight by methods such as dieting, purging, or fasting (Smead, 1984). Thus, as women attempt to diet in order to meet an unrealistic and unhealthy cultural ideal, a self-perpetuating cycle of eating-disordered behavior may emerge.

On a more global level, women's roles and socialization are tied to the prevalence of eating disorders among women. Attaining the thin ideal is important to women because they are socialized to equate self-esteem with body esteem, to see themselves as sexual objects, and to pay vast amounts of attention to their physical appearance in order to "catch" a man (Laidlaw, 1990). Women in our current culture are also socialized to be passive, never angry, nurturant of others, and socially sensitive. Further, women are taught to defer to men and to either put the needs of others before their own or to ignore their own needs altogether (Laidlaw, 1990). Women are also currently expected to achieve professional success while maintaining this ideal image of femininity (Katzman et al., 1986). In short, women are socialized to simultaneously achieve vocational success, focus on their physical appearance, see themselves as objects, and attend to the needs of others.

This socialization is associated with the development of eating disorders on a variety of levels. One of the first theories about bulimia proposed that an overacceptance of the female role was central to the etiology of this disorder (Boskind-Lodahl, 1976). In this view,

215

bulimia is the "struggle to achieve a perfect, stereotypic, female image in which women surrender most of their self-defining behaviors to others" (Boskind-Lodahl & White, 1978, p. 84). More recently, several authors have implicated women's contradictory roles (i.e., the pressure to be simultaneously feminine and career competent) as a risk factor for bulimia (Katzman et al., 1986; Striegel-Moore et al., 1986). According to this viewpoint, young women act out the conflict between success, autonomy, and a more relational orientation through their bodies and eating (Steiner-Adair, 1988).

Although several authors implicate adherence to women's roles as a risk factor in the development of bulimia, in a now classic work, Orbach (1979) suggests that the fat that often results from compulsive overeating represents an attempt to break free from society's sex role stereotypes. Compulsive overeating and fat are seen as a rebellion and protection against powerlessness, objectification and sexualization, and the pressures to be thin, catch a man, and act and look a certain way (Brown, 1985; Orbach, 1979).

Regardless of whether one believes that eating disorders represent an endorsement or rejection of women's roles, the connection between a woman's relationship with food and her role as a self-sacrificing nurturer is difficult to deny. Numerous authors have discussed the relationship between the socialization of women to "swallow" feelings, especially anger, and eating disorders, such as bulimia and compulsive overeating (Weiss, Katzman, & Wolchik, 1986). Food is an instant gratifier that women learn to use to nurture themselves and to deal with feelings such as anger (Laidlaw, 1990). In other words, food and eating behavior may be used as a way of dealing with anger and resentment while maintaining a passive and compliant exterior (Black, 1990). The use of food in this way can become compulsive when real needs and emotions are not acknowledged or dealt with (Laidlaw, 1990; Roth, 1982). Furthermore, because women in our culture are supposed to cook for and nurture others, yet deny themselves food and nurturance, self-feeding becomes associated with guilt and failure. In short, women learn to use food to deal with emotional needs and hungers that are difficult to fulfill in our patriarchal society, yet this use of food becomes tainted by guilt and shame, and for many takes on the air of an obsessive struggle. In sum, there is a strong association between women's roles and socialization, the emphasis on women's physical appearance, and the development and maintenance of eating disorders.

Personal Factors

While the role of cultural factors cannot be denied, the fact remains that not all women develop eating disorders. Hence, a more complete examination of the factors involved in the development of these disorders must also look at the individual woman herself. A focus on cultural factors helps to answer the question of "Why women?", whereas a focus on the characteristics of the woman herself helps to answer the question of "Which women?" (Striegel-Moore et al., 1986). In answering questions regarding the woman herself, previous literature has focused on demographic and personality correlates, unique life history events, and psychodynamic, behavioral, and biological factors.

Biological factors have been posited as contributors to the etiology of eating disorders. Support for this view comes from evidence of a genetic component in affective disorders coupled with high rates of affective disorders in eating-disordered women and their families. In fact, one school of thought classifies bulimia as a form of affective disorder (Dickenson, 1985). However, this theory is controversial, and no conclusions can be drawn at this time (Striegel-Moore et al., 1986).

Another biological factor that may contribute to the development of eating disorders is a woman's metabolism and set point for body weight. "Women who are genetically programmed to be heavier than the svelte ideal will be at higher risk for bulimia than women who are naturally thin" because they will be under even greater pressure to resort to extreme methods to achieve the cultural ideal (Striegel-Moore et al., 1986, p. 254). The biological picture becomes further complicated since, as previously mentioned, dieting itself can lead to binge eating, weight gain, and even lowered metabolism (Striegel-Moore et al., 1986).

Along with research on biological factors, there is a great deal of research aimed at identifying demographic and personality correlates of women with eating disorders. Bulimic women are often described as white, single, college-educated women from middle- to upper middle-class families (Weiss, Katzman, & Wolchik, 1985). There is evidence that this pattern may be changing, with bulimia increasingly cutting across socioeconomic and ethnic lines (Dickenson, 1985). In studies of personality correlates, bulimic women have been found to possess the following characteristics: social dependency, social anxiety, low self-esteem, high need for approval, depression, negative body image, dissatisfaction with their weight, perfectionism, unreasonable self-expectations, difficulty with expressing and recognizing feelings, problems recognizing hunger and satiety, problems with impulse control, high degrees of internal anger, lack of assertion skills, external locus of control, high degree of endorsement of sociocultural values regarding thinness, a belief that others are evaluating and focusing on them and their eating behaviors, and cognitive disturbances such as irrational beliefs, obsessional thinking, and dichotomous reasoning (Gross & Rosen, 1988; Johnson & Holloway, 1988; Katzman & Wolchik, 1984; Mintz & Betz, 1988; Muuss, 1986; Weiss et al., 1985). The personality correlates of binge eaters have been described rather similarly. For example, binge eaters have been described as compulsive, passive, externally focused, and suffering from depression and low self-esteem (Brice, 1981).

Along with describing and listing personality correlates, many authors have focused on the internal dynamics of the woman with an eating disorder or the function that food and eating disorders serve for the individual. In addition to the role of food in dealing with anger that was discussed earlier, dynamic interpretations have pointed to the role of food and eating behavior in easing the pain that comes from the belief that one is bad or defective. Food and eating behavior may also be used to push others away, punish others, punish oneself, and displace energy from other life concerns (Black, 1990; Dickenson, 1985; Striegel-Moore et al., 1986). Food can also be used to gain a sense of control (Black, 1990; Laidlaw, 1990). For many bulimic women, controlling food input and output may be the primary source of feelings of control in the world. To binge and purge (even in secret) is to experience being in control of something.

On both a dynamic and a behavioral level, bulimia and compulsive overeating can be viewed as maladaptive ways of coping with stress (Cattanach & Rodin, 1988). The sources of stress may be the personality and dynamic factors discussed above, such as anxiety, depression, or anger. Eating may provide immediate negative reinforcement by removing feelings of stress and tension. Indeed, many bulimics and compulsive overeaters report a "high" feeling and decreases in tension, boredom, stress, anger, and other negative emotions after binge eating, binge purging, or purging (Muuss, 1986; Weiss et al., 1985). Nevertheless, this decrease in negative affect is often followed by feelings of guilt and self-disgust. Food and eating behavior can thus be immediately reinforcing, but ultimately ineffective methods for women to cope with painful feelings, internal dynamics, and unstructured time.

When examining the life histories of women with eating disorders, it becomes evident that these women often have a number of painful past and current life events. Bulimic women tend to experience more life stress than women without eating disorders (Striegel-Moore et al., 1986). Further, many women with eating disorders have a history of sexual abuse and/or incest (Kearny-Cook, 1988; Root, 1989). For these women, eating-disordered behavior may be a way of keeping memories of the abuse at bay (Root, 1989), as well as a form of self-destructive behavior aimed at dealing with the impaired sense of self and body image problems that result from sexual abuse and incest (Kearny-Cook, 1988). In sum, a variety of personal factors may contribute to the development of an eating disorder in any particular woman, including biological factors, personality correlates, psychodynamic factors, behavioral factors, and life history events.

Relational Factors

Current and past relationship patterns are also related to the etiology and maintenance of eating disorders among women. The women's families of origin often place a great deal of emphasis on weight and appearance and have relational patterns that include overcontrol, rigidity, poor communication, affective overinvolvement or disengagement, and a lack of conflict-resolution and problem-solving skills (McNamara & Loveman, 1990; Stuart, Laraia, Ballenger, & Lydiard, 1990). As mentioned, many eating-disordered women also come from incestuous families, or from alcoholic families and/or families with gambling, drug-abusing, or eating-disordered parents (Black, 1990). In these cases, eating behavior may provide a sense of control, a way to anesthetize pain and shame, or a way to mask family problems (Black, 1990).

Relationships with peers, romantic and sexual partners, and authority figures may also contribute to the development and maintenance of eating disorders. Peer group norms and pressures from teachers, coaches, and other authority figures around appearance and food intake can be critical in the development of eating disorders (Crandell, 1988). Eating-disordered women also often report problems with sexual and romantic relationships. In fact, it is in the context of these relationships that food and eating-disordered behavior are often used as a covert method of attaining power and as a way of expressing anger (Brown, 1985; O'Conner, 1984). In sum, both family of origin and current relational patterns have been implicated as risk factors in the development and maintenance of eating disorders.

Eating Disorders as Multidetermined

While much past writing has taken a unidimensional perspective on the etiology of eating disorders, it is clear that these disorders are multidetermined. Recently, numerous authors have proposed multi-risk, multidetermined models (e.g., Schwartz & Barrett, 1987; Weiss et al., 1985). While each of these models differs, they all acknowledge the interaction of factors that can result in eating disorders. It is important to note that for each eating-disordered woman, the unique constellation of factors and pathways of influence will be slightly, if not significantly, different. The counselor working with an eating-disordered woman will need to be aware of both the factors commonly associated with the etiology of eating disorders and the specific influences and interactions of these factors for particular client.

Multimodal Treatment

Because the cause of eating disorders is both multidetermined and unique to each individual woman, a multifocused treatment approach is most appropriate. The overall treatment goal when working with an eating-disordered woman is to help her feel better about herself and to learn to love herself (Brown, 1985; Weiss et al., 1985). While one goal of treatment is to eliminate the eating-disordered behavior, equally important goals include helping the client to establish a solid sense of self and an identity based on factors other than external appearance.

The treatment of eating disorders must clearly extend beyond disordered eating (Katzman & Wolchik, 1984). Nevertheless, many counselors struggle with how much to focus on eating behavior versus other issues, such as interpersonal relations or incest history. Some clinicians advocate dealing with the behavior first and then pursuing more dynamic work (e.g., Lacy & Moureli, 1986), while others advocate the opposite (e.g., Root, 1989). Our experience is that this decision depends on the severity of the client's eating behavior and the content of the other issues. For a client who is bingeing and purging eight times a day, an initial focus on eating behavior may help increase confidence in herself and in treatment. Conversely, a client who is using eating as a way to cope with childhood trauma may need more intensive counseling to heal from the trauma before she will be able to safely let go of her eating behavior (Laidlaw, 1990). Decisions regarding the focus and balance of treatment can be made in conjunction with the client.

If eating problems are severe, attention to the client's physical health must be the first treatment priority. Because bulimia poses serious, and even life-threatening, physical effects (e.g., electroencephalogram abnormalities, electrolyte imbalances, dental problems, fatigue), it is critical that clients be under the care of a physician who specializes in eating disorders. Early in treatment, the client should be informed about the physical consequences of prolonged bingeing and purging and be referred to a knowledgeable physician. It is important to obtain releases of information, since dialogue with the physician is often useful.

Along with early attention to physical health, we advocate the use of a structured eating disorder intake to gather information about the client's history and current issues and behavior. This intake should cover topics such as weight history, food-related patterns, appearance concerns, medical history, eating disorder history, family history, developmental history, sexual history, sexual abuse history, psychological history, the degree to which the behavior is interfering with current functioning, and motivation to change. Further examples of topics and actual interview formats can be found in Weiss et al. (1985) and Johnson (1985). Such comprehensive intakes facilitate the development of effective, individualized treatment plans.

Many clients benefit from a combination of individual and group counseling, with other modalities and adjuncts being employed as necessary. Effective group and individual treatment incorporates behavioral, cognitive, and insight oriented/affective strategies. One useful behavioral strategy is self-monitoring aimed at identifying situational triggers that lead to bingeing and purging. Clients can, for example, keep a log that includes times, places, and feelings preceding and immediately following binges and purges. Following such identification of situational and emotional triggers, finding and substituting other coping and self-nurturing behaviors is important, although the counselor needs to be careful not to label eating as a unilaterally ineffective self-nurturant strategy (Brown, 1985). Stress management, assertion training, contingency contracting, and response delay strategies may also be effective behavioral strategies. Useful cognitive interventions include thought stopping and cognitive restructuring. Such restructuring should include a gentle challenging of unreasonable expectations, shoulds, and perfectionistic stances and a focus on replacing destructive messages from female socialization with healthier messages (Laidlaw, 1990). Affective and insight-oriented work can focus on identifying underlying emotional hungers and issues (e.g., incest, trauma, loss, loneliness) and on expressing associated feelings in non-food-oriented ways.

Weiss and colleagues (1985) provide a useful manual describing a seven-week psychoeducational group treatment program that incorporates many useful cognitive and behavioral exercises and focuses on topics such as perfectionism, self-esteem, anger, assertion, and cultural expectations for women. A companion workbook for clients is also available (Weiss et al., 1986). While this treatment program is designed for groups, it can also be used within an individual counseling framework. Clients can, for example, use the book as an adjunct to treatment or be assigned specific chapters and homework assignments as relevant to treatment.

While the bulk of treatment will likely be conducted in a multifocused individual or group setting, other adjuncts and modalities may also be useful. Because of the misconceptions about nutrition that many eating-disordered clients have, an emphasis on regular meal intake and information on nutrition and the effects of prolonged dieting are often important treatment components (Mitchell, Hatsukami, Pyle, Eckert, & Davis, 1985; Smead, 1984). While separate work with a dietician is ideal, if this is not possible, the counselor should incorporate nutritional information into individual or group treatment. If the family is involved with the client on a daily basis or if the behavior seems to be a way to distract the family from other problems, family counseling may also be indicated (see O'Conner, 1984; Schwartz, Barrett, & Saba, 1985). While controversy remains regarding the use of antidepressant medication for eating-disordered clients, if the client has a history of depressive disorder or current severe depressive symptoms, an evaluation for medication is warranted (Mitchell et al., 1985). Similarly, in severe cases, the need for inpatient hospitalization should be considered.

Bibliotherapy and support group work may also be useful adjuncts to treatment. Several national eating disorder organizations provide self-help and counselor-focused bibliographies and national support group registries, such as the National Association of Anorexia Nervosa and Associated Disorders in Highland Park, Illinois. A word of caution regarding the use of support groups and

Overeaters Anonymous is warranted. Since such groups differ from region to region, the counselor is responsible for checking on them prior to referring clients. For example, while many clients find the format of Overeaters Anonymous useful, others may find the focus on food as the enemy and a higher power to be less than helpful, or even harmful. As with all treatment decisions, the decision to use such adjuncts must be made on an individual basis and in conjunction with the client.

In sum, the multidetermined and individual nature of eating disorders demands a multifocused and individualized approach to treatment, incorporating various modalities (e.g., group, individual, family), theoretical approaches (e.g., behavioral, insight-oriented, cognitive), and adjuncts to treatment (e.g., nutritional counseling, bibliotherapy, support groups). We advocate that counselors choose and use those modalities and strategies that are effective for a particular client, given her unique constellation of issues.

ADDICTIVE BEHAVIORS

There is a lack of clarity surrounding the definition of addictions. For specific Substance Use Disorder criteria, see the DSM-III-R. For the purposes of this chapter, *addiction* is defined as the continued use of a substance despite evidence that it is causing problems (American Psychiatric Association, 1987). Addiction will be viewed broadly as the use of alcohol, prescription drugs, or illegal substances as a form of coping with distress (Alexander & Hadaway, 1982). The distress can be related to sociocultural factors, personal characteristics, relationship factors, or a combination of the three. Addictive behavior can thus develop for a variety of reasons and can serve many purposes. Women who experience substance abuse problems are a heterogeneous group, and counselors should avoid overgeneralizing or negative stereotyping. While this section will focus on addictions in general, most of the information presented concerns alcohol abuse among women, as alcohol has been the focus of more attention in the literature than have other forms of addictions.

The number of women seeking treatment for alcohol-related problems has increased in the last 10 to 15 years (Litman, 1986). This increase may reflect a rising rate of alcoholism among women or greater visibility of the problem (Fillmore, 1984). While "informed observers agree that alcoholism among women is becoming more prevalent," it is also important to note that this apparent increase may be related to the changing role of women, making problem drinking more visible (Hoar, 1983, p. 253).

It is difficult to accurately estimate the prevalence of alcoholism in women because of the lack of research specific to women's drinking, inadequacies of drinking assessment inventories when applied to women (Beckman & Kocel, 1982; McCrady & Sher, 1983), and the type of help offered to or sought by women. Specifically, women are less likely than men to be referred to treatment by job supervisors (Beyer & Trice, 1981). Women also have fewer arrests and citations for driving while intoxicated, and when arrested are more likely to be escorted home, while men are more likely to be arrested and offered treatment (Blume, 1986; Wilsnack, Wilsnack, & Klassen, 1986). In addition, the type of help sought by women is related to race and socioeconomic status. Black women and women of low socioeconomic status are less likely to seek professional help (Reed & Leibson, 1981), while married women of upper socioeconomic status are more likely to consult with the family physician than with an addiction treatment specialist (Mulford, 1977). In sum, there are unique issues associated with the identification of women who are chemically dependent.

Another barrier to understanding alcohol-related behavior in women is the fact that most current theories of chemical dependence are based on male drinking patterns (Fortin & Evans, 1983). Women are often either overlooked or viewed as more pathological than men (Hoar, 1983). In addition, there is a lack of research concerning the relationship of women's ethnicity and sexual orientation to the etiology, maintenance, and treatment of alcoholism and other addictions (Schmidt, Klee, & Ames, 1990).

Despite a lack of information on women's drinking, there is some evidence that women tend to exhibit different drinking patterns than men. Women tend to have a more rapid development of drinking and drinking-related problems and tend to drink at home and alone more often than do men (Gomberg, 1981; Hill, 1980; Perodeau, 1984). In addition, women may be more likely than men to develop liver damage, cirrhosis, and alcohol-related brain damage (Jacobson, 1986; Saunders, Davis, & Williams, 1981). Not only are women's drinking patterns different than men's, but women also tend to use more prescription drugs than do men (Cooperstock & Sims, 1971). Theories of addiction based on male behavior are therefore inadequate to explain the etiology and treatment needs of women. This section explores the sociocultural, personal, and relationship factors that are relevant to the etiology and maintenance of addictions in women. Treatment strategies and guidelines are also discussed.

Sociocultural Factors

The etiology and maintenance of addictive behavior in women is inextricably interwoven with the socialization of women in our culture. As noted by Reed (1985), "women are women long before they become involved in chemical misuse and dependency" (p. 15). Sociocultural factors provide the context from which women come to view themselves and others, and they present women with unique stressors and challenges. For example, women are devalued and have less economic and political power and therefore fewer resources and options than men. Women struggle with pay inequality, balance multiple roles, and tend to spend more time at home and alone. Problems associated with substance abuse for black women may be even more closely linked to sociocultural factors such as institutional and individual discrimination (Thornton & Carter, 1988). In order to understand the development of addictive behavior in women, it is therefore necessary to understand the impact of sociocultural factors. Two sociocultural factors related to addiction in women are the stress associated with life scripts and identity issues and the tendency for physicians to overprescribe drugs.

Stress Associated With Life Scripts and Identity Issues

Women may use alcohol and other substances as a means of coping with environmental stressors (Johnson, 1982). It is unknown, however, whether these events are the cause or the consequence of problem drinking (Allan & Cooke, 1985). Furthermore, since drinking is a behavior that is socially condemned in women, women may attribute their drinking to specific stressful events in order to avoid condemnation (Dahlgren, 1975). In short, while environmental stressors increase women's vulnerability to use substances as a means of coping, substance abuse is not a simple response to stress.

Stress in women may itself be associated with a variety of roles or life scripts. More specifically, too many roles, conflicts between roles, and even the loss or lack of certain roles have been found to be associated with stress and problem drinking. Problem drinking among women has been associated with the loss of a significant relationship and with being unmarried, divorced, or without children (Dahlgren, 1978; Fortin & Evans, 1983). On the other hand, multiple roles (e.g., being employed and married) have also been associated with higher rates of problem drinking (Johnson, 1982). The woman who combines the traditional role of child-rearer and homemaker with that of employee is faced with the stress of balancing these frequently conflicting roles. Nevertheless, while the stress of multiple roles may be related to problem drinking, the role of employee may serve as a buffer if it provides a source of self-esteem and social support apart from home and family life (Barnett & Baruch, 1985). Clearly, no one role or life script is associated with problem drinking in women. Rather, research has implicated almost every possible life role or combination of life roles, hence making it impossible to draw conclusions regarding the relationship between the stress of specific roles and addictive behavior in women.

For some women, drinking may reduce the stress associated with the conflict between traditionally socialized femininity (i.e., dependence) and new roles and traits available to women (i.e., autonomy) (Beckman, 1978; Benson & Wilsnack, 1983). Indeed, the degree of conflict over the socially prescribed traditional feminine role and the perceived advantages of the masculine role has been found to be related to problem drinking, with the size of this conflict being a critical factor (Scida & Vannicelli, 1979). While sex role conflict has been associated with problem drinking, so have both a more traditional sex role attitude and an undifferentiated sex role identity (i.e., scoring low on both feminine and masculine traits on instruments like the Bem Sex Role Inventory) (Kroft & Leichner, 1987). The female problem drinker who is undifferentiated may drink in order to capture a sense of self (Beckman, 1978; Wilsnack, 1976), while the female problem drinker with a less egalitarian sex role attitude may drink in order to deal with the stress and pain associated with considering herself a second-class citizen. Clearly, the stress associated with certain sex role identities and sex role conflicts faced by women in our culture contribute to problem drinking (Wilsnack et al., 1986).

Overprescription of Drugs

The tendency for women to be portrayed as helpless patients and the overprescription of drugs for women also contribute to addiction in women (Ogur, 1986). Pharmaceutical advertisements depict women as confused, helpless, and passive (Ogur, 1986). It is estimated that 69 percent of all mood-modifying prescriptions are for women (Cooperstock & Sims, 1971; Rosser, 1981). Male physicians prescribe antidepressants to 1 of every 3 women, as compared with 1 of every 11 men (Cooperstock & Sims, 1971; Rosser, 1981). Elderly women appear to be at greater risk for overprescription (Glantz & Backenheimer, 1988), although women of all ages become addicted to drugs they have been prescribed. Clearly, women's lower social status and the power dynamics of the patient-physician relationship contribute to women's addiction to prescription drugs.

In sum, sociocultural variables related to women's social status are significant in terms of understanding the etiology and maintenance of addictive behaviors in women. Women may use substances as a means of coping with stress associated with role overload, role incompatibility, or the loss of roles. Women who feel trapped in the traditional feminine role may be prone to use substances in an effort to gain a sense of self. Women are also more vulnerable to overprescribing and run the risk of developing addictions to prescription drugs.

Personal Factors

A variety of personal factors have been related to addictive behavior. These include biological factors, personality characteristics, and specific life events such as a history of sexual victimization. Evidence of biological factors (i.e., genetic predisposition) in the etiology of addictions comes from the finding that women who abuse alcohol and drugs tend to have an alcoholic parent (Schuckit & Morrissey, 1976). Nevertheless, it is important to note that most studies that have found evidence for a genetic predisposition for alcoholism have focused almost exclusively on men, and the results of studies using female participants have been inconclusive (Goodwin, Schulsinger, Knop, Mednick, & Guze, 1977).

Research aimed at identifying personality characteristics of female alcoholics has been based on the misguided assumption that chemically dependent women are a homogeneous group who share similar personality profiles. Personality differences among alcoholics have traditionally been ignored (Nerviano & Gross, 1983), and research has not supported the notion of an "addictive personality" (Wilford, 1981). Chemically dependent women are a heterogeneous group with a wide variety of personality profiles (Nerviano & Gross, 1983; Schmidt, Klee, & Ames, 1990), and counselors are again cautioned against stereotyping and overgeneralizing.

There are, however, some commonalities among women with substance abuse problems. Chemically dependent women are likely to report low self-esteem, a negative body image, depression, and suicide attempts (Beckman, 1978; Blume, 1986; Gomberg, 1986; Hill, 1980). Female alcoholics have also been found to experience higher neuroticism, more anxiety, and more alienation than both male alcoholics and female nonalcoholics (Beckman, 1978).

Women's minority status, as well as attitudes that devalue women and condone violence, have left women in our culture especially vulnerable to victimization, and there seems to be a clear association between sexual victimization and substance abuse (Coleman, 1987; Evans & Schaefer, 1987; Herman, 1981). One study found that of 50 drug-dependent women, 70 percent had been raped prior to chemical dependency (Wasnick, Schaffer, & Bencivengo, 1980). In another study of 597 adolescent girls in treatment for substance abuse, it was found that those with a history of sexual abuse reported both more shame and more suicidal ideation (Edwall, Hoffman, & Harrison, 1989).

Alcohol and other substances may be used by victims of rape and sexual abuse as a means of coping with posttraumatic stress symptoms (Root, 1989). Perhaps alcohol and drugs help a survivor of sexual violence to block out flashbacks of this violence that may occur during sex. While studies have found that alcohol consumption interferes with sexual relations (e.g., Ames, 1982; Corrigan, 1980), it has also been found that female alcoholics, as compared with female nonalcoholics, reported more desire for and enjoyment of sexual activities after drinking (Beckman, 1979).

Relational Factors

Addictive behaviors are related to both family of origin and current relationships. As stated earlier, women who abuse alcohol and drugs tend to have an alcoholic parent (Schuckit & Morrissey, 1976). While this finding is often taken as evidence for a genetic predisposition, it also constitutes evidence for environmental influences. Along with having an alcoholic parent, alcoholic women are more likely to be married to alcoholic men than are nonalcoholic women (Gomberg, 1981; Wilsnack et al., 1986). In fact, women are likely to be introduced to drugs and alcohol by men. One study of 100 women who use alcohol and prescription drugs found that they were likely to have companions who drank heavily and used prescription drugs (Estep, 1987).

Along with reporting relationships with male abusers, alcoholic women also report a lack of social support in childhood, adolescence, and adulthood (Schilit & Gomberg, 1987). With the exception of black women, who are more likely to drink in groups and in public (Dawkins & Harper, 1983), women who abuse alcohol tend to drink at home alone and to report social isolation (Kagle, 1987). It is unclear, however, whether social isolation and a lack of social support is the cause or consequence of alcohol abuse. A recent study found that social isolation tended to increase with the number of years of drinking (Gomberg & Schilit, 1985). Indeed, a lack of social support may be both a cause and consequence of heavy drinking.

Women in our culture face unique challenges and stressors that contribute to their vulnerability to use alcohol and other substances as a means of coping. Of particular importance are attitudes that devalue women and the impact that these attitudes have on every aspect of women's lives.

Treatment

Most models of treatment and intervention are based on theories of chemical dependence in men (Mandel & North, 1982; Reed, 1987). Men outnumber women in treatment, sometimes as much as four to one (Beckman & Amaro, 1984; Gomberg, 1981). Furthermore, women account for only 7 to 8 percent of research participants in treatment outcome studies (Vannicelli, 1984). Treatment programs are not typically designed to meet women's needs and therefore may not recognize and respond to women's main problems (Reed, 1985). Furthermore, the view of the alcoholic woman as a passive victim is neither accurate nor helpful in treatment and "represents...a demeaning attitude" (Gomberg & Schilit, 1985, p. 314). In order to effectively intervene with and treat women with addictions, it is necessary to understand women's needs within a broader context of gender socialization (Reed, 1985). This section will discuss assessment and treatment setting issues specific to women with addictions, and will then present specific treatment goals and strategies.

Assessment

The treatment of addictions should begin with a thorough assessment. A physical exam by a specialist in the area of addictions should be a standard part of this assessment. The exam should focus on assessing the extent and severity of any physical complications that have resulted from alcohol or substance abuse, as well as the need for hospitalization to treat withdrawal symptoms, which can be fatal in the case of heavy and prolonged alcohol abuse. It is also important to assess for use of and dependency on prescription drugs (Knupfer, 1982). An assessment for depression should also be standard, especially if such depression is associated with prescription and other mood-altering drugs (Naegle, 1988). Finally, since there is a high rate of past sexual victimization among chemically dependent women, a sexual assault history should be a standard part of all intakes (Reed, 1985).

Treatment Setting

While addictions have traditionally been treated through in-patient programs, there is evidence that women tend to prefer outpatient services (Beckman & Kocel, 1982). Because of this preference and evidence that inpatient treatment is no more effective than outpatient treatment (Henderson & Anderson, 1982), practitioners are encouraged to treat addiction the same as any other presenting concern. If hospitalization is not indicated for medical reasons, women's addictions can be treated on an outpatient basis, using standard criteria for hospitalization, such as potential for harm to self or others.

When inpatient treatment is chosen, however, the treatment program must attend to the specific needs of women. Since women in our society tend to carry the primary responsibility for childcare, treatment programs should offer childcare and treatment to children in order to attract and retain women (Beckman & Kocel, 1982). Despite evidence that many addicted women are survivors of sexual abuse, fewer than 20 percent of treatment programs currently offer specialized services to deal with this issue (Yandow, 1989). Specialized services in this area should be provided. Finally, both outpatient counselors and inpatient treatment programs are encouraged to provide career counseling, since many women will need to hone skills or readjust their careers after treatment.

Treatment programs also need to attend to staffing and policy issues. All women's programs offer the advantage of providing a range of female role models and support systems (Reed, 1985). A comprehensive program staffed and run by ethnically diverse women may maximize program effectiveness (Thornton, 1981). In addition, staff need to examine their gender related assumptions and biases, since staff who are unaware of or insensitive to gender related issues are likely to misunderstand women (Reed, 1985). Staff also need to be sensitive to cultural issues and to the value systems of their clients.

Treatment Strategies and Goals

The primary issues of counseling chemically dependent women revolve around identity, self-esteem, shame, and guilt. The chemically dependent woman may not have a clear understanding of her personal values and beliefs and may experience chronic low self-esteem and negative body image. She is also likely to carry a great deal of shame and guilt about her alcohol and drug use. The practitioner can use a variety of strategies to work with these interrelated personal and societally based issues simultaneously.

The chemically dependent woman may need help in identifying personal values and beliefs and in developing an understanding of the societal source of these beliefs (Hoar, 1983). Consciousness raising aimed at increasing understanding of the impact of social status may be particularly helpful in reducing guilt and shame (Reed, 1987). An exploration of the difficulties associated with sex roles, sex role stereotyping, and the difficulties of being female in a sexist society may be beneficial (Mandel & North, 1982). Sports activities, body work, and dance can be utilized in working with body image problems (Reed, 1985). The development of stress management and assertion skills will help enhance the chemically dependent woman's sense of personal power and competence.

The treatment of chemically dependent women will also need to incorporate a focus on relationship issues. Chemically dependent women may lack social support (Schilit & Gomberg, 1987), and thus a focus on developing healthy support networks, particularly with other women, may be beneficial. Since chemically dependent women may be in relationships with chemically dependent partners who are unsupportive of their treatment, a discussion of strategies to deal with this lack of support is critical (Knupfer, 1982). In addition, the client may need help in developing appropriate expectations of healthy, intimate relationships.

Treatment of addicted women should be conducted in a supportive and empowering atmosphere. Traditional confrontational treatment strategies aimed at breaking through denial and resistance may be inappropriate, since rather than being in denial about their problem, women often enter treatment with feelings of guilt and shame. Self-help programs that encourage admission of powerless-ness may also be "very inappropriate and even harmful for many women" (Reed, 1985, p. 35; Underhill, 1986), because many women enter treatment with an intense feeling of powerlessness that may have contributed to the addictive behavior. Thus, while Alcoholics Anonymous (AA) may be helpful to some women in that it can provide a support network and decrease isolation and shame, the emphasis on accepting powerlessness may be adverse and non-therapeutic to women. A thorough exploration of these issues with the client will be beneficial in helping her determine if a particular resource may be helpful.

It is important to involve clients in all stages of treatment, including assessment, planning, and goal setting. This involvement is especially important since many chemically dependent women tend to pay more attention to others' needs and than to their own. In sum, the following are important areas in the treatment of chemi-cally dependent women: (1) a thorough assessment of the extent of use of alcohol and other substances, including prescription drugs; (2) referral for a physical exam; (3) assessment for past sexual victimiza-tion; (4) a focus on self-esteem and identity, including values clarifica-tion, assertion training, all-women groups, consciousness-raising groups, and access to female role models; (5) career services; (6) stress reduction techniques; and (7) attention to or provision of childcare services (Blume, 1986; Mandel & North, 1982; Naegle, 1988; Reed, 1985; Underhill, 1986). Art, music, poetry, dance, and body work, which build on women's expressive strengths, are useful tools in counseling (Reed, 1985). Finally, those working with addicted women need to be sensitive to gender and cultural issues, aware of community resources, and prepared to do outreach and referral (Reed, 1985).

TREATMENT ISSUES FOR WOMEN WITH A HISTORY OF SEXUAL VICTIMIZATION

A critical point of connection between eating-disordered and chemi-cally dependent women is that many (30 to 70 percent) have histories of sexual victimization (Root, 1989). The majority of clients who suffer simultaneously or sequentially from both eating disorders and addictions seem to have a history of sexual trauma (Root, 1989). Whether a woman suffers singly or simultaneously from eating disorders or addictions, if there is a history of sexual trauma, two special treatment issues must be considered. First, the counselor must be knowledgeable about the treatment of sexual abuse, which represents a specialty area within counseling. Second, the counselor must be aware of the issues involved in prioritizing treatment focuses for eating-disordered or addicted women with a history of sexual victimization.

Traditional alcoholism treatment, and some models of eating-disorder treatment, assume that treatment of the problem behavior should take priority. This strategy of establishing abstinence before treating sexual abuse issues may be detrimental and may set clients up for treatment failure (Root, 1989). Rather than requiring abstinence as a prerequisite to treatment of sexual abuse issues, treatment should focus on helping the client to develop new coping skills as she strives to reduce her addictive or eating-disordered behavior. Letting go of the eating or addictive behavior may result in an increase in intrusive and painful memories for many clients. It is thus important for counselors to warn clients about the potential effects of decreasing the behaviors. Treatment must acknowledge the need that sexual abuse survivors may have to maintain current ways of coping until other, more positive ways of dealing with the pain of the abuse are developed (Root, 1989). As abuse and posttraumatic stress symptom issues are addressed and new coping skills developed, there will be less need to rely on food and substances to cope. In sum, for women with a history of sexual victimization, substance abuse and eating disorders are best viewed and treated as a symptom of the primary problem of sexual trauma.

SUMMARY

Many women suffer from addictions and eating disorders. While these are separate disorders, the etiology of both is related to the status of women and the complexity of women's lives and roles in our culture. The relationship of these problems to societal messages, norms, and treatment of women cannot be denied. Similarly, the role of personal and relational factors must also be acknowledged. Effective treatment for both disorders must take a broad yet gender-related perspective. Effective treatment will not only result in a decrease in the problem behavior, but will help the client learn to love and value herself as a strong, capable woman, worthy of love and healthy self-nurturance.

THE EXAMPLE OF HELEN

Helen is a 28-year-old Caucasian woman who presented to our clinic with complaints of depression, vague feelings of uneasiness ("something just doesn't feel right"), and concerns about eating patterns. When questioned about these complaints, Helen stated that she felt constantly low and that she had been bingeing and purging a few times a week for the last two months. She stated that while she had been bingeing and purging sporadically for several years, she was feeling increasingly out of control with her eating, and the frequency of her binges and purges had recently increased dramatically.

At the close of her first session, Helen was asked to return for a two-hour structured eating-disorder intake. It was explained to her that this would be different from future sessions, but that it was necessary in order to gather more information so that treatment would be as effective as possible and tailored to her special needs.

During this intake, information regarding Helen's current situation was gathered. She was currently teaching English at a local junior high school and was very satisfied with her work. She stated that she had several close women friends, one of whom she had met in her inpatient alcohol treatment program, and who attended AA meetings with her. Finally, Helen stated that she had had a series of unsatisfying relationships with men and that she had recently broken up with a man.

During the intake, information regarding Helen's eating and weight history, medical history, drug and alcohol history, developmental history, family history, and sexual history was also gathered. She reported that she had always viewed herself as overweight and that she *hated* her hips and thighs. She also stated that she had been on a diet for as long as she could remember, and that she first began to binge and purge at age 18 during her first year of college. She stated that she was in good physical health, although she had never told a physician about her eating problems. She had been in an inpatient alcohol treatment program eight months ago, and was currently attending AA meetings once or twice a week. She also stated that her father, now deceased, had been an alcoholic and became violent when drinking. When directly questioned regarding sexual abuse, Helen stated that "once in a while when he was drunk, my dad would force me to do things, but it's in the past and is really no big deal and I don't want to focus on this."

After she disclosed her history of sexual abuse, Helen was told that the abuse was probably affecting her life and contributing to her issues with food, alcohol, and depression. She acknowledged that this might be true, but nonetheless stated that she did not want to deal with it in counseling right now. Therefore, the decision was made to focus initially on her eating and to establish a trusting relationship.

The physical complications associated with bulimia were explained to Helen, and she was referred to a local physician who was knowledgeable about eating disorders. It was decided that a psychiatric referral was not necessary at this time since the depression was not severe, and there were no other indicators of the need for psychotropic medication. After assessing Helen's knowledge regarding nutrition, it was decided that separate work with a nutritionist was also unnecessary at this time.

Since establishing trust and getting Helen's eating under control were the first treatment goals, she was asked to keep a log of binges, purges, and feelings preceding and following the binges and purges. These logs revealed a pattern of situational triggers in which the binge/purges occurred at home in the evening, when she was alone and feeling depressed or anxious. Treatment, therefore, focused on alternative coping strategies and thought patterns (i.e., cognitive and behavioral interventions).

During this period of treatment, time was also spent exploring early messages that Helen was given regarding her body, food, and being female in general. Because of her intense body-hatred, cognitive interventions and bibliotherapy aimed at body image and sociocultural pressures to attain an ideal body shape were utilized. It also became obvious that Helen had particularly low self-esteem and lacked assertion skills. Therefore, special attention was given to these areas, and she was helped to develop self-nurturant attitudes and behaviors.

After approximately six weeks of treatment, Helen's bingeing/purging decreased to around once per month and she reported feeling increased ability to control her eating. However, while she was using healthier coping to deal with her feelings, she continued to feel depressed and anxious, particularly at home alone at night. It was at this time that the subject of the sexual abuse was again broached, and Helen was told that this was a likely source of her continued anxiety and depression. She then agreed to focus on her family and abuse history.

As details of the abuse were discussed, Helen began to experience increased panic. During the most intense part of the counseling, she also experienced what she termed "backsliding"—during a two-week period, she got drunk twice and binged/purged three times. This was a crisis period during which Helen was seen for additional sessions. Her use of drinking and eating to cope were normalized, and attempts were made to reinforce healthier coping. She was also urged to use her social support, as she was tending to withdraw from her friends during this period. While this was the most difficult period during her counseling, she did continue to experience a number of periods of intense affect, during which her bingeing/purging would increase. While Helen had the urge to drink during these times, she did not.

After the most intense crisis period had passed, Helen was referred to and began to attend a local support group for incest survivors. Throughout counseling, she was also given several books to read, both on incest and eating issues. She reported getting a great deal of information and support from both the group and the books.

Counseling focused on the sexual abuse and eating for approximately two and a half years, at which time Helen felt more stable and wanted to "take a break from counseling." At the time of termination, she was not depressed, was not drinking, and had experienced four binge/purge-free months. She was warned that in periods of stress, she might be tempted to use eating as a coping strategy. Her new coping strategies were reinforced, and she was invited to contact the counselor at any time.

REFERENCES

Alexander, B. K., & Hadaway, P. F. (1982). Opiate addiction: The case for an adaptive orientation. *Psychological Bulletin, 92*, 367–381.

Allan, C. A., & Cooke, D. J. (1985). Stressful life events and alcohol misuse in women: A critical review. *Journal of Studies on Alcohol, 46*, 147–152.

American Psychiatric Association. (1987). *Diagnostic and statistical manual of mental disorders* (3rd ed. revised). Washington, DC: Author.

Ames, G. (1982). *Maternal alcoholism and family life: A cultural model for research and intervention.* Unpublished doctoral dissertation, University of California, Berkeley.

Barnett, R. C., & Baruch, G. K. (1985). Women's involvement in multiple roles: Role strain and psychological distress. *Journal of Personality and Social Psychology, 49*, 135–145.

Beckman, L. J. (1978). Sex role conflict in alcoholic women: Myth or reality. *Journal of Abnormal Psychology, 84*, 408–417.

Beckman, L. J. (1979). Reported effects of alcohol on the sexual feeling and behavior of women alcoholics and non-alcoholics. *Journal of Studies on Alcohol, 40*, 272–282.

Beckman, L. J., & Amaro, H. (1984). Patterns of women's use of alcohol treatment agencies. *Alcohol Health and Research World, 9*, 14–25.

Beckman, L. J., & Kocel, K. M. (1982). The treatment-delivery system and alcohol abuse in women: Social policy implications. *Journal of Social Issues, 38*, 139–151.

Benson, C. S., & Wilsnack, S. C. (1983). Gender differences in alcoholic personality characteristics and life expectancies. In W. M. Cox (Ed.), *Identifying and measuring alcoholic personality characteristics* (pp. 53–71). San Francisco: Jossey-Bass.

Beyer, J. M., & Trice, H. M. (1981). A retrospective study of similarities and differences between men and women employees in a job based alcoholism program from 1965–1977. *Journal of Drug Issues, 2*, 233–262.

Black, C. (1990). *Double duty.* New York: Ballantine Books.

Blume, S. B. (1986). Women and alcohol: A review. *Journal of the American Medical Association, 256,* 1467–1470.

Boskind-Lodahl, M. (1976). Cinderella's stepsisters: A feminist perspective on anorexia nervosa and bulimia. *Signs: Journal of Women in Culture and Society, 2,* 342–356.

Boskind-Lodahl, M., & White, W. C., Jr. (1978). The definition and treatment of bulimia anorexia in college women: A pilot study. *Journal of the American College Health Association, 27,* 84–86, 97.

Brice, G. (1981). Compulsive overeating: A personality profile. *Australian Journal of Clinical Hypnotherapy, 2,* 1–13.

Brisman, J., & Siegel, M. C. (1984). Bulimia and alcoholism: Two sides of the same coin. *Journal of Substance Abuse Treatment, 1,* 113–118.

Brown, L. S. (1985). Women, weight, and power: Feminist theoretical and therapeutic issues. *Women and Therapy, 4*(1), 61–71.

Bruch, H. (1973). *Eating disorders.* New York: Basic Books.

Bruch, H. (1978). *The golden cage.* New York: Random House.

Cattanach, L., & Rodin, J. (1988). Psychological social components of the stress process in bulimia. *International Journal of Eating Disorders, 7*(1), 75–88.

Coleman, E. (1987). Child physical and sexual abuse among chemically dependent individuals. *Journal of Chemical Dependency Treatment, 1,* 27–39.

Cooperstock, R., & Sims, M. (1971). Mood-modifying drugs presented in a Canadian city: Hidden problems. *American Journal of Public Health, 61,* 1001–1016.

Corrigan, E. M. (1980). *Alcoholic women in treatment.* New York: Oxford University Press.

Crandell, C. S. (1988). Social contagion of binge eating. *Journal of Personality and Social Psychology, 55,* 588–598.

Dahlgren, L. (1975). Special problems in female alcoholics. *British Journal of the Addictions, 70,* 18–23.

Dahlgren, L. (1978). Female alcoholics: III. Development and pattern of problem drinking. *Acta Psychiatrica Scandinavica, 57,* 325–335.

Dawkins, M. P., & Harper, F. D. (1983). Alcoholism among women: A comparison among black and white problem drinkers. *The International Journal of the Addictions, 18,* 333–349.

Dickenson, L. (1985). Anorexia nervosa and bulimia: A review of clinical issues. *Hospital and Community Psychiatry, 36,* 1086–1092.

Edwall, G. E., Hoffman, N. G., & Harrison, P. A. (1989). Psychological correlates of sexual abuse in adolescent girls in chemical dependency treatment. *Adolescence, 24,* 279–288.

Estep, R. (1987). The influence of the family on the use of alcohol and prescription depressants by women. *Journal of Psychoactive Drugs, 19,* 171–179.

Evans, S., & Schaefer, S. (1987). Incest and chemically dependent women: Treatment implication. *Journal of Chemical Dependency Treatment, 1,* 141–173.

Fillmore, K. M. (1984). When angels fall: Women's drinking as cultural preoccupation and reality. In S. C. Wilsnack & L. Beckman (Eds.), *Alcohol problems in women* (pp. 7–32). New York: Guilford Press.

Fortin, M. T., & Evans, S. B. (1983). Correlates of loss of control over drinking in women alcoholics. *Journal of Studies on Alcohol, 44,* 787–796.

Garfinkel, P., & Garner, D. (1982). *Anorexia nervosa: Multidimensional perspectives.* New York: Brunner/Mazel.

Garner, D., & Garfinkel, P. (1985). *Handbook of psychotherapy for anorexia nervosa and bulimia.* New York: Guilford Press.

Glantz, M. D., & Backenheimer, M. S. (1988). Substance abuse among elderly women. *Clinical Gerontologist, 8,* 3–26.

Gomberg, E. (1981). Women, sex roles, and alcohol problems. *Professional Psychology, 12,* 146–153.

Gomberg, E. (1986). Women: Alcohol and other drugs. *Drugs and Society, 1,* 75–109.

Gomberg, E., & Schilit, R. (1985). Social isolation and passivity of women alcoholics. *Alcohol and Alcoholism, 20,* 313–314.

Goodwin, D. W., Schulsinger, F., Knop, J., Mednick, S., & Guze, S. (1977). Alcoholism and depression in adopted-out daughters of alcoholics. *Archives of General Psychiatry, 34,* 751–755.

Gross, J., & Rosen, J. (1988). Bulimia in adolescents: Prevalence and psychosocial correlates. *International Journal of Eating Disorders, 7*(1), 51–61.

Henderson, D. C., & Anderson, S. C. (1982). Treatment of alcoholic women. *Focus on Women, 3,* 34–48.

Herman, J. (1981). *Father-daughter incest.* Cambridge, MA: Harvard University Press.

Hill, S. Y. (1980). Alcoholism introduction: The biological consequences. In *Research Monograph No. 1: Alcoholism and alcohol abuse among women* (pp. 45–62). National Institute on Alcohol Abuse and Alcoholism. Washington, DC: U.S. Government Printing Office.

Hoar, C. H. (1983). Women alcoholics: Are they different from other women? *International Journal of the Addictions, 18,* 251–270.

Jacobson, R. (1986). The contribution of sex and drinking history to the CT brain scan changes in alcoholics. *Psychological Medicine, 16,* 547–559.

Johnson, C. (1985). Initial consultation for patients with bulimia and anorexia. In D. M. Garner & P. E. Garfinkel (Eds.), *Handbook of psychotherapy for anorexia nervosa and bulimia* (pp. 19–54). New York: Guilford Press.

Johnson, N. S., & Holloway, E. L. (1988). Conceptual complexity and obsessionality in bulimic college women. *Journal of Counseling Psychology, 35,* 251–257.

Johnson, P. B. (1982). Sex differences, women's roles, and alcohol use: Preliminary, national data. *Journal of Social Issues, 38,* 93–116.

Kagle, J. (1987). Women who drink: Changing in ages, changing realities. *Journal of Social Work Education, 3,* 21–28.

Katz, J. L. (1990). Eating disorders: A primer for the substance abuse specialist. *Journal of Substance Abuse Treatment, 7,* 143–149.

Katzman, M. A., Weiss, L., & Wolchik, S. A. (1986). Speak don't eat! Teaching women to express their feelings. In D. Howard (Ed.), *Dynamics of feminist therapy.* New York: Haworth Press.

Katzman, M. A., & Wolchik, S. A. (1984). Bulimia and binge eating in college women: A comparison of personality and behavioral characteristics. *Journal of Consulting and Clinical Psychology, 52,* 423–428.

Kearny-Cook, A. (1988). Group treatment of sexual abuse among women with eating disorders. *Women and Therapy, 7*(1), 5–21.

Knupfer, G. (1982). Problems associated with drunkenness in women: Some research issues. In *NIAAA Alcohol and Health Monograph 4: Special population issue.* Rockville, MD: National Institute on Alcohol Abuse and Alcoholism.

Kroft, C., & Leichner, P. (1987). Sex-role conflicts in alcoholic women. *International Journal of the Addictions, 22,* 685–693.

Lacy, J. H., & Moureli, E. (1986). Bulimic alcoholics: Some features of a clinical subgroup. *British Journal of Addiction, 81,* 389–393.

Laidlaw, T. A. (1990). Dispelling the myths: A workshop on compulsive eating and body image. In T. A. Laidlaw & C. Malmo (Eds.), *Healing voices: Feminist approaches to therapy with women.* San Francisco: Jossey-Bass.

Litman, G. K. (1986). Women and alcohol problems: Finding the next questions. *British Journal of Addiction, 81,* 601–603.

Mandel, L., & North, S. (1982). Sex roles, sexuality, and the recovering woman alcoholic: Program issues. *Journal of Psychoactive Drugs, 14,* 163–166.

McCrady, S. B., & Sher, K. J. (1983). Alcoholism treatment approaches. *Medical and social aspects of alcohol abuse.* New York: Plenum.

McNamara, K., & Loveman, C. (1990). Differences in family functioning among bulimics, repeat dieters, and nondieters. *Journal of Clinical Psychology, 46,* 518–523.

Mintz, L. B., & Betz, N. E. (1988). Prevalence and correlates of eating disordered behavior among undergraduate women. *Journal of Counseling Psychology, 35,* 463–471.

Minuchin, S., Roseman, B., & Baker, B. (1978). *Psychosomatic families.* Cambridge, MA: Harvard University Press.

Mitchell, J. E., Hatsukami, D., Eckert, E. D., & Pyle, R. (1985). Characteristics of 275 patients with bulimia. *American Journal of Psychiatry, 142,* 482–485.

Mitchell, J. E., Hatsukami, D., Pyle, R. L., Eckert, E. D., & Davis, L. E. (1985). Intensive outpatient group treatment for bulimia. In D. M. Garner & P. E. Garfinkel (Eds.), *Handbook of psychotherapy for anorexia nervosa and bulimia* (pp. 240–256). New York: Guilford Press.

Mulford, H. A. (1977). Women and men problem drinkers: Sex differences in patients served by Iowa's community alcoholism centers. *Journal of Studies on Alcoholism, 38,* 1624–1639.

Muuss, R. E. (1986). Adolescent eating disorder: Bulimia. *Adolescence, 11,* 257–267.

Naegle, M. A. (1988). Substance abuse among women: Prevalence, patterns, and treatment issues. *Issues in Mental Health Nursing, 9,* 127–137.

Nerviano, V. J., & Gross, H. W. (1983). Personality types of alcoholics on objective inventories: A review. *Journal of Studies on Alcohol, 44,* 837–851.

O'Conner, J. J. (1984). Strategic individual psychotherapy with bulimic women. *Psychotherapy, 21*(4), 491–499.

Ogur, B. (1986). Long day's journey into night: Women and prescription drug abuse. *Women and Health, 11,* 99–115.

Orbach, S. (1979). *Fat is a feminist issue.* New York: Berkeley Books.

Perodeau, G. (1984, Fall). Married alcoholic women: A review. *Journal of Drug Issues,* 703–719.

Reed, B. G. (1985). Drug misuse and dependency in women: The meaning and implications of being considered a special population or minority group. *International Journal of the Addictions, 20,* 13–62.

Reed, B. G. (1987). Developing women-sensitive drug dependence treatment services: Why so difficult. *Journal of Psychoactive Drugs, 19,* 151–164.

Reed, B. G., & Leibson, E. (1981). Women clients in special women's demonstration drug treatment programs compared with women entering selected co-sex programs. *International Journal of the Addictions, 16,* 1425–1466.

Root, M. P. P. (1989). Treatment failures: The role of sexual victimization in women's addictive behavior. *American Journal of Orthopsychiatry, 59,* 542–549.

Rosser, W. W. (1981). Influence of physicians' gender in amitriptyline prescriptions. *Canadian Family Physicians, 27,* 1094–1097.

Roth, G. (1982). *Feeding the hungry heart.* New York: Signet Books.

Rybicki, D. J., Lepkowsky, G. M., & Arndt, S. E. (1989). An empirical assessment of bulimic patients using multiple measures. *Addictive Behaviors, 14,* 249–260.

Saunders, J. B., Davis, M., & Williams, R. (1981). Do women develop alcoholic liver disease more readily than men? *British Medical Journal, 282,* 1140–1143.

Schilit, R., & Gomberg, E. L. (1987, Summer). Social support structures of women in treatment for alcoholism. *Health and Social Work,* 187–195.

Schmidt, C., Klee, L., & Ames, G. (1990). Review and analysis of literature on indicators of women's drinking problems. *British Journal of Addiction, 85,* 179–192.

Schuckit, M. A., & Morrissey, E. R. (1976). Alcoholism in women: Some clinical and social perspectives with an emphasis on possible subtypes. In M. Greenblatt & M. A. Schuckit (Eds.), *Alcoholism problems in women and children* (pp. 5–35). New York: Grune and Stratton.

Schwartz, R. C., & Barrett, M. J. (1987). Women and eating disorders. *Journal of Psychotherapy and the Family, 3*(4), 131–144.

Schwartz, R. C., Barrett, M. J., & Saba, G. (1985). Family therapy for bulimia. In D. M. Garner & P. E. Garfinkel (Eds.), *Handbook of psychotherapy for anorexia nervosa and bulimia.* New York: Guilford Press.

Scida, J., & Vannicelli, M. (1979). Sex-role conflict and women's drinking. *Journal of Studies on Alcohol, 40,* 28–44.

Smead, V. S. (1984). Eating behaviors which may lead to and perpetuate anorexia nervosa, bulimarexia, and bulimia. *Women and Therapy, 3*(2), 37–49.

Squire, S. (1983). *The slender balance.* New York: Pinnacle Books.

Steiner-Adair, C. (1988). Developing the voice of the wise woman: College students and bulimia. *Journal of College Student Psychotherapy, 3*(2–4), 151–165.

Striegel-Moore, R. H., Silberstein, L. R., & Rodin, J. C. (1986). Toward an understanding of risk factors for bulimia. *American Psychologist, 41*(3), 246–263.

Stuart, G. W., Laraia, M., Ballenger, J. C., & Lydiard, R. B. (1990). Early family experiences of women with bulimia and depression. *Archives of Psychiatric Nursing, 4,* 43–52.

Thornton, C. I., & Carter, J. H. (1988). Treating the black female alcoholic: Clinic observations of black therapists. *Journal of the National Medical Association, 80,* 644–647.

Thornton, S. A. (1981). *An evaluation study of Women Incorporated: A substance abuse treatment program for females.* Unpublished doctoral dissertation, Boston University, Boston, MA.

Underhill, B. L. (1986, Fall). Issues relevant to aftercare programs for women. *Alcohol Health and Research World, 11,* 46–47.

Vannicelli, M. (1984). Treatment outcome of alcoholic women: The state of the art in relation to sex bias and expectancy effects. In S. C. Wilsnack & L. J. Beckman (Eds.), *Alcohol problems in women: Antecedents, consequences, and interventions* (pp. 369–412). New York: Guilford Press.

Wasnick, C., Schaffer, B., & Bencivengo, M. (1980, September). *The sex histories of fifty female drug clients.* Paper presented at the National Alcohol and Drug Coalition, Washington, DC.

Weiss, L., Katzman, M., & Wolchik, S. (1985). *Treating bulimia: A psychoeducational approach.* New York: Pergamon Press.

245

Weiss, L., Katzman, M., & Wolchik, S. (1986). You can't have your cake and eat it too: A program for controlling bulimia. Saratoga, CA: R & E Publishers.

Wilford, B. (1981). *Drug abuse: A guide for the primary care physicians.* Chicago, IL: American Medical Association.

Wilsnack, R. W., Wilsnack, S. C., & Klassen, A. D. (1986). Antecedents and consequences of drinking and drinking problems in women: Patterns from a U.S. national survey. *Nebraska Symposium on Motivation, 34,* 85–158.

Wilsnack, S. C. (1976). The impact of sex-roles on women's alcohol use and abuse. In M. Greenblatt & M. Schuckit (Eds.), *Alcoholism problems in women and children* (pp. 37–83). New York: Grune and Stratton.

Yandow, V. (1989). Alcoholism in women. *Psychiatric Annals, 19,* 243–247.

THE IMPACT OF INTERNALIZED MISOGYNY AND VIOLENCE AGAINST WOMEN ON FEMININE IDENTITY

Karen W. Saakvitne and Laurie Anne Pearlman

INTRODUCTION

As noted earlier in this book, violence against women occurs in the context of deeply rooted cultural beliefs about the relative value and power of women and men. Cultural misogyny, the pervasive devaluation of feminine traits and the hatred of women, is learned and internalized by men and by women in our society. Women, as well as men, then perpetuate misogyny through their interactions with girls and other women and through their judgments of themselves, which are formed on the basis of internalized misogyny and resultant shame. Misogyny both leads to and is reinforced by violence against women. This chapter addresses the cultural underpinnings of internalized misogyny, its implications for women's identity development and self-esteem, and the prevalence of violence against women. It attempts to integrate the current literature and to examine how women can begin to challenge and change societal and personal misogyny and thus counter the cultural acceptance of the inevitability of violence against women.

Theoretically, this chapter reflects the blend of interpersonal, object relational theories of personality development with the recognition of broader sociocultural influences that provide the context for each individual's development. This blend of individual psychodynamic psychology with social psychological context is described in more detail in constructivist self-development theory (McCann and Pearlman, 1990). In this chapter, the role of early key relationships in shaping later attitudes about oneself and others is discussed.

Finally, this chapter focuses on counseling and psychotherapy practice. Our extensive experience as clinical psychologists working with adult female survivors of sexual abuse and other emotional and physical violence is the basis for this discussion of both the context of women's lives and the role of counseling and the counselor in women's recovery from traumatic events.

THE CONTEXT FOR VIOLENCE AGAINST WOMEN

Teaching the Devaluation of Women

When she enters the world with a cry, a baby girl is still likely to be met with disappointment: "Oh, a girl," rather than the triumphant, "It's a boy!" In a society that values men and maleness, the simple fact of being female can set the stage for a lifetime of devaluation.

The cultural beliefs that permeate our surroundings shape our identities, which in turn shape our behaviors (Burke, Stets, & Pirog-Good, 1988; Stryker, 1980). Children born into a family and a culture that values them and all of their abilities and potentials will, over time, internalize this positive view, learn to value themselves, and develop positive self-esteem. Of course, the opposite is also true; a child born into a world that does not accept her, will, over time, come to devalue herself. When what is devalued is as central as the child's gender and all of its related meanings, the negative impact of this devaluation is pervasive; it permeates all aspects of the child's identity and experience of self, her behavior, and her interactions. Thus, in a society that often equates "feminine" with weak, passive, ineffectual, and inferior (Spence & Helmreich, 1978), women face a tremendous personal challenge in developing a positive sense of self.

The interpersonal relationships in which we learn about feminine roles, identities, and relative worth and power exist within a patriarchal society that values men over women. Both in intimate family settings and in the context of the larger culture, girls are given explicit and implicit messages about femininity that determine their concepts of what is normal and acceptable for females. They internalize society's models and rules and apply them to themselves. Violence against women is simply the end-point of a continuum of messages about gender that begins with the devaluation of femaleness. As Herman (1984) notes, the "pathology" of most sex offenders is "simply an exaggeration of accepted norms of male dominance" (p. 3), gender norms that are taught to everyone.

This teaching takes place consciously and unconsciously in all contexts, including family, community, school, media, and the larger society. Girls learn from men and women to denigrate their femaleness. A female's worth is always determined in relation to males; girls learn to evaluate and see themselves in relation to others in all environments. The negative cultural beliefs about femininity and femaleness are transmitted within families through acts of omission and commission: failure to encourage or active discouragement; a lack of compliments or cruel contempt; and behaviors that range from neglect to abuse (Russell, 1986). A girl learns as she observes her mother and other female relatives speak their minds or maintain silence, care for themselves or focus on others; as she sees them treated either with respect and love or with disrespect and violence by male family members (Chodorow, 1978).

As a child leaves home, opportunities arise for the messages that were learned at home to be either confirmed or contradicted. All the ways that girls are treated differently from boys and the overt and covert messages they are given are internalized as part of their female identity. When girls are given different toys, activities, or roles in games, they are being taught the limits of their abilities and options. "Don't do that; you'll get dirty"; "that's for boys"; "you're too little for that" are all very powerful messages to young girls.

Adults' responses to incidents of violence against or denigration of girls provide clear and powerful messages about girls' inherent worth and right to respect. The mother who discounts or disbelieves her daughter's reports of sexual abuse confirms the girl's fear that she is making trouble for the perpetrator or the family, who are more important and deserving of protection than she.

Messages in school about academic and nonacademic skills impart important values. Girls tend to become silenced by the time they reach junior high school (American Association of University Women, 1992; Gilligan, 1989); this silencing results from internalizing values that girls should not be too smart. Girls learn early that they need to protect male egos, and this lesson leads to later beliefs about interpersonal responsibility. Women are taught to feel responsible if they threaten men's egos or tempt men's libido or aggressions, as though a prime responsibility for women were to make men feel good about themselves, feel smart, strong, competent, and manly (Lerner, 1988). This understanding is consistent with the Stone Center for Development Services and Studies' view that women's lives have traditionally focused on facilitating the growth and development of others (Miller, 1987). Taken to an extreme, this orientation leads to women taking the blame for men's sexually assaultive behavior: "you wanted it"; "you shouldn't dress so seductively"; "you tempted him."

In the larger culture, feminine identity is taught through media portrayal of women and their contexts (i.e., societal institutions, the legal system, the government, employment patterns, and financial power) (Faludi, 1991; MacKinnon, 1989). American media are notorious for the paucity of positive role models for women. These media profit enormously from images of men perpetrating violence against women as entertainment, thus normalizing battering, assault, rape, and murder of women before millions of viewers daily.

Finally, the structure and organization of the culture teach girls that women are disempowered, that power is unfeminine, and that women should be grateful for what little power or control they have. It is as subtle as language use (Lakoff, 1975; Lerner, 1988) and as blatant as televised Senate hearings that discredit a woman's word against that of a prominent man.

Violence Against Girls and Women

It is a short step from pervasive devaluation of women to violence against them (Smith, 1990; Wertz, 1984). Given the generally sanctioned aggression in our society and the tendency for insecure dominant groups to devalue those who are different and then target these different others for violence (Staub, 1989), it follows that women are often the objects of verbal and physical assaults. Because the differences between men and women are based on sexual difference, and because sexuality is culturally linked to power, it is not surprising that these assaults are often sexual in nature (Scher & Stevens, 1987).

Violence against women is sanctioned by our patriarchal society at all levels and in countless ways (Hilberman, 1980; MacKinnon, 1989). These sanctions are evident in laws, policies, and social institutions, such as marriage (Haavind, 1984) and the church (Alsdurf, 1985), that perpetuate cycles of violence against women, but perhaps even more destructively in the lack of outrage and outcry, by either men or women, about sexual victimization of women. The passive acceptance of violence against women makes both the violence and its effects pernicious and difficult to address (Haavind, 1984; Swift, 1987).

Culturally sanctioned violence against children epitomizes devaluation and disrespect (Greven, 1991); sexual abuse of girls communicates powerful negative messages about vulnerability, sexuality, and femininity. According to Russell's (1984) excellent research, one in three women in the general population has unwanted sexual experiences before the age of 18, and most of the abusers are male. In addition, almost as many girls as boys are victims of nonsexual physical abuse (Finkelhor, 1979, 1984; Straus & Gelles, 1986); much of the physical and sexual abuse occurs within the context of emotional abuse and neglect (Vissing, Straus, Gelles, & Harrop, 1991).

To the extent that this abuse is ignored, denied, or even sanctioned by society, its meanings are incorporated with little questioning into the female child's sense of herself as unworthy, toxic, bad, or dirty. The specific meanings of sexual abuse often include the sense that one's sexuality and gender are shameful, that being female is the reason for being abused.

The violence does not stop with assaults against children. Adult women face a 25 percent chance of being raped at some time during their lives (Russell, 1984). Over 2 million women were battered by their spouses in 1985 (Straus & Gelles, 1986). In this society, women cannot move about freely, either outside or within their homes, without risking sexual and other physical assault (Browne, 1987).

Women come to accept the inevitability of violence and the restrictions of living in fear (Gordon & Riger, 1989) without a sense of outrage, because of the social context that condones violence against women (Haavind, 1984). Both men's and women's views of women contribute to the perpetuation of violence against women. The subtle social sanctioning of victim-blaming is found in such widely held assumptions as "people get what they deserve," which Lerner and Miller (1978) term the "just world" hypothesis. For victims of sexual assault, this attribution quickly translates into guilt, shame, and rage at oneself (Burke et al., 1988; Kristiansen & Giulietti, 1990; Roth & Lebowitz, 1988).

THE MALE VIEW OF WOMANHOOD: HOW DO MEN SEE WOMEN?

The patriarchal culture that provides the broad context of our lives informs fundamental assumptions about the relative importance of women's and men's needs. Because of the greater valuing of men, men learn that they are entitled and expected to want and wield power over others, especially women (see O'Neil and Egan's chapter).

While this imbalance certainly has many etiological threads, one important psychological thread is a deep, strong fear of powerful women. Several authors have written about the difficulties faced by the developing male child as he struggles to separate from his mother to form his own, separate male identity (Chodorow, 1989; Rubin, 1983). The terror this boy experiences as he struggles against the possibility that his individuation may not succeed, as well as the rage he may feel at the necessity of separating from the mother and her resources, can readily transform into hatred of the powerful mother. The developmental task requires him to recognize his differences from his mother and reconcile the narcissistic loss—that he is not and can never be the same as her. In addition, he must reconcile his adoration and idealization of her with his growing awareness of the cultural devaluation of women.

This complicated separation and individuation process can often result in conscious and unconscious envy, devaluation, and hatred of women. While the process of male individuation and identity development differs for each boy, depending on many developmental variables, one common shaping factor is the patriarchal and misogynist culture in which this development takes place (Spretnak, 1983). This culture and its values clearly inform the resolution of identity and separation issues for men as well as women.

The culture of boys is one in which girls and women are denigrated. The classic locker-room talk that objectifies and maligns women is a developmental ritual through which few men pass unaffected. In certain subcultures (e.g., male adolescents) and situations (e.g., men in an all-male work situation), to refrain from deriding women or girls conveys an impression of weakness or, even worse in a homophobic society, emasculation.

This process results in a variety of personality characteristics in men. Part of the fallout of deep-seated misogyny is that men come to despise their own more feminine characteristics, such as vulnerability, sensitivity, tender feelings (or in many cases, feelings in general), creativity, and nurturing. Many men have difficulty accepting their own need for connection and, repeating the childhood pattern, despise and reject the women who love them and upon whom they depend in adulthood.

Quite understandably, these characteristics lead to relationship difficulties. Women often complain about husbands who won't talk to them, can't express their feelings, and treat them disrespectfully, and about a society in which men assault women verbally, physically, and sexually. Recent theory and research suggest that abusive men are those who are least secure in their own male gender identities (Groth & Burgess, 1980).

HOW DO WOMEN SEE THEMSELVES?

A woman in this culture internalizes a sense of self as "less than," a sense of herself as "only a woman." She develops a deep, internalized, at least partly unconscious hatred and denigration of her femaleness.

This internalized misogyny is the single most powerful weapon against women in this culture. It is through this deep self-hatred and woman-hatred that as women we fail one another. We agree with men in blaming and devaluing women. Internalized misogyny plays a critical role in the perpetuation of violence against women.

HOW INTERNALIZED MISOGYNY
PERPETUATES VIOLENCE AGAINST WOMEN

Often women—mothers, grandmothers, and others—are the central purveyors of the male culture, and their teachings are based on internalized misogyny. Adult women do not know how to teach girls to love in themselves that which adult women have learned to fear and hate: their femininity, their femaleness, their feminine powers.

How does this teaching actually work? First, through women's roles with each other, they convey beliefs about feminine role expectations. Mothers are powerful role models, and mothers' self-esteem and ability to value aspects of their daughters' femininity indelibly affect daughters' beliefs about womanhood. Therefore, the seeds of victimization can be planted in subtle ways in the early maternal relationship. This can occur through mothers' violence toward daughters, a subject about which research and writing are just beginning to appear (Allen, 1990; Sroufe & Ward, 1980); through their inability to protect their daughters from violence; through their active denigration of their daughters; through their denigration of themselves; through their depression, paralysis, low self-esteem, and fears; through their own victimization at the hands of a violent spouse or partner, or at the hands of a denigrating social or employment system. Both active assaults and passive modeling of self-disrespect contribute to a mother's lessons to her daughter about shame and femininity.

What women teach and fail to teach is influenced by their own fear and ignorance. For example, many mothers fail to teach their daughters about their bodies; mothers name boys' external genitals, but for girls, they name only the vagina, an internal, unseeable organ, failing to give names to the seeable, touchable vulva, clitoris, and labia (Lerner, 1988). This omission gives a fundamental message of shame and mystery about a female body. On a more general level, failures to question limited role choices for girls, or to encourage girls to speak out, to take chances, to know their strength and competence, and to value their intuition and capacities to connect, nurture, and create also teach girls silence and shame. Women fail in their formal and informal education of girls to value women's ways of knowing (Belenky, Clinchy, Goldberger, & Tarule, 1986) and their unique capacities. The route to self-pride is not for a woman to be more like a man; positive self-esteem requires valuing oneself as a woman and the unique gifts one has as a woman.

WOMEN'S SUSCEPTIBILITY TO VIOLENCE

Internalized misogyny plays a critical role in the perpetuation of violence against women in several ways. The more negative a woman's relationship to herself as a woman is, the more susceptible she can be to assault, both from herself and from others. One area of assault commonly seen in women clients is self-loathing. A woman's internalized misogyny emerges consciously as pervasive shame, hatred of her female body, low self-esteem, a view of herself as damaged and inadequate, a sense of uncontrollable vulnerability, and a belief that she deserves abuse and contempt, all because she is female. This unquestioned self-denigration is seen clearly in many clients who are survivors of sexual abuse.

In addition to these psychological assaults, women learn to assault themselves physically. Internalized misogyny is an important component and etiological factor in such self-destructive behaviors as harmful dieting (Spitzack, 1992), anorexia and bulimia, excessive plastic surgery, substance abuse, and the more widely recognized self-mutilative behaviors of cutting, burning, and self-battery. These self-assaults set the stage for and maintain a woman's identity as a deserving victim of abuse; one's self-esteem and self-care inform the standard of care one expects from others.

Another realm of women's violence toward women is evident in lesbian battering relationships. Lesbians are subjected not only to cultural misogyny but also to cultural homophobia. They are silenced, made invisible, and isolated. When they internalize misogyny, they can project their self-hatred onto or take out their frustration and discontent on their partners.

Because of their internalized misogyny, women are also susceptible to violence from others. Rape, battering, childhood sexual abuse, and femicide (the murdering of women) provide violent, vivid lessons in women's powerlessness and female shame. Both childhood and adult victimization create and reinforce internalized shame and hatred for femininity. Femaleness is causally associated with vulnerability to harm, rape, and humiliation and therefore is experienced as hateful and dangerous. Many adult survivors of sexual assault have profoundly conflicted feelings about their femaleness; many try to deny feminine aspects of the self. Sometimes this conflict is conscious, but often it is an unconscious, automatic process of negative gender identity.

As a woman learns to expect and anticipate abuse, she is less likely to protect herself. The lack of natural self-protective responses of "signal anxiety," outrage, and the feeling that one is entitled to respect makes a woman more vulnerable to sexual harassment, denigration, verbal abuse, battery, acquaintance rape, and emotional abuse. If a woman has little or no access to a sense of power or entitlement as a woman, she has little defense against such unacknowledged violence. In fact, she is unconsciously resigned to accepting the inevitability of such abuse and the role of victim of predictable violence. The fact that women's power is often seen by women as unfeminine and therefore is degraded reflects the effects of internalized denial of women's strengths and rights.

This culture has traditionally held women responsible for their sexual victimization, blaming the victim for her own rape, battering, and sexual harassment (Ryan, 1971). Women are not responsible for men's actions against them; no one is responsible for another's violence toward her. Women need to believe and teach one another that they are entitled to respect and safety and that they do not deserve denigration and violence. We want to be very clear that we are not blaming women for their victimization; rather, we are supporting women's power to know how they are victimized and how they are taught to accept victimization in a misogynist culture, and we are supporting women's rights and power to question and reject those teachings.

A related issue is the invitation for women to blame other women, one form of which is "mother-bashing." Women have often been invited (not infrequently in the context of counseling or therapy) to blame their negative childhood experiences and low self-esteem on their mothers alone without stepping back to look at the larger picture (Herman & Lewis, 1986). If women fail to understand the context in which their mothers developed their self-concept and beliefs about feminine identity, they cannot truly know themselves and their historical roots. Truly, mothers can inflict serious hurt on their daughters. Mothers can be both consciously and unconsciously hurtful, malicious, and cruel. Mothers can incestuously abuse their daughters (Allen, 1990). However, mothers are also products of a misogynist culture, who teach their daughters only what they know. By experiencing grief for their mothers, women can be freed to claim more entitlement than their mothers were allowed rather than having to continue the cycle of deprivation, guilt, and resentment.

The unconscious association of femaleness with victimization and weakness is consistent with another common sequela to abuse, the need to dissociate and remain in confusion. In fact, the edict to remain unaware of one's experience of abuse, which is so clearly evident in women who have been traumatized, is a critical part of women's powerlessness and oppression. Notably, it is a central feature in the diagnosis of hysteria, so much more commonly assigned to women. This unawareness reflects cultural prohibitions against women's knowledge and awareness. For survivors of child abuse, this edict is disturbingly familiar, as it echoes their families' pathological, pathogenic denial. When a child cannot know that her sexual abuse was wrong, she decides that *she* is wrong and bad in order to make sense of her discomfort and pain. When she cannot know that the abuse occurred, she must dissociate and deny in order to survive. When she cannot know that incest had any effect or meaning for her, she attributes all her feelings and behaviors to being crazy.

PSYCHOLOGICAL CONSEQUENCES OF VIOLENCE

The specific psychological sequelae of sexual violence are only now being investigated systematically. The consequences of this violence range from acute psychiatric and physical symptoms, including those encompassed by the Diagnostic and Statistical Manual of Mental Disorders (DSM-III-R) (American Psychiatric Association, 1987) diagnosis of posttraumatic stress disorder, to changes in fundamental ways of experiencing oneself and the world (McCann & Pearlman, 1990). In fact, numerous recent research reports indicate that 43 to 96 percent of individuals in various psychiatric treatment samples have a history of childhood sexual or physical abuse (Coons, Bowman, & Milstein, 1988; Herman, Perry, & van der Kolk, 1989; Jacobson & Richardson, 1987; Mas, 1992; Mills, Rieker, & Carmen, 1984; Westen, Ludolph, Misle, Ruffins, & Block, 1990). These patients' diagnoses include borderline personality disorder, multiple personality disorder, posttraumatic stress disorder, dissociative disorders, major depression, and schizophrenia. Indeed, many of these patients (mainly women) have been given multiple diagnoses; our inability to perceive and acknowledge the underlying trauma has left counselors and clients with a list of symptoms without a sensible framework. The massive assault that childhood sexual abuse inflicts upon the developing self has a formative role in disrupted abilities to tolerate strong affect, to moderate self-loathing, and to maintain a sense of connection with others, as well as shaping distorted psychological needs and disrupted beliefs about self and others (McCann & Pearlman, 1990).

Because of the pervasiveness of sexual violence against women, many women seeking psychotherapy or counseling will have experienced sexual violations in childhood or adulthood, whether or not they view these violations as the reason for seeking treatment. The wide variety of presenting problems that may relate to a history of sexual abuse is a reflection of individual differences in adaptation. Individuals presenting for counseling or therapy may demonstrate difficulties in any or all of the following five areas: cognitive, behavioral, emotional, biological, and interpersonal (McCann, Sakheim, & Abrahamson, 1988). Some of the most common psychological problems in female survivors of violence include depression, eating disorders, substance abuse, dissociation, low self-esteem, difficulties in interpersonal relationships, sexual dysfunction, and anxiety (Gelinas, 1983). In addition, many women present initially through medical clinics with a variety of physical symptoms (Hilberman, 1980).

In addition to these clinical symptoms, women experience a wide variety of more generalized aftereffects of victimization as they try to understand and cope with their traumatic experiences. These aftereffects are more fully described elsewhere (McCann & Pearlman, 1990). Of particular interest here are those that relate to the disruptions in a woman's meaning system, or frame of reference.

Disruptions in frame of reference include distorted beliefs about oneself, or identity, and about others, or worldview. Examples of these disrupted schemas might include the belief that a woman is responsible for her victimization, that women are inferior, that men are entitled to more esteem than women, that women are fated for tragedy, that the world is fundamentally malevolent, and that the future is bleak. The implications of these beliefs are evident in women's life choices and their relations with self and others.

IMPLICATIONS FOR COUNSELING

Working With Survivors of Violence

Perhaps the most significant part of healing for all victims of violence, including adult survivors of sexual trauma, is the creation of meaning in their lives, the transformation of the victimization into something different, a development beyond the self. For women in counseling, this process can include understanding their individual experience to be part of a larger context—the political, social, and familial context of women's lives (Laidlaw, Malmo, and Associates, 1990). For many, this process also includes a spiritual or transpersonal component, allowing oneself to be open to joy, hope, gratitude, wonder, forgiveness, love, faith. The specific forms this component takes, as with all aspects of treatment, depend upon the individual client. To neglect this component of recovery, however, may be to abandon clients at the threshold of true transformation, as well as to deprive counselors of one of the most rewarding aspects of doing trauma work.[1]

When the client herself holds a devalued view of womanhood, what are the tasks and strategies for the counselor? To begin with, the role of a counselor is to invite the woman client to notice and know what she believes about women. This includes, over time, identifying the components of her ego ideal, what kind of woman she wants to be. Self-esteem issues can be looked at in the context of a feminine ego ideal; a client's self-esteem is the result of her comparison between who she thinks she is and who she wants to be.

One step in this process is for the client to notice what she has been taught about being female, particularly what messages she heard within her family about femaleness. This process includes examining what she has been taught by observing her mother and remembering the messages, implicit and explicit, given by her mother and other members of her family. Once a client has been given permission to notice these messages, long ago internalized, she can begin to reinterpret her personal history and reevaluate her beliefs.

This awareness allows her to work toward developing a more positive internal ego ideal of self as woman. In this process, a client will need to examine her underlying negative assumptions about femaleness and her feminine identity. This examination often involves reframing womanly aspects of the self as positive rather than negative attributes, for example, seeing "dependency" as a press for connection rather than as weakness (Surrey, 1985) and feelings as strengths rather than liabilities. Many childhood beliefs and myths are called into question in this process. The work may take considerable time, as the client is being asked to reconsider her most fundamental beliefs.

The role of the counselor in this process is critical and varies according to gender. A woman counselor is first and foremost a role model. She treats herself and her clients with respect and gentle strength. This means she is able to protect herself by maintaining

---

[1] We thank Dr. Leslie Nowinski for her thoughts on the place of spirituality in psychotherapy with incest survivors.

appropriate boundaries and limits, and she is able to value her women clients as women. Further, a woman counselor is inevitably called upon to rework some of the client's historical interactions with maternal figures. This role includes giving permission and valuing the client's feminine qualities—liveliness, rebelliousness, and uniqueness. It is important to emphasize that a woman counselor must examine these issues in her own life, or else she will unconsciously repeat to her clients the negative messages she may have received. This work asks a counselor to give permission to her clients that may well have been denied her in her own childhood.

For male counselors, the task is complicated in different ways. Again, a woman client will look to the male counselor expecting to hear both in the present and transferentially from the past familiar messages about her worth and loveability as a female. The client will assume that the counselor will require her to sacrifice herself or parts of herself to protect his esteem and power just as the culture has taught her. A male counselor must be unconflictedly supportive of a woman client's move toward self-focus and self-acceptance. The counselor's capacity to take delight in his client developing a positive sense of self as a woman is a powerful component of the therapeutic holding environment. His support for the client's quest for knowledge and personal power inherently mitigates against a culture that denies both. For the male counselor, this work will stir his own identity issues and beliefs about himself in relation to women.

In addition to providing a positive nurturing environment for this growth, a male counselor must actively notice assumptions the woman client brings into the relationship. By trying to make conscious and open to observation assumptions that are unconscious and automatic, he breaks the cycle of silent acceptance and invites the client together with him to rethink gender stereotypes. Again, when he is invited to reinforce messages received from important males in his client's past, he can notice with her what she has learned about herself as a female in these important early relationships.

Both male and female counselors and therapists need to reexamine their own gender socialization and beliefs in this process. No one is immune to internalized stereotypes about gender roles learned from a patriarchal society that fears feminine power and characteristics. This task is not an easy one, and counselors need support to question such basic assumptions about identity and self-worth. Only if counselors have the courage to do so can they be reasonable guides for clients engaged in this important and challenging process.

Finally, it is important to address issues of internalized misogyny in counseling with women who have been victims of violence, whether from childhood or adult abuse. However, on a cautionary note, a counselor meeting with a survivor of severe childhood abuse needs to be aware that treatment can be lengthy and difficult. Some clients present with a complicated diagnostic constellation and severe symptomatology and distress. These clients may need to be referred to an experienced psychotherapist trained in trauma therapy.

Of course, the first priority in working with victims of violence must be their safety and stabilization. Once the client is in a safe physical environment and her acute symptoms have been addressed, the counseling can move to an exploration of the social, cultural, and personal meanings of violence and of her womanhood. From the beginning, counseling should focus on examining the counseling relationship—the ways the client experiences the counselor's responses to her, including both transferences from earlier relationships and the current realities of this counseling relationship. Counseling provides the opportunity for the client to rework her experiences with men and women in authority, to learn to accept her need for support, and to develop a feeling of safety in a significant one-to-one relationship. Over time, the client can internalize the counselor's respect and concern for her, although this process may take a very long time in incest survivors, whose trust has been deeply violated by others who purported to care for them (Saakvitne, 1990).

When working with a trauma survivor client, a counselor must always be sensitive to the unique meanings of the traumatic events for the individual client. While the literature often lists characteristic responses of all trauma survivors, incest survivors, rape victims, and so forth (Burgess & Holmstrom, 1974; Finkelhor & Browne, 1986; Gelinas, 1983), it is important to remember that every individual will experience and understand her life experiences in the context of her own history, personality, social-cultural context, and circumstances (McCann and Pearlman, 1990). The counselor must listen for her story; what about her experiences was traumatic, important, and meaningful to her?

Gradually, references or a notable absence of references to a client's identity as a woman and her beliefs about women and men will emerge. Over time, as the counselor and client explore these issues in the context of identity, esteem, trust, intimacy, control, and safety (constructivist self-development theory, McCann & Pearlman, 1990), they can explore the role of traumatic events, sexual and physical violence, in the formation of her beliefs and feminine identity.

Female survivors of childhood sexual abuse learn about relationships and themselves in relation to others from their experiences. Thus, a survivor may deduce from her experience that she can only get her affectional needs met by being sexual, or by being hurt. Another woman may believe that love equals sex and that she has to pay the price of sex in order to be held. When a child is humiliated, hurt, and denigrated as part of the abuse, she may come to believe that she deserves such treatment because she is female. Another may believe that being female made her vulnerable to abuse and may come to hate her femaleness. She may try to eradicate her womanliness by starving herself to destroy physical evidence of femaleness or by covering her feminine body in a layer of disguising fat or baggy, nondescript clothes. She may behave in ways that deny vulnerability or allow her to forget that she has a gender. These patterns need to be opened up for exploration in the context of a safe, respectful counseling relationship. It is impossible to resolve issues of self-esteem and self-loathing when someone despises her gender, a basic component of identity. Reclaiming a right to a positive feminine identity is part of the task of psychotherapy for survivors of childhood sexual abuse.

Of course, one major task of the therapeutic work with a survivor is to uncover, explore, challenge, and eventually change pervasive negative beliefs or schemas about women and womanhood.

This work involves the counselor posing gentle challenges to those beliefs that impede the client's growth; helping the client experience herself and her relation to others differently in the counseling relationship; identifying and creating opportunities for positive experiences of self and others outside of counseling; and working with the client to find new meaning in her life. This work requires an exploration not only of the personal and cultural origins of the client's self-denigrating and anti-female beliefs, but also the self-protective functions of these beliefs. How does a woman's self-blame protect her connection to others? Schemas or beliefs which seem negative or distorted to the counselor must not be challenged prematurely or without a solid understanding of their adaptive value for this client; to do so would be an empathic failure. In this process counselor and client begin to assess the costs these beliefs impose on the woman and her development. What would be the implications of shifting these beliefs to view the perpetrator as guilty? What might be lost? The self loathing experienced by many women and the cultural messages not to know, not to feel the losses, not to acknowledge their truths are powerful, and they make the counseling process frightening and often threatening. Changes in frame of reference are painful, even if ultimately liberating.

In working with women in counseling on issues related to feminine identity and sexual violence, the counselor's task with respect to men's internalized misogyny is to help the woman recognize and place it in a context. This is not to say that violence against women or misogyny is acceptable. Rather, women can become stronger self-advocates and develop more positive relationships with men if they learn to understand the roots of male attitudes and behaviors. To move beyond hating men, women must understand the deep-seated fears underlying male misogyny. In this process, the female client must also come to terms with the implications of her new realizations. Women may experience a great sense of loss, underlying their own rage, about living in a culture, and perhaps in a relationship, that despises powerful women. However, the understanding of context allows her to work toward change by addressing the central underlying issues. The grief may be intense as a woman comes to understand the implications of being hated for something she would like to learn to cherish: her femininity and her strength.

SUMMARY

Violence against women occurs in a cultural context of devaluation of femininity. This devaluation is shared by men and women and passed from one to another in a variety of ways. Misogyny is thus internalized by both sexes and creates the foundation for the epidemic of violence against women in this culture. Violation is not limited to physical and sexual assaults, but includes emotional and spiritual assaults on self-worth and personhood through devaluation and apathy (Shengold, 1989). Psychological abuse damages women profoundly and contributes significantly to their vulnerability to physical and sexual violence and violation (A. Miller, 1983; J.B. Miller, 1988), which then further damages women's self-esteem and identity. This cycle of misogyny starts at birth and is perpetuated throughout a woman's life; its effects, however, can be mitigated by making the process conscious and by challenging the negative assumptions, beliefs, and identity components.

An understanding of misogyny then provides the basis for any psychotherapy and the context through which a counselor and a client understand her identity and experience (Laidlaw et al., 1990). Within the safety and respect of the therapeutic relationship, a client can herself identify the cultural and familial context for both her feminine identity and her relationship to herself as a woman. As she recognizes the range of messages she has received and internalized about her gender, she can actively question, challenge, and rework her negative internalized assumptions. This process allows a woman to develop an alternative self-concept and feminine ego ideal.

This examination of feminine identity is, of course, not the only aspect of treatment with an abuse survivor or a victim of violence. However, it is a crucial component of such counseling. In the process of creating meaning from experience, female victims of violence develop stable identities and worldviews that themselves perpetuate victimization and self-hatred. The trauma of violence against women always includes the meaning of being a woman, and that meaning must be examined as part of the healing process.

THE EXAMPLE OF DARLENE

Darlene is a 30-year-old white single woman presenting with issues of low self-esteem, parenting difficulties with her son, and despair. (Note: this case description represents a composite of many people with whom we have worked over the years and does not reflect any specific person.) In her family of origin, she is the youngest of four children. Darlene's mother was a homemaker whom Darlene describes as alternately available and somewhat supportive, and depressed and angry. Their conflicts intensified during Darlene's adolescence. Years later Darlene learned that her mother was sexually abused by her maternal uncle in childhood. Darlene's father was a career military officer whom Darlene describes as strict, running the family in an efficient, military way. She constantly yearned for his approval, which he rarely expressed. Darlene was sexually abused by her oldest brother from ages 8 through 15. The boys were all physically abused by the father, and the youngest brother was also abused by the older two boys, especially when he stood up for his sister.

At 17, Darlene became pregnant; she married and left her parents' home. Her husband was emotionally immature, alternately dependent and explosive and episodically physically abusive. She worked part-time as a nurse's aide while raising their son. When Darlene was 27, her husband hit their 9-year-old son when he was enraged with her for attending to her son's needs before his own. This event prompted Darlene to leave her husband; she and her son went to a battered women's shelter. The shelter staff referred her for counseling because of their concerns about Darlene's low self-esteem and her parenting difficulties with her son.

Darlene described herself as "a marginal person living a marginal life." She viewed herself as an inevitable and probably deserving victim in any interpersonal relationship or situation. Although she liked her work, she struggled to get through each day and had no sense of meaning or purpose in her life. She was surprised when another woman at the shelter said Darlene had helped her by talking to her. She acknowledged that she worked hard at her job, but was very self-critical and therefore surprised when she received praise from her supervisors or patients.

Her son was extremely important to her, but she worried constantly about him and about her parenting. She found him difficult to control and worried that she was both too critical of him and too permissive with him; although she could be harshly critical, she had great difficulty saying no to him. He was often disrespectful to her and would ignore her or walk away when she was speaking, which enraged her and increased her self-criticism.

Darlene had no positive sense of herself as a woman. She tended to dress in drab, functional clothes, and was critical of her looks and her weight, describing her average-sized body as "gross and fat" and her delicate features as "mousy and unattractive." She envied women who seemed self-confident, but was also contemptuous of women in general, feeling they were fundamentally weak and vulnerable. She had two close women friends whom she had known since high school, and she knew one woman at work with whom she talked. In general, Darlene viewed the world as an unsafe, difficult place and believed that people were usually untrustworthy, out for themselves, and often actively malevolent. She had a chronic sense of vulnerability, stating early in therapy that she felt there was no safe place for her, physically or emotionally.

At the same time, she did not feel she could rely on herself or her judgment. She had often placed herself and her son at risk by relying on people who ultimately harmed her. Her self-esteem was very low and she experienced intense self-loathing at times, culminating in despair and shame. She was frightened of her strong feelings and tried to keep herself calm by staying numb or keeping busy. She had little sense of her interpersonal resources, either internally or externally. When in distress, she could not imagine a comforting connection with anyone; she felt utterly alone and believed that it was up to her to manage whatever she was feeling.

Darlene's initial statement to her female counselor was, "I don't see how you can help me. It's hopeless. I'm probably a hopeless case."

She appeared demoralized and depressed. The therapy focused first on assessing her safety and setting a frame for the therapy relationship. The counselor established that Darlene's living situation was physically safe and that she was not in danger of harming herself. The shelter staff was working on problems of daily living, such as helping Darlene find a safe place to live, manage her finances, and get her son settled into a new school. Darlene assumed that her counselor was the authority and would tell her what she had done or was doing wrong and then tell her what to do. She was bewildered and uncomfortable when the counselor invited her to talk about what she noticed and felt, wanted, and needed from the counselor. The counselor explained the process of psychotherapy and addressed the structure and frame of their relationship.

An early challenge in this therapy was helping Darlene develop a sense of confidence and trust in the counselor. Darlene expected the counselor to criticize her for her difficulties, agree that she was a hopeless case, and abandon her by refusing to work with her anymore. Slowly Darlene experimented with allowing herself to rely on the counselor. She considered using the counselor as a resource, for example, trying to think of her counselor and their conversations when feeling alone and overwhelmed.

As Darlene's confidence in herself and in the therapeutic relationship grew, her counselor was gradually able to draw their attention to Darlene's attitudes about herself, which stemmed from her experiences as a girl and as a woman. She remembered how her father expressed contempt for women, whom he described as "stupid, self-centered, and worthless." She remembered her mother's self-criticism and her passivity in the face of her father's verbal abuse. Her mother would always support her father or her brothers over Darlene, saying, "That's just the way men are; we have to humor them," which was what her mother had learned in her old-world family of origin. Through these family attitudes and as a result of her own sexual abuse, Darlene had come to feel that women were weak and contemptible and that power resided with men, an observation that was reinforced by the predominance of men in power in the military context of her development, as well as in the larger society.

She explored the lessons she had learned about herself, her feminine identity, and her relationships in the context of sexual abuse by her brother. She recognized how desperately she had needed approval and nurturance at that time in her life, and eventually she empathized with herself as a young girl facing an impossible dilemma of being required to suffer violation to get what little attention was available in a critical and violent family. As she allowed herself to forgive herself, she was able to acknowledge her anger at and disappointment in her brother. In time, she decided to talk to him about her feelings, and she felt empowered by her ability to break the family silence.

The therapy provided Darlene with opportunities to experience a woman counselor who was a positive role model, who was nurturing and supportive while self-confident and clear about boundaries. As Darlene was able to notice what she admired and liked about the counselor, she began to experiment herself with different ways of being. One day when she came to session wearing a colorful new dress, she commented on how she liked her counselor's use of color in her wardrobe. She was moved by her counselor's admiration of her newfound ability to experiment with self-image, and she remembered how critical and envious her mother had been of any of Darlene's attempts to be pretty or feminine. She began to think about and ultimately question the messages she received, and continued to give herself, about liking her body, her right to experience pleasure, and her right to enjoy being a woman.

As Darlene's trust grew, she became able to consider that she herself might have some positive qualities, for example, that her ability to nurture her son was valuable rather than, in her husband's words, "pitiful babying." She felt more comfortable requiring that her son treat her and himself with respect and dignity, and she was able to set appropriate boundaries and limits with him as well as with friends and colleagues. She accepted a promotion to a full-time supervisory position at work and was able to explore her fear of her counselor's anger or envy about her success. She realized that she had never felt supported by anyone for her successes as a professional woman and therefore had learned to fear success as leading to rejection. As she experimented with ways of asserting her abilities and her power, she came to understand the profound disempowerment of her girlhood context.

She came to understand the context for her intense feelings of shame and self-loathing and began to take in her counselor's gentle approval and permission giving. She started to preface positive self statements with, "I thought about what you would say." She found herself able to reach out to women friends differently, and she was pleased to notice how she could get her needs met in these relationships in ways she had never thought were possible.

In summary, over the course of about three years, Darlene dealt with issues of self-esteem and despair as they related to her personal context of sexual and emotional abuse as well as the larger social context. Her parenting ability improved, and she was able to develop more fulfilling relationships with women and men based on mutual respect and appreciation. Through her relationship with her female counselor, she was able to explore her feelings about herself as a woman and about women in general and to avail herself of the interpersonal context of her world in new and different ways.

REFERENCES

Allen, C. A. (1990). Women as perpetrators of child sexual abuse: Recognition barriers. In A. L. Horton, B. L. Johnson, L. M. Roundy, & D. Williams (Eds.), *The incest perpetrator: A family member no one wants to treat* (pp. 108–125). Newbury Park, CA: Sage.

Alsdurf, J. M. (1985, Winter). Wife abuse and the church: The response of pastors. *Response*, 9–11.

American Association of University Women (1992, Spring). *AAUW Outlook*. Washington, DC: AAUW.

American Psychiatric Association (1987). *Diagnostic and Statistical Manual of Mental Disorders* (3rd ed., rev). Washington, DC: Author.

Belenky M. F., Clinchy, B. M., Goldberger, N. M., & Tarule, J. M. (1986). *Women's ways of knowing: The development of self, voice, and mind*. New York: Basic Books.

Browne, A. (1987). *When battered women kill*. New York: Free Press.

Burgess, A. W., & Holmstrom, L. L. (1974). Rape trauma syndrome. *American Journal of Psychiatry, 131*, 981–985.

Burke, P. J., Stets, J. E., & Pirog-Good, M.A. (1988). Gender identity, self-esteem, and physical and sexual abuse in dating relationships. *Social Psychology Quarterly, 51*(3), 272–285.

Chodorow, N. (1978). *The reproduction of mothering: psychoanalysis and the sociology of gender.* Berkeley: University of California Press.

Chodorow, N. J. (1989). *Feminism and psychoanalytic theory.* New Haven, CT: Yale University Press.

Coons, P. M., Bowman, E. S., & Milstein, V. (1988). Multiple personality disorder: A clinical investigation of 50 cases. *The Journal of Nervous and Mental Disease, 176*(9), 519–527.

Faludi, S. (1991). Backlash: The undeclared war against American women. New York: Crown Publishers, Inc.

Finkelhor, D. (1979). *Sexually victimized children.* New York: Free Press.

Finkelhor, D. (1984). *Child sexual abuse: New theory and research.* New York: Free Press.

Finkelhor, D., & Browne, A. (1986). The impact of child sexual abuse: A review of the research. *Psychological Bulletin, 99,* 66–77.

Gelinas, D. J. (1983). The persisting negative effects of incest. *Psychiatry, 46,* 312–332.

Gilligan, C., Lyons, N., & Hanmer, T. (Eds.). (1989). *Making connections: The relational worlds of adolescent girls at Emma Willard School.* Troy, NY: Emma Willard School.

Gordon, M. T., & Riger, S. (1989). *The female fear.* New York: Free Press.

Greven, P. (1991). *Spare the child: The religious roots of punishment and the psychological impact of physical abuse.* New York: Alfred A. Knopf.

Groth, A. N., & Burgess, A. W. (1980). Male rape: Victims and offenders. *American Journal of Psychiatry, 137*(7), 806–810.

Haavind, H. (1984). Love and power in marriage. In H. Holter (Ed.), *Patriarchy and the welfare society* (pp. 136–167). Norway: Universitetsforlaget.

Herman, J. L. (1984). *Sexual violence.* (Work in Progress No. 8). Stone Center Working Papers. Wellesley, MA: Stone Center for Developmental Services and Studies.

Herman, J. L., & Lewis, H. B. (1986). Anger in the mother-daughter relationship. In T. Bernay & D. W. Cantor (Eds.), *The psychology of today's woman: New psychoanalytic visions.* Cambridge, MA: Harper & Row.

Herman, J. L., Perry, C., & van der Kolk, B. A. (1989). Childhood trauma in borderline personality disorder. *American Journal of Psychiatry*, *146*(4), 490–495.

Hilberman, E. (1980). Overview: The "wife-beater's wife" reconsidered. *American Journal of Psychiatry*, *137*(11), 1336–1348.

Jacobson, A., & Richardson, B. (1987). Assault experiences of 100 psychiatric inpatients: Evidence of the need for routine inquiry. *American Journal of Psychiatry*, *144*(7), 908–913.

Kristiansen, C. M., & Giulietti, R. (1990). Perceptions of wife abuse: Effects of gender, attitudes toward women, and just-world beliefs among college students. *Psychology of Women Quarterly*, *14*, 177–189.

Laidlaw, T. A., Malmo, C., & Associates (1990). *Healing voices: Feminist approaches to therapy with women*. San Francisco: Jossey-Bass.

Lakoff, R. (1975). *Language and woman's place*. New York: Harper & Row.

Lerner, H. G. (1988). *Women and therapy*. Cambridge, MA: Harper & Row.

Lerner, M. J., & Miller, D. T. (1978). Just world research and the attribution process: Looking back and ahead. *Psychological Bulletin*, *85*, 1030–1051.

MacKinnon, C. A. (1989). *Toward a feminist theory of the state*. Cambridge, MA: Harvard University Press.

Mas, K. (1992). *Disrupted schemata in psychiatric patients with a history of childhood sexual abuse on the McPearl Belief Scale*. Unpublished doctoral dissertation, California School of Professional Psychology, Fresno.

McCann, I. L., & Pearlman, L. A. (1990). *Psychological trauma and the adult survivor: Theory, therapy, and transformation*. New York: Brunner/Mazel.

McCann, I. L., Sakheim, D. K., & Abrahamson, D. J. (1988). Trauma and victimization: A model of psychological adaptation. *The Counseling Psychologist*, *16*(4), 531–594.

Miller, A. (1983). *For your own good*. New York: Farrar, Straus and Giroux.

Miller, J. B. (1987). *Toward a new psychology of women*. Boston: Beacon Press.

Miller, J. B. (1988). Connections, disconnections, and violations (Work in Progress No. 33). Stone Center Working Papers. Wellesley, MA: Stone Center for Developmental Services and Studies.

Mills, T., Rieker, P. P., & Carmen, E. H. (1984). Hospitalization experiences of victims of abuse. *Victimology: An International Journal*, *9*(3–4), 436–449.

Roth, S., & Lebowitz, L. (1988). The experience of sexual trauma. *Journal of Traumatic Stress, 1,* 79–107.

Rubin, L. B. (1983). *Intimate strangers: Men and women together.* New York: Harper & Row.

Russell, D. E. H. (1984). *Sexual exploitation: Rape, child sexual abuse and workplace harassment.* Beverley Hills, CA: Sage.

Russell, D. E. H. (1986). *The secret trauma: Incest in the lives of girls and women.* New York: Basic Books.

Ryan, W. (1971). *Blaming the victim.* New York: Pantheon Books.

Saakvitne, K. W. (1990). *Psychoanalytic psychotherapy with incest survivors: Transference and countertransference paradigms.* Paper presented at American Psychological Association Annual Convention, Boston, MA.

Scher, M., & Stevens, M. (1987). Men and violence. *Journal of Counseling and Development, 65,* 351–354.

Shengold, L. (1989). *Soul murder: The effects of childhood abuse and deprivation.* New Haven, CT: Yale University Press.

Smith, M. D. (1990). Patriarchal ideology and wife beating: A test of a feminist hypothesis. *Violence and Victims, 5*(4), 257–273.

Spence, J. T., & Helmreich, R. L. (1978). *Masculinity and femininity: Their psychological dimensions, correlates and antecedents.* Austin: University of Texas Press.

Spitzack, C. (1992). *Confessing excess: Women and the politics of body reduction.* Ithaca: State University of New York Press.

Spretnak, C. (1983). Naming the cultural forces that push us toward war. *Journal of Humanistic Psychology, 23*(3), 104–114.

Sroufe, L. A., & Ward, M. J. (1980). Seductive behavior of mothers of toddlers: Occurrence, correlates, and family origins. *Child Development, 51,* 1222–1229.

Staub, E. (1989). *The roots of evil: The origins of genocide and other group violence.* Cambridge, England: Cambridge University Press.

Straus, M. A., & Gelles, R. J. (1986). Societal change and change in family violence from 1975 to 1985 as revealed by two national surveys. *Journal of Marriage and the Family, 48,* 465–479.

Stryker, S. (1980). *Symbolic interactions: A social structural version.* Menlo Park, CA: Cummings.

Surrey, J. L. (1985). *Self-in-relation: A theory of women's development.* (Work in Progress No. 13). Stone Center Working Papers. Wellesley, MA: Stone Center for Developmental Services and Studies.

Swift, C. F. (1987). *Women and violence: Breaking the connection.* (Working Papers No. 27). Stone Center Working Papers. Wellesley, MA: Stone Center for Developmental Services and Studies.

Vissing, Y. M., Straus, M. A., Gelles, R. J., & Harrop, J. W. (1991). Verbal aggression by parents and psychosocial problems of children. *Child Abuse & Neglect, 15,* 223-238.

Wertz, D. C. (1984). Women and slavery: A cross-cultural perspective. *International Journal of Women's Studies, 7*(5), 372-384.

Westen, D., Ludolph, P., Misle, B., Ruffins, S., & Block, J. (1990). Physical and sexual abuse in adolescent girls with borderline personality disorder. *American Journal of Orthopsychiatry, 60*(1), 55-66.

CONCLUSION: HELPING WOMEN HEAL, TODAY AND TOMORROW

Ellen Piel Cook

We are accustomed to considering gender as a property of the individual, present from birth and responsible for a host of personality characteristics, preferences, life choices, and social behaviors. Recent perspectives on gender agree that biological sex shapes but does not preordain our eventual life paths. The nearly universal belief across cultures that biological sex should dichotomize human beings' characteristics and roles sets into motion a complex, lifelong interaction between an individual's personal characteristics and the sociocultural environment. The consequence is that women and men end up with more significant differences between them than their essential shared humanness would suggest. Gender differences are paradoxically both artificial, in that we humans create them for ourselves, and yet natural in that they are fundamental to how we routinely see ourselves and others. There is nothing illusory about the fact that women today are still subject, by and large, to expectations, options, and experiences that are different from those facing men.

As the chapters in this book have amply illustrated, the popular truism that the sexes are separate but equal in privilege and esteem is a myth (Hare-Mustin & Marecek, 1990a). Examples abound, most obviously in continued occupational sex discrimination and sexual harassment, and the shocking frequency of violence against women. Performing women's traditional roles well can have negative consequences, including depression and low self-esteem, eating disorders and substance abuse, and endurance of battering relationships. Despite increasing awareness of gender issues, counseling texts still often discuss women's problems under the category of "special populations." In Hare-Mustin and Marecek's (1990c) words, "as long as male behavior remains the standard in the culture, women's differences from men will be regarded as deficiencies" (p. 14).

Things *have* changed enough in the past two decades so that writers in the counseling literature no longer feel the need to persuade readers that traditional gender prescriptions can be hazardous to one's mental health. The question today, instead, is how should counselors conceptualize and intervene in women's lives to enable them to live more personally rewarding lives?

The authors of the chapters in this book have provided ideas for counselors working with specific problem areas clients present in counseling. Certain common themes emerge, among them (1) profound self-esteem and personal identity issues; (2) relationships in women's lives as both a cause and a cure for women's distress; (3) the prevalence and effects of sexual violence; and (4) attitudes of significant others as well as those in the broader sociocultural environment. Such problems do not lend themselves to simple answers. As I suggested in the Introduction, how counselors understand the role of gender in women's lives may have a major impact upon how they work with women today.

In this final chapter, I will expand upon this argument in several directions. First, I will briefly summarize some of what we have learned about gender in women's lives today from the other contributors to the book. Next, as implied in the Introduction, where we locate the responsibility for the causes for and changes in women's lives can be ultimately empowering or disempowering for our clients. I will discuss this idea by briefly exploring topics of diagnosis and the economic context of women's lives. Finally, gender is generally seen as breaking the human population into two dichotomous groups of female and male. The degree to which we espouse such a conception of gender can also make a difference in how we view an individual woman seeking our assistance. The presence of multicultural issues in the gender literature exemplifies this point.

REVIEW OF GENDER IN WOMEN'S LIVES

Authors were instructed to consider the role of both the sociocultural context and individual factors in explaining varieties of women's issues today. It quickly became evident that distinctions between levels of analysis and types of problems are difficult to maintain. For example, the broader sociocultural context embodies certain attitudes and norms about women's value and expected role within society, but these standards are transmitted to individual women through relationships they have with others (e.g., in school, at home) as well as by what they experience more indirectly (e.g., through the media). Relationships with others shape a woman's self-concept and self-esteem. The relational perspective suggests that women define themselves via their relationships with others. Thus, the self-versus-other distinction maintained in much of modern psychology may be an inaccurate portrayal of the connection between an individual and others. How a woman thinks about herself and her role in the world influences the nature of her daily interactions with others; the manner in which she invests herself in society via the life roles she adopts for herself; and the degree to which she is psychologically vulnerable to abusive interpersonal expressions of the broader sociocultural devaluation of women. And, the life choices women make today, variously prompted or punished by the context of their own unique lives, will help to collectively define the perceptions and values about women facing their children in the future. In all of these ways, factors associated with the broader sociocultural environment and the individual are intermingled.

In terms of the types of problems women face, there is also significant overlap. A number of issues are likely to occur in a woman's background regardless of her presenting problem: disappointing or destructive relationships, depression, low self-esteem, inhibited ability to take action on one's behalf, eating disorders (or more mildly, disordered eating) and addictive behaviors, a loss of a sense of meaning in life, role conflicts, experiences of discrimination, and experiences of violence including rape, battering, and incest. Thus, readers will probably find a combination of chapters useful in understanding most women clients.

Several major themes unite discussions about women's lives today. The level of agreement about these themes within the gender literature probably attests both to the essential truth of these themes in our society today and to the inevitable power of the theoretical zeitgeist to channel our thinking along similar paths.

The first major theme is the continued existence of broad sociocultural attitudes that restrict women's possibilities and injure their sense of themselves as individuals. Patriarchy and sexism are fundamental principles responsible for the differential socialization of the sexes and the prevalence of gender-related devaluations, restrictions, and violations perpetrated by others and women themselves. Cultural misogyny fosters violence against women, and when internalized by women makes them open to multiple forms of victimization throughout their lives. The widespread oppression of women helps to explain the high incidence of depression in women, and its effects are multiplied for women experiencing oppression also because of their sexual orientation or race/ethnicity.

The prevalence of daily life stressors characterizing the lives of many women is linked to the roles they are mandated to play and how they are treated by others and society at large. The frequency with which women encounter these life stressors speaks to the power of the gendered context of women's lives. Women employed outside the home continue to struggle with partners reluctant to share equitably in home and childcare responsibilities and with employers who view child-care facilities, flextime arrangements, and parental leaves as expensive and unnecessary luxuries (Cook, 1992). Many lesbian and bisexual women must be constantly vigilant to hide essential aspects of their identity and life-styles from others to avoid opprobrium. Women are overwhelmingly the targets of sexual violence and battering relationships; daily life for many women means fending off further abuse and coping with the wrenching life disruptions caused by the violence of others. As I will discuss later, poverty is a burden increasingly experienced by women and their children.

Balancing recognition of the power of the environment is the emphasis on women's identity issues. This emphasis is consistent with

Western psychology's predominant conceptualization of the human being as a self-contained agent of action. This book highlights the strengths of the modal identity believed to describe women's selves, while pointing to its dark side. How women see themselves as individuals influences a vast array of personal characteristics and choices: juggling of roles in the present and over time; choices about childbearing and birth control; consumption of food and other substances; and willingness to act on behalf of their own interests and life goals, to name a few.

Relationships define the priorities and choices of many women today. The relational perspective discussed in this book is appealing partly because it provides a powerful antidote to the pervasive devaluation of women. In recent years, writers have perpetuated this devaluation by portraying women's traditional socialized characteristics as inferior to those characteristic of men as a group. Thus, women have been enjoined to become more career oriented/more assertive/less caretaking in relationships/more like men in general to gain self-respect and social power. Such changes may indeed be salutory for women in some circumstances. The relational perspective, however, has highlighted the essential human strengths born out of a commitment to nurturing relationships with others and the pain engendered by a society that regards such activities as private and secondary in importance.

Yet experts have described the psychic costs to many women of such a relational identity. Women may choose to surrender their very selves in order to preserve important relationships. The role women adopt as self-sacrificing nurturer can lead to eating disorders and addiction as well as depression. Women convinced of their destiny as mothers can experience real anguish when confronted by infertility or a pregnancy at the wrong time or with the wrong partner. Feelings of guilt, shame, and low self-esteem can accompany strained or failed relationships because of the responsibility women often take to ensure relational success. Women can even learn from their mothers to hate themselves as women.

Correspondingly, counselors need to explore the nature of women's relationships in order to understand their distress. For proponents of the relational perspective, this exploration of relationships helps in understanding how women currently perceive themselves as individuals as well as what went wrong in important relationships. Many psychologically troubled women have experienced abusive relationships with significant others in their lives—fathers, other relatives, lovers, and friends. Divergent communication patterns may be at the root of relationship stress. Social support appears to be critical to women's ability to manage stressful situations and make changes in their lives, encompassing coping with addictions, violence, infertility, or discrimination against them.

Not surprisingly, the key to therapeutic change is the provision of an empathic helping relationship. A variety of strategies were proposed in this book depending on the counselors' theoretical orientation, including cognitive and behavioral strategies, couples counseling, attention to here-and-now relationship issues between the counselor and client, and use of peer support or counseling groups.

The first step in the counseling process is problem conceptualization or diagnosis. For counselors unaware of the role of gender in clients' lives—as well as its role in conditioning our attitudes about clients—this step is laden with pitfalls. Diagnosis can be used in ways that ultimately empower or disempower clients.

DIAGNOSIS

All counselors operate on the basis of some more or less explicit formulation of why the client needs counseling at this time. Increasingly today, counselors are likely to use a formal diagnostic system such as the DSM-III-R, adopted as the standard by mental health practitioners across fields. At their best, such formal diagnostic systems provide a common language for professionals, a convenient shorthand for summarizing a complex of symptoms, and a guide for intervention. Such systems inevitably embody the sensitivities of the time, however. A number of experts have pointed out recently that diagnostic practices today can paint potentially biased pictures of women clients' distress.

Mental health counselors know that there are large sex differences in rates of diagnosing certain psychological problems, for example, depression in women. Simply diagnosing a particular disorder more frequently in one sex is not automatically a sign of sex bias. Women and men may be differentially exposed to stressful life events related to development of certain psychological problems, as in the case of greater numbers of men than women diagnosed as having a posttraumatic stress disorder (PTSD) after fighting in the Vietnam war. Women are less likely to exhibit PTSD symptoms for battle- related reasons, although they may do so for other reasons (e.g., sexual abuse). In this manner, differences in rates of diagnosis by sex may simply mirror the reality of life experiences.

A more pressing question is whether practitioners' gender-related expectations and values and those embodied in the diagnostic tools they use cause them, however innocently, to apply different standards to identify psychological problems in each sex. One way this has occurred, according to Kaplan (1983), is that, because feminine characteristics are devalued in our society, simply behaving in a feminine stereotypic manner is enough to earn a woman a diagnostic label (e.g., histrionic or dependent personality disorder). Kaplan argued that women may be diagnosed as "disordered" for behaving in a way that they are socialized to do—being a "good woman" in the traditional sense—whereas men are not. This difference reflects an equating of masculine characteristics with mental health and a corresponding devaluing of feminine characteristics as somehow deficient or immature. Particularly in the case of the personality disorders, where application of diagnostic criteria requires greater interpretation than more behaviorally referenced problems, gender bias may shape what practitioners label as disordered (Hamilton, Rothbart, & Dawes, 1986).

These observations do not discount the appropriateness of applying certain diagnoses to clients. However, counselors must seriously ask what it means when a disproportionate number of women clients receive a particular diagnosis. Is it possible that such diagnostic patterns say more about our own views of women than about their lives? Are women prone to certain types of problems by their own nature or by the nature of their lives? Or both? Are we more likely to label as problematic a woman's "overfunctioning" in a family system than her partner's emotional unavailability? What does it mean if we identify most women clients as "codependent"? Do we punish challenging clients by labeling them as seriously disturbed because they irritate us or threaten our sense of competence (Brown, 1992; Stiver, 1985/1991)?

A second gender-related problem associated with diagnosis is an error of omission: Counselors may also develop a limited view of women's problems when they fail to consider gender-related factors contributing to certain types of problems. An all-too-common example is failure to detect and appreciate the consequences of sexual abuse, including rape, incest, and battering. As the chapter authors have made abundantly clear, sexual abuse is prevalent enough to be considered normative in women's lives and can result in lifelong struggles over self-worth and trust. Although certainly not all women survivors of abuse seek counseling, sexual abuse is a common background factor in women suffering psychological distress (cf. Carmen, Rieker, & Mills, 1984). Victimization may contribute to diagnoses of personality disorders and depression, which often coexist (Hamilton & Jensvold, 1992). Some symptoms labeled as signs of personality disorders may be behaviors skillfully designed to facilitate survival under repetitive abuse (Brown, 1992). Battered women may present symptoms identified as indicative of schizophrenia or borderline personality disorder, although in their cases such symptoms may be quite realistic responses to their lives (Rosewater, 1985). Such misdiagnoses may be particularly likely for minority women, who must contend with multiple forms of discrimination (Brown, 1992).

In cases of survivors of abuse, the difference a diagnosis makes should be obvious: Do we treat such a woman primarily as a victim of her environment or of her own disordered psyche? Yet in other cases as well, the choice of diagnosis makes a difference precisely for the reasons that many counselors avoid formal diagnosis wherever possible. Each diagnosis carries with it certain connotations of severity, chronicity, and likability of the client bearing such a label. How we see the client as a snapshot of her life history can determine whether we believe she can be empowered to change her life and how successfully we are able to work with her toward such a goal.

THE ECONOMIC CONTEXT OF WOMEN'S LIVES

A second illustration of the effects of our gender-related conceptualizations of clients' problems is how we approach economic issues with women. Poverty is a disturbing feature of many women's lives. The phrase "feminization of poverty" reflects the relationship between economic status and being a woman in our society today, particularly for minority women. Factors contributing to the feminization of poverty are diverse. Female heads of households with young children are particularly prone to experience poverty, and increasing numbers of women cannot rely on a man's financial support of his family (Smith, 1986). Each additional child increases the financial burden, because public resources provide little substantial support (Bianchi & Spain, 1986; Zopf, 1989). Divorce means poverty for many women, including women who were reasonably affluent before divorce. Weitzman (1985) has demonstrated that "gender-neutral" divorce laws assuming that the partners are equally, able to support themselves economically after divorce contributes to the impoverishment of women. This assumption of equality does not take into account essential differences in opportunities for the sexes as a result of typical role allocation in marriages and sex differentiation of the work force. The high rate of noncompliance with child support arrangements (Weitzman, 1985), which are often insufficient to begin with, means that many women take sole financial as well as custodial responsibility for children after divorce. Women working outside the home often face employment discrimination; limited job opportunities because of their skills, caretaking responsibilities, or lack of mobility; and expensive or inadequate daycare (Cook, 1992). Root (1992) recommends that poverty be thought of as exposure to cumulative trauma over time, with major consequences for a woman's psychological functioning.

Again, how we view poor women in the gendered context of their lives is important. In one sense, women may be poor because of the life choices they have made: for example, pregnancy at an early age, failure to pursue an education, lack of transferable job skills because of adopting a homemaker life role. Yet viewing such choices with an awareness of gender dynamics can suddenly alter our view of their choices: Young women may become pregnant partly because gender dynamics make open negotiation of birth control difficult. Poor women may drop out of school because there is no one else to care for the children, and our society does not consider subsidized child care to be a priority. Homemakers may have successfully acted out a life role that they, their husbands, and society at large viewed as their major responsibility—and then the rules changed after divorce. To paraphrase Bem and Bem (1973), what does it mean to be allowed to vote on your life's direction when the ballot has already been marked for you?

As I have argued elsewhere (Cook, 1992), counselors' views about poor women can influence the counseling interventions they deem most appropriate. For some women, focusing on personal deficiencies using a skills-oriented problem-solving approach may work well; for example, helping women overcome inadequate educational and career development by career exploration, job skills training, and so on. For other women, such an individualistic perspective may be doomed to failure unless the counselor incorporates consideration of the gendered context of their lives, such as caretaking responsibilities and lack of support in meeting them and experiences that have influenced clients' perceptions of the possibilities open to them (e.g., discriminatory educational or employment experiences, abuse in relationships). Counselors must also be aware of factors that may interact with or supersede gender, such as race/ethnicity.

Paradoxically, surrendering some personal responsibility for one's problems can be liberating. As McWhirter (1991) stressed, empowering perspectives help clients to be aware of broader systemic factors outside their control while developing concrete alternatives to their lives as they see them. Women clients typically do not need to feel more responsible for and guilty about their lives. Such self-attributions of blame are very common among women. Instead, they need to be empowered to explore and enact personally meaningful responses to the particulars of their lives, some of which are likely to be beyond their control. Such responses can range widely, from self-exploration leading to discovery of their own possibilities to social activism. Counseling and other community resources can either serve or negate such efforts. Women need to feel that they have a right to utilize (or not) community resources, that such resources can extend rather than replace their own strengths, and that there are systemic reasons why many women need such services (Cook, 1992). The goal is a commitment and ability to pursue personally meaningful relationships and individual achievements, with dignity and respect for self and others. Empowerment to do so is most likely to come from a counseling process that is able to see women as responsible—in the sense of capable of responding—within a world that frequently views them as powerless and unimportant.

DIVERSITY IN WOMEN'S LIVES

Counselors today readily acknowledge the importance of multicultural influences in individuals' lives. A recent special issue of the *Journal of Counseling and Development* (Pedersen, 1991) illustrates how sophisticated our understanding of these issues promises to become. Yet the literature on gender and multicultural influences is surprisingly sparse. Little is written on the gender-relevant experiences and problems of women of color. Authors face the vexing dilemma of whether to omit discussion of such influences entirely (an unacceptable solution for many), to say what little we know about these issues and lament the limitations of our understanding (an often unsatisfying solution), or, based on their own experience and knowledge, to speculate on the nature of such differences (a potentially perilous solution).

Such omissions concerning multicultural issues in the gender literature have received more attention recently. For example, Brown (1990) roundly criticized feminist theory and research as white, Western, and classist. Our descriptions of women's lives are culture bound, not recognizing the diversity of roles, family structures, and personal interpretations of external realities (see *Women and Therapy*, 1990, vol. 9 for a two-part series discussing such issues). According to Brown, it is incorrect to assume that gender is even of central importance in all women's lives; other realities such as their race or economic standing may hold greater salience for them (see also Lott, 1990).

The diversity of lesbian women's experience is also gaining more attention. Counselors are slowly coming to understand that because of their oppressed status, lesbian women's lives can differ from those of heterosexual women in far more than their choice of partners. Failure to acknowledge the unique life paths of lesbian (and gay) individuals can "separate clients from their souls" (Ritter & O'Neill, 1989, p. 11). Recent accessible references for counselors include special issues of the *Journal of Counseling and Development* (Dworkin & Gutierrez, 1989) and *The Counseling Psychologist* (Fassinger, 1991).

Part of the lack of attention to diversity in women's lives is unfortunately attributable to our own ignorance and bias. Being sensitive to how exclusionary processes work in the case of gender does not make us immune to cultural ethnocentrism, racism, or heterosexism. Members of a dominant group (in our society, white/middle or upper class/heterosexual/male) are prone to consider their own privileged status as the norm. Such a standard ignores how many privileges accrue from having the favored characteristics and relegates everyone else to the position of being exceptions to the rule who merit acknowledgement only in passing. Counselors need to routinely educate themselves about the limitations of their own worldviews, the validity of others different from theirs, and the likely presence of still others presently invisible to them.

The lack of attention to diversity in women's lives may also point to the power of our gender ideology to dichotomize the human world into two entirely separate groups, thus overlooking the overlap between the sexes and the enormous variability in characteristics within each sex. When we emphasize between-sex differences, as both traditional and relational perspectives tend to do (Hare-Mustin & Marecek, 1990b), we can minimize the existence of considerable differences within each sex and similarities between the sexes. For example, we should expect at least some men to be relational in

286

nature and some women to adopt an autonomous mode in relationships. Similarly, expecting women from different cultural and social backgrounds to be alike simply because they are women can be presumptuous and devalues the importance of multicultural influences in human beings' lives. Yet Hare-Mustin and Marecek (1990b) caution that dismissal of gender differences as inconsequential can backfire when women's special needs (e.g., for recovery after childbirth) or socially determined differences between the sexes (e.g., in partners' earning potential after dissolution of a traditional marriage) are not considered.

Any counseling intervention that does not take seriously differences in expectations, opportunities, and rewards characterizing the gendered context of our world is likely to perpetuate rather than correct women's disadvantaged status. For some examples, women interested in climbing the corporate ladder need more than career information and credentials; they must be prepared to deal with both subtle and overt exclusionary practices maintaining the glass ceiling (Ragins & Sundstrom, 1989). Many women in the labor force and in higher education need information and support in dealing with sexual harassment in its many forms (e.g., Hotelling, 1991; Salisbury, Ginorio, Remick, & Stringer, 1986). Battered women lacking economic resources or social support are unlikely to leave their partners. Programs providing job skills to poor women, or chemical dependency treatment programs, may fail if they do not provide childcare for participants.

While respecting the diversity among individual women in identity, life history, and worldview, we must recognize that such characteristics are not subject to easy change—nor should they be. Individual characteristics, shaped as they are by years of life experience, are tenacious and resistant to change. Simplistic brief interventions (e.g., day-long workshops on overcoming codependency) risk leaving women confused and feeling more guilty rather than empowered. Counselors need to recognize women clients' concerns as representing resilience: determined efforts to cope the best they can with often daunting life circumstances, even though such efforts may prove to be unsuccessful or self-defeating. Respect for the resilience and dignity of women clients is healing as they struggle to empower themselves in a world that has traditionally viewed women's concerns as less important than those of men.

At its best, counseling can assist women to actualize new ways of thinking, feeling, and acting that they did not even envision as possibilities before. Because such a change process occurs within a rich relational context, counselors as well as clients can find the process to be a joyous and life-affirming one.

REFERENCES

Bem, S. L., & Bem, D. J. (1973). Training the woman to know her place: The social antecedents of women in the world of work. Division of Pupil Personnel Services, Bureau of Instructional Support Services, Pennsylvania Department of Education.

Bianchi, S. M., & Spain, D. (1986). *American women in transition.* New York: Sage.

Brown, L. S. (1990). The meaning of a multicultural perspective for theory-building in feminist therapy. *Women and Therapy, 9,* 1–21.

Brown, L. S. (1992). A feminist critique of the personality disorders. In L. S. Brown & M. Ballou (Eds.), *Personality and psychopathology: Feminist reappraisals* (pp. 206–228). New York: Guilford.

Carmen, E., Rieker, P. P., & Mills, T. (1984). Victims of violence and psychiatric illness. In P. P. Rieker & E. Carmen (Eds.), *The gender gap in psychotherapy: Social realities and psychological processes* (pp. 199–211). New York: Plenum.

Cook, E. P. (1992). Empowering women: Gender issues in adulthood. In J. A. Lewis, B. Hayes, & L. Bradley (Eds.), *Counseling women over the lifespan* (pp. 133–154). Denver: Love.

Dworkin, S. H., & Gutierrez, F. (Eds.) (1989). Special issue: Gay, lesbian, and bisexual issues in counseling. *Journal of Counseling and Development, 68.*

Fassinger, R. L. (Ed.) (1991). Counseling lesbian women and gay men. *The Counseling Psychologist, 19.*

Hamilton, J. A., & Jensvold, M. (1992). Personality, psychopathology, and depressions in women. In L. S. Brown & M. Ballou (Eds.), *Personality and psychopathology: Feminist reappraisals* (pp. 116–143). New York: Guilford.

Hamilton, S., Rothbart, M., & Dawes, R. M. (1986). Sex bias, diagnosis, and DSM-III. *Sex Roles, 15,* 269–274.

Hare-Mustin, R. T., & Marecek, J. (1990a). Beyond difference. In R. T. Hare-Mustin & J. Marecek (Eds.), *Making a difference: Psychology and the construction of gender* (pp. 184–201). New Haven: Yale University Press.

Hare-Mustin, R. T., & Marecek, J. (1990b). Gender and the meaning of difference: Postmodernism and psychology. In R. T. Hare-Mustin & J. Marecek (Eds.), *Making a difference: Psychology and the construction of gender* (pp. 22–64). New Haven: Yale University Press.

Hare-Mustin, R. T., & Marecek, J. (1990c). On making a difference. In R. T. Hare-Mustin & J. Marecek (Eds.), *Making a difference: Psychology and the construction of gender* (pp. 1–21). New Haven: Yale University Press.

Hotelling, K. (1991). Sexual harassment: A problem shielded in silence. *Journal of Counseling and Development, 69,* 497–501.

Kaplan, M. (1983). A woman's view of DSM-III. *American Psychologist, 38,* 786–792.

Lott, B. (1990). Dual natures or learned behavior: The challenge to feminist psychology. In R.T. Hare-Mustin & J. Marecek (Eds.), *Making a difference: Psychology and the construction of gender* (pp. 65–101). New Haven: Yale University Press.

McWhirter, E. H. (1991). Empowerment in counseling. *Journal of Counseling and Development, 69,* 222–227.

Pedersen, P. B. (Ed.) (1991). Special issue: Multiculturalism as a fourth force in counseling. *Journal of Counseling and Development, 70.*

Ragins, B. R., & Sundstrom, E. (1989). Gender and power in organizations: A longitudinal perspective. *Psychological Bulletin, 105,* 51–88.

Ritter, K. Y., & O'Neill, C. W. (1989). Moving through loss: The spiritual journey of gay men and lesbian women. *Journal of Counseling and Development, 68,* 9–15.

Root, M. P. P. (1992). Reconstructing the impact of trauma on personality. In L. S. Brown & M. Ballou (Eds.), *Personality and psychopathology: Feminist reappraisals* (pp. 229–265). New York: Guilford.

Rosewater, L. B. (1985). Schizophrenic, borderline, or battered? In L. B. Rosewater & L. E. A. Walker (Eds.), *Handbook of feminist therapy* (pp. 203–213). New York: Springer.

Salisbury, J., Ginorio, A. B., Remick, H., & Stringer, D. M. (1986). Counseling victims of sexual harassment. *Psychotherapy, 23,* 316–324.

Smith, J. (1986). The paradox of women's poverty: Wage-earning women and economic transformation. In B. C. Gelpi, N. C. M. Hartsock, C. C. Novak, & M. H. Strober (Eds.), *Women and poverty* (pp. 121–140). Chicago: University of Chicago Press.

Stiver, I. P. (1985/1991). The meaning of care: Reframing treatment models. In J. V. Jordan, A. G. Kaplan, J. B. Miller, I. P. Stiver, & J. L. Surrey (Eds.), *Women's growth in connection: Writings from the Stone Center* (Work in Progress No. 20) (pp. 250–267). New York: Guilford.

Weitzman, L. J. (1985). *The divorce revolution: The unexpected social and economic consequences for women and children in America.* New York: The Free Press.

Zopf, P. E. (1989). *American women in poverty.* New York: Greenwood Press.

INDEX

9365